American Confluence

A History of the Trans-Appalachian Frontier

Walter Nugent and Malcolm Rohrbough, eds.

American Confluence

The Missouri Frontier from Borderland to Border State

STEPHEN ARON

INDIANA UNIVERSITY PRESS BLOOMINGTON & INDIANAPOLIS

This book is a publication of

Indiana University Press
601 North Morton Street
Bloomington, IN 47404-3797 USA

http://iupress.indiana.edu

Telephone orders 800-842-6796
Fax orders 812-855-7931
Orders by e-mail iuporder@indiana.edu

The paper used in this publication meets the minimum requirements of American National Standard for Information Sciences—Permanence of Paper for Printed Library Materials, ANSI Z39.48-1984.

Manufactured in the United States of America

Library of Congress Cataloging-in-Publication Data

Aron, Stephen.
American confluence : the Missouri frontier from borderland to border state / Stephen Aron.
p. cm. — (A history of the trans-Appalachian frontier)
Includes bibliographical references and index.
ISBN 0-253-34691-6 (cloth : alk. paper)
1. Missouri—History—18th century. 2. Missouri—History—19th century. 3. Frontier and pioneer life—Missouri. 4. Missouri River Region—History—18th century. 5. Missouri River Region—History—19th century. 6. Frontier and pioneer life—Missouri River Region. 7. Indians of North America—Missouri River Region. I. Title. II. Series.
F466.A76 2006
977.8'01—dc22
2005018951

1 2 3 4 5 11 10 09 08 07 06

FOR

Daniel and Jack

Contents

Acknowledgments

Since this book is about the compromises and collaborations that once characterized the frontiers at the confluence of the Missouri, Mississippi, and Ohio rivers, it is appropriate that I acknowledge the accommodations and adjustments made for me by many individuals and institutions. Thanks to Walter Nugent and Malcolm Rohrbough for engaging me to write a book about frontier Missouri and accepting a book whose geography challenged the definitions of their series. Along with Walter and Mac, Robert Sloan proved patient and flexible in waiting for the belated delivery of the manuscript and in allowing me the title of my choosing. My thanks as well go to Elaine Durham Otto for her superb copyediting.

For the last eight years, a period that coincides with the research and writing of this book, the University of California, Los Angeles has provided me with a wonderful academic home. I am grateful to the History Department, whose faculty provided stimulating intellectual companionship and spirited athletic competition. Three chairs—Ron Mellor, Brenda Stevenson, and Teo Ruiz—deserve special recognition for making the department so invigorating and for being so obliging when I asked permission to split my appointment between UCLA and the Autry National Center. To this list should be added Scott Waugh, who as dean of social sciences made possible my dual appointment and generously supported my research.

Over the past two and a half years, I have complained that my dual appointments seem like dueling ones, especially on days when the freeways of Los Angeles don't cooperate. Certainly, the complications of holding two positions delayed the completion of this book. Still, on most days I feel that with one foot at

UCLA and one at the Autry, I enjoy the best of both university and museum worlds. For this opportunity, I owe much to John Sussman and John Gray, who brought me to the Autry, taught me how museums work, and adjusted to the peculiarities of my schedule. Above all, being at the Autry has renewed my faith in the importance of history, and I hope that comes through in the pages that follow.

The ideas that animate the following pages trace to more publications and conversations than I can remember or possibly cite in the book's endnotes. John Mack Faragher and Richard White, I hope, will appreciate how their scholarship has inspired and informed this book. The same is true for Joyce Appleby, Hal Barron, Alfred Bush, Ellen Dubois, Janet Fireman, John Gray, Eric Hinderaker, Thomas Hines, Peter Mancall, Karen Merrill, Melissa Meyer, John Murrin, Gary Nash, Walter Nugent, David Myers, Robert Ritchie, Malcolm Rohrbough, Virginia Scharff, Sharon Ullman, Joan Waugh, Mark Wetherington, and Henry Yu. Although I have had only one or two brief meetings with Carl Ekberg, William Foley, and Walter Schroeder, much of what I know about the Missouri frontier builds from their work.

Invitations to lecture or conduct seminars at California State University, Northridge, the Claremont Graduate School, the Colorado Historical Society, the Constitutional Rights Foundation, the Filson Historical Society, the Missouri Conference on History, the University of California, Santa Cruz, the University of Utah, the University of Nevada, Las Vegas, Washington University, Western Illinois University, and Western Kentucky University gave me opportunities to present portions of the book to a variety of audiences and gained me extremely valuable feedback. So, too, were the responses from hundreds of students at UCLA, who listened (usually patiently) to the sometimes half-baked ideas that I tested out in various courses. Among those students, I am most in debt to the members of WHEAT and to the splendid research assistance provided by Greg Beyrer, Mike Bottoms, Cynthia Culver, Lawrence Culver, Nat Sheidley, Allison Varzally, and Lissa Wadewitz.

As I explain in the introduction, my work on a world history textbook profoundly altered the ambitions of this book, and I am grateful to my coauthors—Jeremy Adelman, Stephen Kotkin, Suzanne Marchand, Gyan Prakash, Michael Tsin, and Robert Tignor—for broadening my historical vision. More than any individual, my collaborations with Jeremy Adelman have enriched my understandings of frontiers and borderlands and have shaped this book.

There would be no shape (and no book) at all without access to and assistance from the Autry Library, the Braun Research Library, the Filson Historical Society, the Huntington Library, the Mudd Library at Princeton University, the Missouri Historical Society in St. Louis, the State Historical Society of Missouri in Columbia, and the UCLA Library. Generous support from the UCLA Academic Senate paid for numerous trips to Missouri, and fellowships from the Filson Historical Society and the Friends of Princeton University Library underwrote my research in those archives.

Finally, no list of commendations would be complete without an acknowledgment of the accommodations made by close relatives and close friends. Of greatest value are those of parents, siblings, in-laws, spouse, and children. So to Tom, Marilyn, Paul, Nicole, Carl, Ruby, Amy, Daniel, and Jack, thank you for showing me how the compromises, collaborations, and love of families make for the best confluences.

Introduction

In the heart of North America, the continent's three greatest rivers come together. As the crow flies, only about 135 miles separate the points where the Missouri and the Ohio join the Mississippi. Together, the three rivers drain a vast portion of North America, uniting waters from west, north, and east on a journey to the south in a region that I have designated the "American confluence."

This book examines the history of the lower Missouri valley and the whole of the "confluence region" as it extended back on both sides of the Mississippi, principally, though not exclusively, between the mouths of the Missouri and Ohio rivers. The boundaries of the confluence region are left deliberately vague, for the area was characterized by its fluid borders through much of the period under study. Focusing on the last two-thirds of the eighteenth century and the first third of the nineteenth, the book explores the meetings of peoples, or frontiers, that evolved within the area where the rivers met. This history of multiple frontiers accents the American confluence's transition from a place of overlapping borderlands to one of oppositional border states.

In its original incarnation, this book pursued a single frontier demarcated along more conventional lines. It began as a history of "frontier Missouri," one in a series of new surveys of the frontier experiences of trans-Appalachian states. When I took on the assignment, I anticipated a straightforward project: to trace how the area that became the state of Missouri emerged from its precolonial origins, how a frontier opened when colonists contested with natives for occupancy, and how its development led to its admission as one of the United States, the expulsion of Indian peoples, and the closing of the Missouri frontier. Telling the history of frontier Missouri this way made for an obvious sequel to the book that I had written on frontier Kentucky. After all, the westward migrations of Kentuckians had landed many in Missouri, including Daniel Boone, who in my previous book had served as a synecdoche for pioneers moving across the Appalachians. Initially, I conceived the Missouri book as the next chapter in "a greater western history" that narrated and connected the conquest, colonization, and consolidation of one American West after another. Since my conception of a greater western history posited that patterns of conquest, colonization, and consolidation repeated themselves as American expansion proceeded westward, Missouri seemed the best place to look for a replay of what had happened to its east.[1]

But a few years of reading, researching, and teaching have revised this book's ambitions and directions. Of great import has been my collaboration on a recently published world history textbook. Writing world history prompted me to rethink the framework for understanding the history of frontier Missouri. From the perspective of world history, the area that became the state of Missouri has little significance if it is only one of fifty such chapters in the expansion of the United States. Within a world history, what made Missouri matter were the connections between the experiences of its peoples and those who occupied frontiers, not just within the present-day United States but across the Americas and beyond. Instead of contributing to a "greater western history," the project became an opportunity to explore what Herbert Bolton termed a "greater American history." And so the history of one state (within the history of one nation-state) evolved into a more complicated contemplation, involving multiple polities and overlapping colonialisms and speaking to a comparative and common history of the Americas. Framed this way, patterns and repetitions that moved from east to west lose their exclusivity. Instead, processes of conquest, colonization, and consolidation can be seen to travel along multiple trajectories.[2]

No matter how broadly framed or variously vectored, writing a frontier history for one state remains an obstacle-filled enterprise. First are the problems associated with the concept of frontier. Despite its frequent usage, historians do not really agree about the definition of *frontier*. Over time, the term has acquired many meanings, and historians have employed it promiscuously. At best, say critics, vague and shifting definitions diminish analytical precision; at worst, the frontier is fatally wounded by its ethnocentric heritage. Of concern, too, are the issues raised by taking state boundaries to demarcate frontier histories. For much of the period that falls within the parameters of frontier Missouri, there was no state of Missouri. To refer, as I have done in each of the preceding paragraphs, to "the area that became the state of Missouri" reads frontier geography and history backwards from borders that were fixed only in the early nineteenth century. Most history, of course, is written this way. Although historical narratives typically move forward in time, their analytical tracks follow backward-looking reflections. As historians, we know what happened; it is our great advantage over those who lived in the times about which we write. Yet it also puts us at a disadvantage, for it encourages us to explain only what did happen, to identify a single line running straight from past to present. In the case of the area that became the state of Missouri, this puts the focus on elucidating how these borders came to be, how one particular political outcome triumphed. Other possibilities get lost entirely or gain entry only in terms of their failings, of how and why alternative mappings of the area did not hold.[3]

I have tried to tackle these problems by reconsidering the meaning of frontier, reconceiving the geographic boundaries of the project, rethinking the conventional periodization, and resolving to write history forwards. Regarding the first issue, I define *frontier* most simply as a meeting point. To be sure, that is a vague designation that can be applied to almost every place at any time. As such, or as "an intergroup contact situation," a "cultural cross-roads," or a "zone of interpenetration," frontiers have no spatial or temporal boundaries. These definitions tell us little about the territorial or chronological reach of particular meeting points. Adding a few words to meeting point can set some limits and bring greater analytical precision. Heeding Howard Lamar and Leonard Thompson, I envision a frontier as a meeting point *between peoples of differing ways and from distinct polities.* It opens, as Lamar and Thompson have asserted, "when the first representatives of the intrusive society arrive" and enter into sustained contact with indigenes; "it 'closes' when a single political authority has established hegemony over the zone."[4]

Helpful as this addition is, Lamar and Thompson presume an order and simplicity that frontiers often lacked. In North America, a single indigenous group rarely had exclusive possession or usage of a clearly bounded territory. With precolonial and colonial histories of Indian groups distinguished by continuing migrations, overlapping claims predominated. In almost any "zone of interpenetration" were found both more recently arrived and longer established peoples. Compounding the confusion was the absence in Indian North America of centralized states, in lieu of which all politics was truly local. Thus where Lamar and Thompson posit a monolithic indigenous entity, North American frontiers more typically featured multiple polities. Just as important, European colonial intruders did not respect one another's maps. Like those whom Lamar and Thompson would lump together as "indigenes," the invaders did not always march into a frontier zone in a neat, single file. Just as often, they represented different polities with competing colonial schemes.

To address the complexities that accompanied overlapping colonial claims, Jeremy Adelman and I have proposed that we supplement the term *borderland* to our frontier histories. By *frontier,* we understand a meeting place of peoples (in which no single political authority has established hegemony and fixed control over clearly demarcated borders). We reserve the designation of *borderland* for the contested boundaries between colonial domains. This pairing of the intercultural and the intercolonial, we hope, will allow the differences of European rationales and styles to come to the fore, as well as the shifts in those rationales and styles. Equally significant to the history of borderlands and frontiers are the ways in which Indians exploited these differences and compelled these shifts. By our usage, then, meetings of peoples create(d) frontiers, meetings of empires create(d) borderlands, and this project can serve as a case study of the interaction of frontiers and borderlands in one part of the Americas.[5]

Contrary to my original intentions—and perhaps to the objectives of the series for which this book is intended, I no longer define that place simply as Missouri, and I try to avoid references to the area that became the state of Missouri. That is, to escape from writing anachronistic or presumptuous history, I have eschewed borders that are prematurely assigned. Instead, in an effort to write history forward, I have chosen to reorient this book as a study of the confluence region. By this, I refer to the lands adjacent to the conjunction not only of the Missouri and Mississippi rivers, but also of the Ohio River with the Mississippi. The center of the confluence region, the stretch on the Mississippi between the mouths of the Missouri and Ohio rivers, is clear enough. But its perimeter I leave deliberately vague. I do so, because until well into the eighteenth century, the rivers that were the chief geographic feature of the confluence region functioned more as corridors than as borders. For thousands of years, these waterways facilitated the movement of peoples and objects to and through the center of the confluence region. No other location in North America saw such traffic from points near and far. Hence, my decision to designate this greatest of meeting points as the American confluence.

Both *confluence region* and *American confluence* are terms of my invention. Neither would have any resonance with the historical occupants of the area. Yet in this respect, confluence region is no worse than talking about the area that became the state of Missouri. In fact, the fluid character and boundaries of the American confluence make it more suitable for frontier historians, who should be wary of retrospectively imposed borders.

Indeed, confluence is an ideal metaphor for frontier studies. What is a frontier but a coming together of two or more streams of people? In some cases, the confluence, like the meeting of the Missouri and Mississippi rivers, was a turbulent one. Above the mouth of the Missouri, as numerous European explorers noted, the Mississippi was relatively calm and clear. The Missouri, however, was widely described as murky and turbid. Where the Missouri hit the Mississippi, violent spumes swelled, and below their intersection, the joined rivers took on a murkier and rougher cast. So, too, frontiers within the confluence region (and elsewhere) sometimes engaged cohabiting peoples in destructive conflict, and minglings almost always muddied cultural waters. By contrast, the Ohio River was often referred to as "the beautiful river," and its meeting with the Mississippi produced a gentler union. Likewise, the frontiers within the confluence region (and elsewhere) generated creative adaptations and constructive accommodations that allowed peoples to mix and meld more peacefully. At the American confluence, then, the coming together of rivers and peoples involved both collisions and collusions. The result, in Colin Calloway's phrase, was the emergence of "new worlds for all." The emergence of new peoples of mixed ethnic ancestry most obviously manifested the altering power of frontier interactions. Subtler, and sometimes more ephemeral, were the blending of ways and blurring of distinctions that were also a by-product of frontier cohabitation. Such "cultural fusion between native and settler cultures," suggest historians John Mack Faragher and Robert Hine, was "one of the most notable—and least understood—developments of early American history."[6]

What makes the lands adjacent to the confluence of the Missouri, Ohio, and Mississippi rivers particularly noteworthy for students of frontiers is what happened with the entrance of Europeans and the formation of borderlands. At one time or another and sometimes at the same time in the last half of the eighteenth century, the area played host to each of North America's major colonial powers: France, Spain, England, and the United States. Thus the meeting of rivers provides a single setting in which to explore the meetings of peoples and empires and to compare how overlapping forms of colonialism mapped multiple frontiers.

The first four chapters of this book examine how changes in colonial maps influenced intercultural relations. On the east side of the confluence region, territory passed from France, to England, to the United States. On the west side, imperial conflicts and bargainings shifted lands from France, to Spain, back to France, and then to the United States. Although these four chapters focus on the impact of these remappings, they do not break at the transfer of a colony from one empire to another. To have done so would adhere too closely to a conventional periodization that assigns too much import to the cartography of colonialism. Through the eighteenth century and the first decade of the nineteenth, the maps drawn by empire builders and keepers provided only a limited guide to the borders that existed on the ground. Again and again, the programs designed by distant metropolitan officials and the edicts issued by local colonial authorities could not be implemented or enforced, especially on Indian peoples who maintained the power to draw their own borders and protect their own rights. The history of the confluence region, then, demonstrates how the practices of colonialism were the products of intercultural negotiations.

Into the nineteenth century, the strength of Indian inhabitants and the play of imperial rivalries deflected frontier relations away from prior histories. As competition between European rivals heated up, what had been divergent patterns of intercultural relations on the part of French, Spanish, English, and American regimes converged. Especially for Spanish, English, and American representatives, the shift in the character of frontiers meant unprecedented accommodations with Indian cohabitants. So long as European colonial domains brushed up against one another, Indians who occupied the contested lands between were better able to deflect imperial powers from their original purposes and devise economic, diplomatic, and personal relations that, if not entirely on Indian ground, at least rested on more common ground.

This argument for a confluence of accommodationist frontiers near the confluence of rivers runs against one of the older currents in early American history. That course involves the assignment of essential and static features to colonial societies and their frontiers. The source of this view flows back to the seventeenth and eighteenth centuries, although it was most strikingly voiced by one of nineteenth-century America's most famous historians: "Spanish civilization crushed the Indian; English civilization scorned and neglected him; French civilization embraced and cherished him." So Francis Parkman summarized the divergent patterns that characterized North America's major colonial frontiers. On most subjects, Parkman's work, even more than Frederick Jackson Turner's, has been discredited by withering attacks. Yet Parkman's encapsulation of immutable frontier relations surprisingly survives and, in a modified version, still informs the opening chapters of many American history textbooks. In challenging this "neo-Parkmanism," I do not mean to discount persisting differences in frontier relations. But the lesson of frontiers and borderlands in the confluence region spotlights an alternative trajectory in which intercultural relations shifted and for a time flowed together.[7]

The tide of intercultural relations turned in the years after 1800. In the first decade of the nineteenth century, the Louisiana Purchase gave the United States control over both the east and west banks of the Mississippi River. The confluence was now truly American, although this transfer quickly jeopardized the region's status as the true American confluence. For a few years after the takeover by the United States, foreign intrigue, particularly the continuing interest of the British in the region, preserved a quasi-borderland situation and promoted a degree of accommodation between Americans and Indians in the middle of the continent. The book's final two chapters, however, describe how the balance of power in the confluence region shifted decisively away from its various Indian inhabitants. After the War of 1812, the focus of imperial rivalry swung far to the west, and Indians lost European partners to play off against Americans. Very rapidly, the eclipse of borderlands doomed the accommodations that had characterized eighteenth-century frontiers in the confluence region. The interplay of collisions and collusions that had marked previous frontiers tipped decisively toward the former. Rather than inclusive relations born of delicate negotiations, Americans increasingly dictated their exclusive occupations. During the 1820s and 1830s, as newcomers continued to pour into the region and as Indians were evicted from the meeting point of rivers, the American confluence ceased to be the meeting point of peoples that it had long been.

Coincident with the demise of borderlands was the emergence of the region as a place of border states. With the achievement of statehood for Missouri in 1821 and the removal of Indians from within its borders during the 1820s, the Missouri frontier closed. The state of Missouri shifted from *being* a frontier to *having* a frontier. But in the years immediately before Missouri entered the American union and in the decades that followed, it became the focal point of the strife between "free" and "slave" states. Missouri's entrance into the United States nearly split the American republic in two. The state remained on the front lines in the gathering conflict between "North" and "South," while also serving as the chief staging ground for continuing American expansion to the west. Historically the place where north, south, east, and west connected, the American confluence looked more and more like it would be the site at which the United States divided.

Note on Terminology

Although "American confluence" and "confluence region" are terms of my invention, I have, for the most part, adopted contemporary designations for the various groups that moved to and through the area in the eighteenth and nineteenth centuries. That decision, I realize, brings its own set of naming problems. As Stuart Banner points out, "It is no longer in fashion, for instance, to limit the term 'American' to English-speaking people from the United States—and there were at that time a few groups in the area who might have had equally plausible claims to the name." To be fairer to the other groups whom we now see as equally American, I toyed with employing Frank Lloyd Wright's term for those from the United States—"Usonians." Alas, Wright's designation has never caught on and, more problematic, it would clash with contemporary usage that did exclusively assign American to people from the United States. Likewise, following contemporary usage and now conventional historical practice, I label French-speaking colonists as "French," which is what they usually called themselves, even though, as Banner also notes, many had lived in North America their entire lives.[8]

American Confluence

I.

Openings

Not until the end of the seventeenth century did European colonists establish a permanent presence on the east bank of the Mississippi River between the mouths of the Missouri and Ohio rivers; not until the middle of the eighteenth century did Europeans found a town on the western side of the Mississippi in the confluence region. But a frontier history of the American confluence need not wait for the arrival of colonizers from overseas. Long before the intrusion of Europeans, Indians moved up and down the rivers and in and out of the region. With waterways acting as conveyors, their confluence became North America's most prominent meeting point. From these minglings emerged new peoples and new ways.

Too often, frontier histories dismiss the precolonial past as mere prehistory. That is unfortunate, for it leaves so much of the history of the place and its people out. Just as Europeans who came to the confluence of the Missouri, Ohio, and Mississippi drew on discrete regional cultures and divergent prior colonialisms, so, too, the Indians of the area came from different places at different times, speaking dissimilar languages and bearing disparate traditions. In short, like Europeans from various kingdoms, these Indians of diverse backgrounds brought

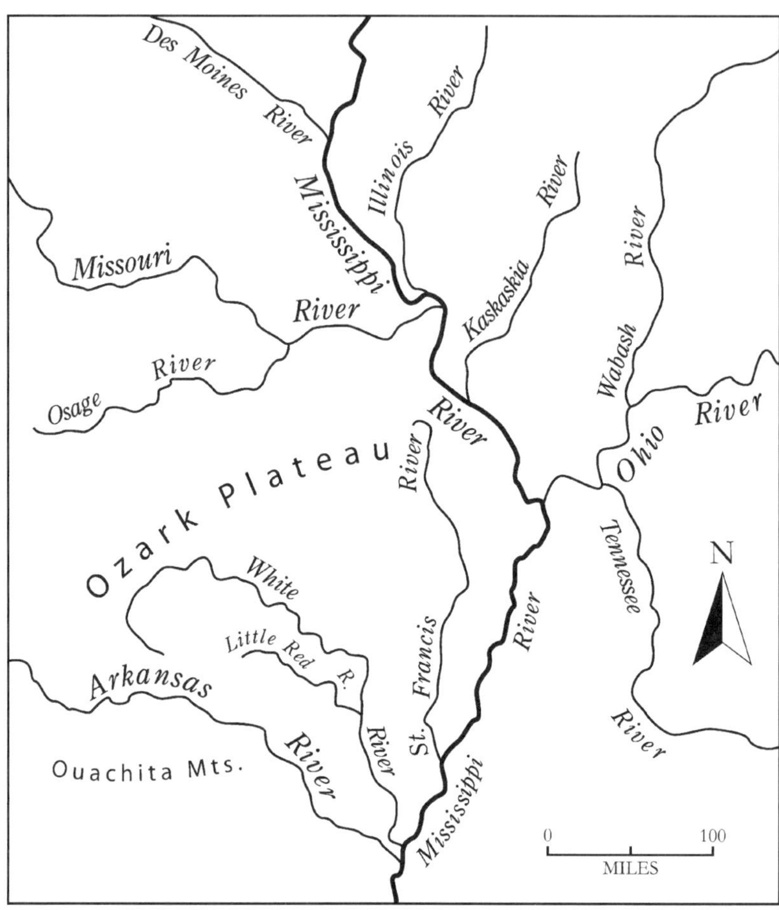

Map 1. Physical Geography of the Confluence Region.

distinct histories that later molded their responses to colonial intruders.

Close encounters in the period before direct and sustained colonization also shaped the frontiers that opened between Indians and Europeans. In the 1540s, Spanish seekers ventured near the confluence region. The impact of European things reverberated across the area in the seventeenth century, although only in the 1670s did French explorers find the Mississippi and its major tributaries. In the decades that followed, a few hundred Frenchmen settled on the eastern side of the Mississippi, while a handful of missionaries and fur traders crossed the river and traveled up the Missouri. These settlements and explorations laid the basis for immense French claims in the Mississippi valley. Vast claims, however, in no way signaled colonial domination of the confluence region before the middle of the eighteenth century. Rather, the Osages, benefiting from their positioning between woodlands and grasslands, between Indians to their east and west, and between French and Spanish orbits, made themselves the foremost power in the lower Missouri valley.

Prior Occupants

When Europeans first came into the area where the Missouri and Ohio rivers join the Mississippi, they found Indians living in scores of villages. In what is now Illinois lived a loose confederacy of Algonquin-speaking tribes who later gave their name to the state. The Illinois, whose domain stretched into parts of what are now Iowa, Missouri, and Wisconsin, inhabited more than sixty towns. Included within the confederacy, which had no formal political structure, were Kaskaskias, Cahokias, Peorias, Michigameas, Moingwenes, and Tamaroas. Neighboring groups to the north, south, and east included Sac and Fox, Shawnees, Kickapoos, Mascoutens, Piankashaws, Weas, and Miamis. Across the Mississippi in what is now Missouri lived various Siouan-speaking peoples: Otos, Iowas, Quapaws, Missouris, and Osages. At the entrance of Europeans, the last of these, the Osages, were the most populous and powerful nation in the confluence region.[1]

Viewing the confluence region's Indians as people without history, European newcomers slighted the dynamism of the precolonial past. Before Europeans arrived in the confluence region, people came and went, and cultures rose and fell. What drew the earliest inhabitants was an environment rich in wildlife. By 8000 BCE, however, changes in climate along with the activities of human predators had resulted in the extinction of a number of species of large mammals upon which hunters had previously depended. As the supply of certain game thinned, some people moved on, while others made do. Archaeological records suggest that in the ensuing "archaic" period inhabitants displayed more diversity and developed a heightened sense of territoriality. The region warmed and cooled and experienced long periods of drier and wetter times. These changes continued to force people to adapt. Yet, even in this distant past, inhabitants did not simply let the "environment" happen to them; they also changed it, most dramatically by burning forests to improve their yields from hunting and gathering. Even more decisive changes came about two thousand years ago during a cooler and wetter period with the introduction of the cultivation of seed crops. From about 300 BCE to 300 CE, an elaborate ceremonialism developed among the cultivators of the Mississippi valley. The climate again entered a less favorable era, bringing smaller yields and diminished ceremonialism. Around 900 began several centuries of generally wetter and cooler years, which triggered a new wave of comings and goings and ushered the rise of a more complex culture.[2]

Climatic change supported the growing of maize, which after spreading from Mesoamerica to North America became the centerpiece for what has come to be called "Mississippian" culture. At its peak in the eleventh and twelfth century, Mississippian sites stretched from the Atlantic Ocean and the Gulf of Mexico north into the Ohio River valley and west beyond the Mississippi into what is now Oklahoma. No political bonds linked villagers across this vast domain, but the exchange of products and ideas fostered cultural similarities. At the base of these commonalities was a subsistence that drew heavily on the cultivation and consumption of maize. Although related to today's corn, the Mississippians' maize possessed a higher proportion of minerals and vitamins and packed a greater caloric punch. That allowed Mississippians a more secure subsistence and facilitated the development of more complex and stable polities and more urbanized societies.[3]

Along with maize, mounds distinguished Mississippian culture. By the tenth century, various Indian groups had constructed large earthen works at a number of locations in the Mississippi and Ohio valleys and across what is now the southeastern United States. These mounds came in three basic shapes: ridgetop, conical, and platform. The last of these most closely resembled the great pyramidal platforms of Mesoamerican societies, suggesting that architectural forms had spread north along with agricultural techniques. As in Mesoamerica, these platforms likely served as elevated bases for religious ceremonies.[4]

The largest cluster and most immense mounds were found in the heart of the confluence region. On the west bank of the Mississippi, just south of the mouth of the Missouri, at the site of St. Louis, were twenty-six man-made earthworks that later provided the metropolis with one of its nicknames, "Mound City." Yet the dirt pyramids on the west bank of the Mississippi were dwarfed in number and size by the 120 mounds located just across the river. This was Cahokia, the largest Mississippian site in eastern North America, indeed, at its peak, by far the largest urban center north of Mexico. Estimates suggest that Cahokia's mounds contained fifty-five million cubic feet of dirt. The biggest, Monk's Mound, alone rested on twenty-two million cubic feet of earth and rose almost one hundred feet up from its more than seven hundred thousand square foot base. Moving so much earth was obviously a massive undertaking that required hundreds of thousands of hours of labor. Such a task could only have been accomplished by a considerable population. This Cahokia certainly had, for in the eleventh and twelfth centuries, it was home to between ten and twenty thousand people spread across a five square mile metropolis.[5]

Sustaining such a dense population required an immense amount of food, and demand eventually strained local resources. Maize was the most important element in Cahokia diets, although the subsistence of residents also depended on the cultivation of other seed crops, the gathering of wild plants, and the hunting of wildlife. Through the eleventh and twelfth centuries, this mixture met the needs of Cahokia's bulging population. Already, however, some vital resources were showing signs of wear or becoming more scarce. Wildlife populations diminished, soils deteriorated, and, perhaps most immediately visible, forests thinned. Having cleared the bottomland closest to their town of most of its trees, Cahokia's residents began gathering their firewood and constructing their houses from the oaks and hickories that grew in adjacent uplands. Adding to the pressure on wood supplies, Cahokias built a series of stockades, again made of oak and hickory logs, around the perimeter of their settlement in the twelfth century. Extending for miles, these fortifications consumed tens of thousands of trees and further depleted surrounding forests.[6]

Drawing resources from neighboring regions was not new in Cahokia; in fact, Cahokias had long depended on exchanges not only with nearby villages but also with people at considerable distance. In the vicinity of Cahokia were perhaps fifty villages scattered across the area's lowlands. Many were in present-day Illinois; others were across the Mississippi in what is now Missouri. On both sides, the river was a corridor, not a border, and villagers looked to Cahokia as a ceremonial center. From deer remains excavated at Cahokia, which included few lower limb, skull, or neck bones, archaeologists have concluded that the animals were likely killed away from Cahokia, with only prime cuts transported to the great city. This, they suggest, may have been a tribute payment made by subordinated people to the religious and political authorities at Cahokia. Although the terms of exchange remain unclear, the extent of the trade networks that radiated from Cahokia are more certain—and very impressive. In addition to meat from neighboring settlements, Cahokia received a variety of exotic goods from greater distances. From sites around Cahokia, digs have recovered at least nineteen kinds of marine shells that originated in the Gulf of Mexico and Atlantic Oceans. As Cahokia's population grew in the tenth and eleventh centuries, the quantity of these shells, which were used to decorate clothing and ornaments, also increased. Important as these imports from the south and east were, Cahokia's trade to the north and west was of a greater volume, with the Mississippi, Missouri, and Illinois rivers serving as the primary avenues of long-distance exchange.[7]

For reasons that have engendered much speculation, if no definitive explanation, Cahokia's trade and population began to drop around the middle of the twelfth century, and these declines steepened during the thirteenth century. No evidence has been found of a single event that started Cahokia's fall. The construction of stockades indicates the possibility of a military threat, but the enemy has not been identified, nor have archaeologists recovered records of a decisive battle. More likely, changes in climate and reduction of resources contributed to a gradual decline. A warming trend from the mid-twelfth to the mid-thirteenth centuries followed by a substantial cooling period undoubtedly caused problems for Cahokia's farmers. Apparently, some of Cahokia's neighbors adapted more readily to changes in the growing season by planting new varieties of corn and mixing in beans. By contrast, Cahokia's growers kept to old ways, leading to diminished corn harvests and depleted fields (which lacked the nitrogen that beans would have returned to the soil). As food supplies decreased and other necessities, such as game and timber, became harder to find, the glory days of Cahokia faded. Through the thirteenth and fourteenth century, its population dwindled, not by starvation but by emigration. To where, we do not know, although some ex-Cahokias probably assimilated into neighboring villages. Others likely ventured further, lured by the ample bison herds that had spread across the grasslands west of the Mississippi River (including into the western parts of what is now Missouri). By the end of the fourteenth century or the beginning of the fifteenth, Cahokia had been entirely depopulated, its magnificent mounds abandoned.[8]

In crossing the Mississippi, refugees from Cahokia moved among some people with whom they had long-standing trade and kinship ties and others who were less familiar to them. By the fifteenth century, the area that became Missouri was home to a variety of groups, including possibly the Osages. According to the Osages' creation myth, their origin traced to the mating of the first Osage man, who came down from the sun, and the first Osage woman, who hailed from the moon. This coupling produced six offspring, three boys and three girls, who in pairs explored the wilderness in all directions. Subduing the other people they encountered, the progenitors of the Osages came to call themselves the *Wha-sha-she* (daring men) and that became the name of the people who followed them (at least until the eighteenth century, when Europeans started referring to them as the Osages). But although the Osages explained their arrival in the Missouri valley this way, historians generally subscribe to a different tale in which the Osages, along with other Dhegiha speakers of the Siouan language family, migrated from the east. Supporting the theory of a joint westward migration are the linguistic similarities between the Osage, Omaha, Ponca, Kansa, and Quapaw and their shared oral traditions of a great move. In one version, more powerful Indians pushed the Dhegihan speakers from their homelands east of the Mississippi; in another, the lure of game pulled them west. In both, a split occurred upon reaching the river. The Quapaw went south, making a new homeland along the Arkansas River. The other groups continued up the Missouri, with the Osages breaking off to establish towns along the river that still bears their name. Yet scholars disagree about just when this relocation occurred. Some suggest the move took place as early as the eighth century, even before Cahokia had emerged as a major center. Other scholars, however, date the migration much later (perhaps as late as the seventeenth century), in which case the Osages and related groups lay outside of Cahokia's orbit and provided no haven for those who left it.[9]

Certainly, though, by the middle of the seventeenth century, the Osages were in place in what is now central and southwestern Missouri. After the relocation, their way of life combined traditions brought from the east with adaptations to new environs. Ecologically, the region into which the Osages had moved was a transition zone between eastern forests and western plains. Thanks to nearby forests, the Osages were able to retain many of their woodland customs. In contrast to most prairie dwellers who favored earthen lodges or buffalo-skin tipis, the Osages continued to build wood-framed longhouses. In personal appearance as well, the Osages maintained many of their woodland ways. Men, for example, stuck with the scalp-lock hairstyles that were typical among many eastern Indians. Women still cultivated the familiar mix of maize, beans, squash, and pumpkins. At the same time, the Osages altered some routines to take advantage of grassland resources. If dwellings were still wood-framed, they were now covered with mats made of woven marsh grasses. Seasonal routines also shifted. After planting crops in the spring, the

Osages left their villages to hunt buffalo on the plains during the summer and fall. In the woodlands, extended hunting had been confined to the fall and winter months. But in the Missouri valley, Osage men, with assistance from women and children, pursued buffalo and a variety of other animals over longer periods of the year. This was a pattern more typical of plains Indian groups, although the Osages never gave up cultivating the soil as their more nomadic western neighbors had. That the Osages sometimes referred to themselves as the "Children of the Middle Waters" was fitting, for the blending of woodland and grassland ways made theirs a culture in between.[10]

As it would in coming centuries for other Indian groups and American pioneers, the Osages' move west brought significant changes to their way of life and sense of selves. As hunting took on a greater role—both in terms of time spent doing it and in terms of its contribution to diets, the relations among men and between men and women shifted. As hunters, men gained power as their realm gained importance. True, Osage women accompanied hunters and played crucial roles skinning and butchering animals, but these were secondary roles. Their chief concern and authority remained the cultivation of crops and the preparation of food. If this work took less of the Osages' time than it had in the east, it still consumed a good deal of the annual calendar and still provided a large chunk of their subsistence. The hunt, though, was the primary domain of men, and leadership of it was left to men. At first, these hunt leaders were also the headmen of clans or moieties. Westering again brought gradual change, however: as hunting became more prominent, leadership, at least on the hunt, passed to individuals chosen for their particular skills.

What stayed the same was the Osages' commitment to sharing, reciprocity, and limited material accumulations. In buffalo hunting, for example, the man who killed an animal claimed it. Successful hunters, however, did not hoard their take. For one thing, Osage hunters recognized that theirs was a communal activity and that killing game required coordination among groups of men, while preparing it depended on the assistance of groups of women. For the Osages, as for their neighbors in both the woodlands and the prairies, hunters earned status by making gifts of meat to men who had not killed an animal and to families who had no hunters to support them. By contrast, lack of generosity cost men (and women) the respect of fellow villagers. Besides, if not shared, much meat would otherwise go to waste. That ethos and that logic carried over to the possession of other property. Moreover, frequent travels dampened desire for the acquisition of excess belongings. Most families traveled on foot with just their essentials, which were generally limited to some clothing and small tools.

Sharing and reciprocity did not mean that all were equal among the Osages. Prior to contact with Europeans, the Osages acknowledged no centralized tribal authority, but they had developed an elaborate clan system in which specific obligations and positions were tied to specific clans. Hereditary lines also largely determined the selection of village leaders, with each Osage town having two *Ga-hi-ge* (chiefs). These two held equal status and dominion in internal matters, although in dealings with outsiders, one assumed greater authority in times of war, while the other oversaw peaceful intercourse. The power of *Ga-hi-ge* was, however, hardly absolute. A council of respected elders weighed in on most decisions, and leaders understood that building consensus was essential before any enforceable commands could be issued. Moreover, while *Ga-hi-ge* and other persons of high status did keep a few additional sacred items such as pipes, shells, and medicine bundles, the accumulation of these possessions was not the measure of exalted position. Instead, rank and respect derived from the ability to give goods away to fellow villagers and from successful leadership of male endeavors such as hunting. For women, too, rank had its obligations. Ranking women assisted during births, illnesses, weddings, and feasts.

The mix of change and persistence served the Osages and their neighbors well. This was true for both long established groups and more recent migrants from the east. But already by the seventeenth century, the pressure for change was building as the impact of the European invasion of the Americas touched the Osages' homeland. For the Osages, their history of selective adaptations prepared them for the possibilities and dangers introduced by European colonialism, though only partially.

Prior Colonialisms

Not until the last decades of the seventeenth century did persons of European descent glimpse the abandoned mounds of Cahokia or wander into the countries of the Osages and their neighbors. By then, however, their distant presence had brought opportunities and disasters to the people who inhabited the region in which North America's major rivers converged. By then, too, the previous colonial experiences of the first Europeans prepared the ground for their encounters with the Osages and their neighbors. As with Indians, though, the prior colonialism of European intruders only partially equipped them for life at the intersection of the Mississippi, Missouri, and Ohio rivers.

As early as the 1540s, Europeans had come close to the confluence region. In 1541, the Spanish explorer Hernando de Soto had taken a party of Europeans, Africans, and Indians north and west from Florida into the lower Mississippi valley. Like other Spanish explorers in North America, de Soto hoped to duplicate the treasures found—and taken—by Cortez in Mexico and Pizarro in the Andes. Indeed, de Soto was a veteran of the conquest of the Incas. About the same time that de Soto set out to search the lands north and west of Florida for cities filled with silver and gold, Francisco Vásquez de Coronado conducted a similar expedition that went north from Mexico to the Rio Grande valley, and then on to the western plains. But Coronado's quest for the riches of the fabled Seven Cities of Cibola reached an end at a modest Indian village in what is now western Kansas, still some distance from the country of the Osages. Likewise, de Soto's party stopped well south of Cahokia's abandoned mounds.[11]

Finding no precious metals, Spanish explorers pulled back, though not before they instigated great changes among the Indians they encountered—and among many, including the Osages, who as yet had no direct contact with any Europeans. First and worst were the diseases Europeans brought with them and which then spread ahead of them through nonhuman carriers like birds, bugs, and squirrels. These microbes had been a decisive factor in the Spanish conquest of the Aztecs, and diseases wreaked demographic catastrophe among many of the Indians in and around de Soto's path. Waves of epidemics resulted in sharp declines of the Indian population of what is now the southeastern United States in the last half of the sixteenth century. For the moment, the Osages and their immediate neighbors escaped the ravages of smallpox and other deadly illnesses. To an extent, they benefited from the reduction of other people to the south and east of them. In those settled areas that had become virtual no man's lands, fewer hunters now pursued prey, allowing the population of deer and other game to increase.[12]

What allowed the Osages to hunt more effectively and at greater distance from their villages was another import from Europe: the horse. Like germs, horses moved beyond the spheres of European colonizers. And like germs, their spread was not controlled by those who introduced them back to the Americas. Early in the seventeenth century, the Spanish colony in New Mexico became a target for Apache and Comanche raiders, with horses being a favorite target. Some of these stolen horses became wild and proliferated on the plains. Others moved along the circuits of intertribal trading and raiding by which the Apaches and Comanches exchanged goods with plains Indians. Horses came to the Osages during the seventeenth century and opened up remarkable opportunities. On horseback, Indian hunters could travel farther, carry heavier loads, and kill more game, especially buffalo.[13]

With horses, Osages enjoyed a more abundant life, but this prosperity posed a challenge to established ways. Compared with some plains people, who became nomadic hunters after they acquired horses, the equine revolution was less far-reaching for the Osages. As in earlier times, Osage women cultivated fields, and all stayed near their villages for months at a time. In adapting horses, the Osages sought to fit a fresh element into a familiar context. In referring to the horse as *ka-wa*, meaning "mystery dog," they showed this trait. Yet a familiar frame did not make horses and dogs the same, and it did not eliminate the cultural change that horses instigated. On horseback, small bands of hunters could pursue game more swiftly and killing became more of an individual, as opposed to a group, activity. No longer did whole villages need to be enlisted in the actual hunt, and no longer did the activity require the previous degree of coordination and leadership. As in pre-equestrian times, Osage hunters remained committed to sharing meat, but they did not distribute horses equally. Some men had more, others less, introducing a new form of inequality into Osage life.[14]

If the arrival of horses presented opportunities and challenges, the appearance of Europeans multiplied these manifold. From the Spanish, at least indirectly, had come deadly microbes, wondrous horses, and perhaps even a few other exotic items of European origin. But Spanish explorers had never reached the Osages' villages, and Spanish colonial settlements and missions remained far to the southeast in Florida and to the southwest in New Mexico. Direct contact between the Indians of the lower Missouri valley and Europeans arrived only in the last decades of the seventeenth century. These newcomers, however, came from the north, not the south, and they represented France, not Spain.

In many respects, the colonial designs of Spain and France started out alike and, through the seventeenth century, continued to resemble one another in certain respects. The Catholic monarchs who ruled both countries hoped their American empires would yield riches, preferably in the form of gold and silver. In this scheme, colonies enriched monarchies, but they were not meant to attract large numbers of colonists from the mother countries. Among those who were given official encouragement and royal support were missionaries of various Catholic orders, dispatched by both Spain and France to bring Christianity to the Indians. Lacking such inducements, relatively few lay men—and far fewer lay women—migrated from Spain and France to the Americas. Accordingly, colonial populations were small, occupying tiny pockets of the vast territorial empires that Spain and France each claimed to rule. In fact, across the hinterlands that Spain and France presumed to possess, Indian groups still predominated and could dominate presumptuous colonizers who ventured too far or behaved too haughtily.[15]

Differing circumstances of colonization, however, created divergent colonial regimes. For Spain, the expectations of empire were largely fulfilled during the sixteenth and seventeenth centuries. The conquest of Aztecs and Andes produced an enormous bonanza, and the discovery of rich silver mines in northern Mexico further swelled the royal treasury. Subsequent northward expansion had not been as profitable. Because it boasted no precious metals, seventeenth-century New Mexico remained a sparsely populated outpost, subject to frequent raids by Apaches and Comanches and periodic rebellions by Pueblo villagers. Still, even on this isolated periphery of Spain's empire, missionaries, primarily Franciscans, worked assiduously to convert natives, and with great success, or so it seemed from the impressive numbers of baptisms that priests recorded in the first half of the seventeenth century. France, by contrast, had less to show for its initial colonization. In terms of gold and silver, Canada was no Mexico. It was, in fact, more like New Mexico. The chief settlement, Quebec, had been founded about the same time as Santa Fe in New Mexico, and throughout the seventeenth century it, too, was an unimpressive outpost.[16]

Beyond their shared isolation, important differences distinguished Spain's northern periphery (New Mexico) from both the core (Quebec) and hinterlands of New France. In New Mexico, as in Mexico, Spanish colonists tended to reside in towns and place their fields around these clustered dwellings. This pattern diminished the isolation of Spanish colonists from one another, if not from the distant capital of New Spain. French colonists in Canada, by contrast, did not cluster in towns. Most *habitants* lived on farmsteads that extended along both sides of the St. Lawrence River in narrow strips.[17]

The French also showed greater willingness to venture into an expanding hinterland. By the middle of the seventeenth century, a few Frenchmen had made their way to and around the Great Lakes or what was called the *pays d'en haut* (upper country).

Many were Jesuit missionaries. Their ends—turning Indians away from "heathenish" practices and converting them to Christianity—were the same as Franciscans, but their means were not. Both Spanish and French missionaries spoke of "reducing" Indians to Christianity and civilization. But where the Spanish tended to bring Indians into missions and treat them as subjugated people, French Jesuits displayed more flexibility in trying to save Indians who had in no way been reduced. Founding missions in regions where Indians recognized no colonial domination, French fathers had to be more subtle as they went about undermining indigenous beliefs and native spiritual leaders.[18]

Others who traveled up rivers and across the Great Lakes were traders, and these, too, interacted with Indians in ways that were quite unlike the patterns of Spanish colonists. Some of these traders were *habitants* who supplemented their income by wintering in Indian villages. But these *hivernants* were soon outnumbered by full-time traders, both *voyageurs*, who were sanctioned by French officials, and *coureurs de bois*, who operated outside the bounds of colonial authority. With or without licenses, these traders spent much of their time in Indian villages, where they lived not as *conquistadors* but as consorts.

Because European-born women were a small minority of both colonial populations, sexual relations became entwined with cross-cultural relations. The most obvious signature of these contacts was the growing number of mixed-race offspring in both New Spain and New France. Spanish suitors, however, often coerced the native partners who mothered *mestizo* children. Not so the French traders in the upper country. In search of furs, and dependent on Indians to provide them, French traders knew they had to cultivate close ties with native suppliers. In this, they understood that sexual relations were part of broader relationships. A native wife's work—in cultivating the soil and preparing skins—was crucial to the subsistence and commerce of traders. She also facilitated the connections by which a French trader successfully exchanged his wares for the skins proffered by his wife's kin. For their part, the wives of traders gained prestige as a conduit for European manufactures.

From these unions, too, were born *métis* offspring, who themselves became crucial intermediaries in intercultural trade and diplomacy.[19]

Although French officials frequently complained about the uncontrolled goings and dealings of traders, the political relations between the crown's agents and Indian allies paralleled and, indeed, played off the personal connections between traders and their wives' kin. In the first place, intercultural diplomacy was closely linked to intercultural economics. Finding no precious metals around Quebec or the Great Lakes, the French state remained dependent on fur exports for the revenues to underwrite colonial ventures. Fortunately, these lands boasted abundant populations of many mammals, especially the most coveted of all, beavers. No less than private traders then, the French state needed Indians to trap and truck. But here the interests of the state and of French traders did not always mesh with those of Indian partners. From the beginnings of French colonization in the St. Lawrence valley and extending across the Great Lakes region, Indians showed an eagerness to acquire various European goods and contraptions. But they were determined to conduct exchange by their own rules and for their own ends. That meant subordinating purely economic considerations to broader personal and political ties. And it meant French officials had to participate in elaborate rituals of exchange and intercultural diplomacy that displayed the mutual respect and generosity expected between family members.[20]

To be sure, French officials were by no means entirely happy with the extensive protocol and expensive offering of gifts that accompanied their dealings with Indian partners. In other circumstances, they might have preferred to follow the Spanish example of settling among, missionizing, and extracting labor from subjugated Indians. If not through outright domination, the French would at least have liked to impose terms of trade that diminished the cost of presents and put exchanges on a sounder and more straightforward commercial footing. But along the St. Lawrence and even more so around the Great Lakes, the French operated under circumstances that demanded they accommodate Indian expectations about intercultural relations.

Thanks to common interests born of mutual weakness and creative misunderstandings turned to constructive purposes, these accommodations reached a new level in the western Great Lakes. Here the frailty of the French, so few in number, was obvious. But many of the Indians with whom the French interacted were also newcomers to the region and were also in a weakened position. Like the Osages, these Indians, lumped together as Algonquians, had been driven in the late seventeenth century from homelands to the east. Their numbers diminished by warfare with Iroquois invaders, refugees had scattered, before regrouping in the lands south of Lake Superior and west of Lake Michigan. But unlike the Osages, who kept their kinship lines intact while moving west, the various Algonquian villagers who reassembled between the Great Lakes and the upper Mississippi valley did so in towns that were far more diverse than those they had left behind. In many cases, existing kinship ties and established lines of authority had fragmented, leaving already depleted tribes even more vulnerable. Under these circumstances, the French appeared not only as a supplier of exotic goods, but also as a useful mediator of inter-Indian disputes. Conveying their desires through kinship metaphors, Algonquians turned to the French "father" for assistance. For French officials, who fashioned ties with refugee communities, the language suggested the authority of the French king and his agents over allied Indians. Algonquians, however, understood a father's position not as an omnipotent patriarch but as a generous provider. Such misunderstandings threatened to undermine peaceful relations and political bonds between French and Algonquians. At times, it did. And yet, in the last decades of the seventeenth century, French and Algonquians seemed to have found considerable common ground in the western Great Lakes.[21]

Close Encounters of the First Kind

Even as these symbiotic relations emerged in the western Great Lakes, French eyes fastened on new lands for missionaries and traders to work. Behind official support for exploration and expansion lay hopes of finding finally a source of precious metals or the long sought water route across the North American continent. For the French crown, the profits from controlling a waterway to the Pacific were far more attractive than any that might come from duties on furs. Every river and lake, it was hoped, would prove a "Northwest Passage" to the riches of Asia. Thus when French traders and missionaries in the Great Lakes passed on word of a great river to the west, colonial officials were eager to learn more about where these waters flowed. From Lake Superior, one priest wrote that local Indians referred to this river as "Messipi." Its source was unknown, although some speculated that its mouth was back at the English settlements in Virginia. Others guessed more optimistically that the Messipi, or what became known as the Mississippi, an Algonquian designation for the "father of waters," emptied into the Pacific.[22]

Prospects were alluring enough to overcome the long-standing objections of French authorities to westward explorations and colonial expansions into the interior of North America. Before the 1670s, Jean-Baptiste Colbert, the French minister of the marine, who oversaw the development of overseas colonies, resisted such moves. Colbert feared that the diversion of resources and manpower to the Great Lakes and beyond left the still underdeveloped St. Lawrence heartland of New France even more vulnerable to attack from neighboring English settlements. But while furs alone did not entice French imperial officials, word of a possible waterway across the continent encouraged a change of view. And so in May 1673, an expedition set out from the Straits of Mackinac in search of this river of dreams.[23]

Combining secular and religious impulses, the expedition was led by an experienced trader, Louis Jolliet, accompanied by a Jesuit priest, Father Jacques Marquette, and a few boatmen. Following Lake Michigan south, the party found its way to the Illinois River and then reached the Mississippi. In two birchbark canoes, they then proceeded downstream. Very quickly, the explorers learned that birchbark canoes, so well suited to travel on the Great Lakes, were less satisfactory on the Mississippi. One problem, according to Marquette, was that the fish in the Mississippi were "so big," that, in the event of a collision, one's "Canoe was like[ly] to be broke[n] into Pieces." Big fish, however, did not deter the party, as it passed the points where the Missouri and Ohio rivers joined the Mississippi. What did stop them was the determination that the Mississippi flowed neither toward Virginia nor to the Pacific but rather to the Gulf of Mexico. Concerned that going on would put them in a sea of unwelcoming Spaniards, the explorers turned back north in mid-July.[24]

In addition to fish of considerable size, the Jolliet–Marquette expedition encountered numerous Indians during their brief journey down the Illinois and Mississippi rivers. For his part, Marquette, like fellow Catholic missionaries, introduced himself by proclaiming his faith in Christ. These vocal declarations were fused with dramatic gesturing by the mysteriously black-robed, cross-wielding missionary. How much Marquette's audiences understood of this vocal and visual display, we do not know. Nor can we truly discern what Indians made of Jolliet's professions of the power of the French king. For their part, Indians may have been impressed by some of the objects carried by Marquette and his confederates, but they were not awed by the newcomers. Perhaps, even in their first direct encounter with Frenchmen, Indians in the confluence region recognized their potential as purveyors of exotic goods and as protectors against Iroquois, Sioux, and Osage enemies. But any incorporations of French spiritual powers and material products were to be done on Indian terms. That meant introducing the French to the protocols of Indian diplomacy, which in the confluence region focused on the calumet ceremony. Accordingly, as Marquette recorded, Indians performed elaborate songs and dances upon greeting the French expedition. In time, the calumet, a long-stemmed feathered pipe, emerged. Next, the dancers "salute[d] the Manitou" by "inhaling the smoke" and blowing it "upon the Manitou, as if . . . offering it incense." Marquette (and following missionaries) did not fully appreciate the symbolic meanings of these rites, but French newcomers understood that Indians attached great import to the singing, dancing, smoking, gift giving, feasting, and *sharing* of the pipe. Time-consuming though the ceremonies were, participation was essential. Failure to do so risked offending Indian hosts, in which case hostilities might be provoked, souls unsaved, and negotiations about political and commercial relations aborted.[25]

Nine years after the Marquette–Jolliet corps retreated from the confluence region, the French mounted a more ambitious expedition down the Mississippi under the command of René Robert Cavelier, Sieur de la Salle. A protégé of the governor of New France, La Salle was granted a monopoly over the fur trade on the Mississippi and its tributaries, if he, at his own expense, followed the great river to its mouth. With a party of fifty-four French and Indian men, La Salle reached that destination on April 9, 1682, claiming possession of the river and its tributaries for France. Impressive on maps, the vast new colony, which La Salle named Louisiana for Louis XIV, had unknown boundaries and no colonists. After returning to France to promote the colony and recruit colonists, La Salle planned to come back to Louisiana, this time by sailing directly to the mouth of the Mississippi. But the small fleet that he led into the Gulf of Mexico in 1685 missed the entrance to the river and landed instead on the coast of Texas. Wandering north and east for two years in a vain search for the Mississippi, La Salle's starving crew mutinied and assassinated him in March 1687.[26]

So ended La Salle's journeys but not France's interest in the Mississippi and its tributaries. After La Salle's death, the colony of Louisiana became the responsibility of a crown-chartered "Company of the West." The company gained La Salle's monopoly on trade in and out of the Mississippi River and, in return, pledged to secure France's hold by settling six thousand whites and three thousand blacks in the colony. As these plans for peopling the lower Mississippi valley took shape, adventurers continued to scout the upper reaches of the river. These explorers, too, were a mixed lot with mixed motives; mineral seekers, fur traders, and soul savers sometimes shared canoes. All remained mindful of the possibility that, if not the Mississippi, then perhaps one of its western tributaries might prove the long desired waterway to the Pacific.

Of the streams that flowed into the Mississippi from the west, none generated more excitement than the broad river that Father Marquette claimed was known by local Indians as "Pekitanoui." That term meant "muddy water," which seemed to Marquette and subsequent French explorers an apt description for a river whose turbid color contrasted sharply with and then disturbed the Mississippi's clearer flow. Indian informants at the point where Pekitanoui entered the Mississippi told him it came "from very far in the northwest." From these Indians, who Marquette knew as the Missouri ("people of the canoes"), the Jesuit learned that one of the tributaries of the Pekitanoui flowed out of a small lake. This body of water was also the source of another river that ran west to the ocean, which Marquette hopefully concluded must be the "Red or California sea." La Salle spoke as well with Missouri Indians, from whom he passed on a slightly amended version about its source. A "ten or twelve days" voyage upriver, he was told, took one to "a mountain where it rises," and from there, one "saw great ships."[27]

Although the explorers who followed Marquette and La Salle did not find their way to the Pacific, they did gather information about the Pekitanoui. For the most part, explorers continued to repeat the view that the river had its origins in "a great lake, which has still another outlet" that "falls into the Western sea." Still, further explorations, including forays upriver, did change ideas about the Pekitanoui, not least its name, which was more frequently given as the "river of the Missouris" or simply the Missouri River. Speculating on the Missouri's source, its considerable flow, and the way its waters muddied the Mississippi, more than one traveler suggested that perhaps the Mississippi was, in fact, a tributary of the Missouri. Much attention also fastened on the animals along the river, especially the buffalo, whose "abundance," according to a 1709 account, "exceeds all imagination." Even more consideration fell on the fourteen "very populous tribes" who lived along the river. Of particular interest were their relations with one another and with the Spanish to the south and west. By 1700, the French had learned that the Pawnees and the Wichitas, whose villages were situated to the west of the Missouri's northward turn, had horses with

Spanish brands. That caught the attention of French traders who hoped the river would provide a convenient route, if not to the Pacific, then at least to Spanish settlements in New Mexico.[28]

Conjecture about the Missouri's course and the connections to be made upstream continued to animate early eighteenth-century discussions, but of more immediate interest to the French were the peoples and products of the lower valley. These Indians, primarily the Missouri with villages near the lowest part of the now eponymous river and the Osages a bit further upstream, came into the earliest and most sustained contact with French adventurers. That made them the easiest targets for missionary efforts and the most likely candidates to be drawn into an economic and political alliance of the kind that French and Algonquians were creating in the western Great Lakes.

Of the two principal nations that occupied the lower Missouri valley, the Missouris seemed more willing to embrace the French. As Chiwere Siouan speakers, the Missouris' language was more closely related to the Iowas, Otos, and Winnebagos than to the Osages, whose tongue belonged to the Dhegihan branch of the Siouan language family. Still, in other respects, the Missouris and Osages resembled one another. Most obvious were the similar subsistence mix and seasonal calendars that each group maintained. Missouris and Osages also found common cause against common enemies, principally Algonquian-speaking groups across the Mississippi. Warfare with the Illinois nation took a toll on both the Osages and the Missouris, who, according to a French observer in the 1680s, were now "glad to keep on the good side" of their former adversaries. This, added the observer, opened an opportunity for French traders, for the Osages and Missouris were "in need of hatchets, knives, and awls, and other necessary things." But the latter, being fewer in number, had the greater need, not only for trade goods but also for the protection that a French-mediated alliance might afford them against Algonquian enemies.[29]

The first French traders arrived in 1683, and the following years saw increasing numbers of *coureurs de bois* visiting Missouri towns. For the Missouris, as for other Indian groups brought into European exchange networks, the goods offered by

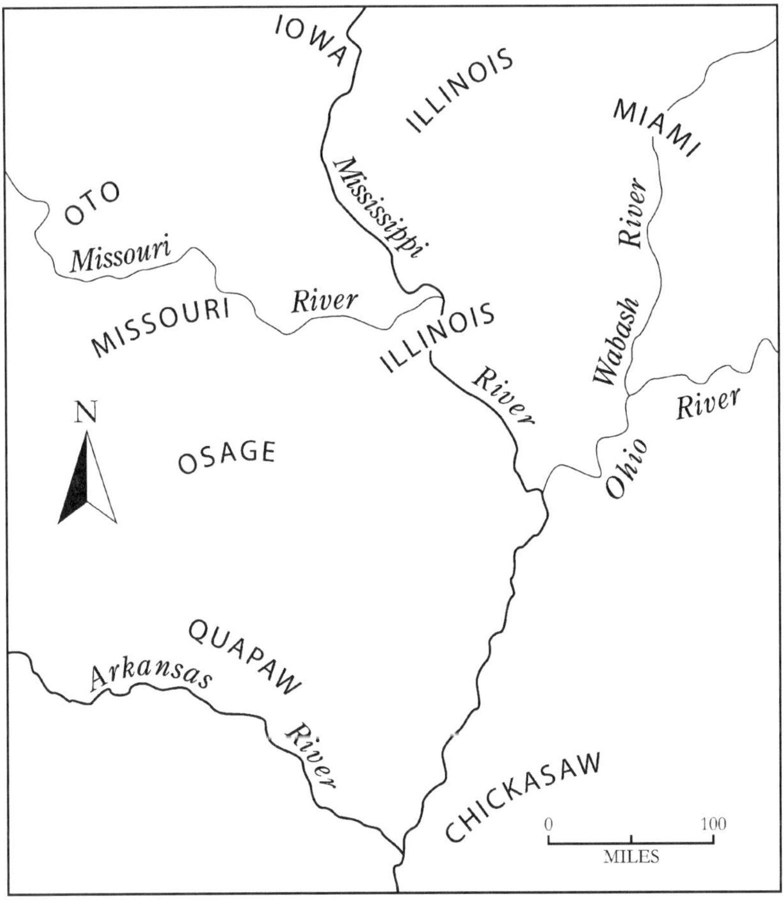

Map 2. Major Indian Nations in the Confluence Region, c. 1700.

French traders appealed for both symbolic and practical reasons. Glass beads, metal bells, and pieces of jewelry were attractive adornments, made more so by their exotic character. At the same time, iron implements, hoes, and pots eased burdens for women in cultivating soil and preparing food. Increasingly even more necessary for men were firearms, gunpowder, and lead balls. Without these the Missouris were at a disadvantage against enemies to the east who had access to French weapons. In return, the French wanted skins, especially beaver. Turned into hats, beaver pelts were much in fashion among western Europeans, who found them a useful and attractive adornment, made more so by their exotic character. Unfortunately, the lower Missouri valley did not boast winters that were long enough or cold enough to produce beavers with the thick, dark pelts that were most in demand. So instead of beavers, the Missouris principally supplied deerskins in great numbers, for it took twenty skins to secure a single musket.

The Osages also welcomed trade in these same items, but they enjoyed certain advantages that enabled them to resist being exclusively tied to French goods and a French alliance. First were numbers. With a population in various villages totaling more than five thousand, the Osages were considerably larger than the Missouris, and they outnumbered other neighboring groups as well. Second was geography. The first Osage villages on the west side of the Mississippi River were located close to the mouth of the Missouri, near where the Missouris had settled. Under pressure from Illinois Indians, who also crossed the river to hunt these lands, the Osages had moved west and south. Relocating their towns during the seventeenth century along what came to be called the Osage River, the Osages gained a buffer against attacks from the east. That situation also positioned them between French-connected groups to their east and Spanish-contacted ones to their west.[30]

Being between became the central fact of Osage life. Ecologically, as has been noted, the Osages adjusted their subsistence schedule to make use of the resources of both woodlands and grasslands. With firearms from French traders, Osage hunters and warriors could control game-rich territories to the west, whose Indian inhabitants—Wichita, Caddo, Pawnee, Kansa, and Quapaw—had less access to European-manufactured weapons. That dominance, in turn, gave the Osages more access to bison, which emerged as an increasingly significant element of Osage life. The buffalo remained secondary to deerskins as a trade commodity. More important for exchange purposes were the horses and mules that Osages took from plains people, and the people themselves, who were sold as slaves to the French. This represented something of a change, for previously the Osages ei-

Figure 2. Exotic items, such as this magnifying glass found at a Miami Indian site in present-day Illinois, were prominent in eighteenth-century trade between Europeans and Indians in the confluence region. Courtesy of the Autry National Center.

ther killed their captives (as part of mourning rituals) or adopted them (to "cover" the dead and replenish numbers).[31]

Staying between required that the Osages prevent French travelers and traders from making contact and initiating direct exchanges with nations up the Missouri and to their west. Thus in 1719, when Claude Charles DuTisné thought of going on to the Wichitas and Pawnees, the Osages thought otherwise. Only after DuTisné threatened to cut off all trade did the Osages allow him to go. But asserting their own power, the Osages let the departing party take only three muskets, and they sent a messenger ahead to warn the Pawnees that DuTisné was looking to enslave them. Evidently, the Pawnees believed the warning, for DuTisné received a hostile reception. Twice in four days among the Pawnees, angered Indians had "raised the tomahawk above my head," reported a shaken DuTisné.[32]

In spite of this and other incidents, which inspired some French officials to label the Osages "treacherous," the French and Osages found their own middle ground in the early decades of the eighteenth century. Trade was crucial to this accommodation. So was the military campaign that Osage warriors launched against the Illinois-based Fox in 1712. This was shortly after the Fox had attacked the French post at Detroit. Of course, the Osages went to war with the Fox for their own reasons. The Fox, after all, had been among the Indians who trespassed on what the Osages considered their Missouri valley hunting lands. But by joining the French, the Osages strengthened their claims for additional gifts, especially firearms. Here and throughout the eighteenth century, Osage leaders demonstrated the canny intercultural diplomacy that kept them between and not beneath any colonial power or rival Indian nation.[33]

French Footings and Imperial Maneuverings in the Age of the Osages

Establishing peaceful and profitable relations with the Osages was one of many interrelated issues with which French colonial officials wrestled. To secure French control over the Gulf Coast and the mouth of the Mississippi, posts were established at Biloxi in 1699, Mobile in 1702, and New Orleans in 1718, the last emerging as the capital of France's vast Louisiana colony. In the same years, but without the official imprimatur that guided French colonization in the lower Mississippi valley, *coureurs de bois* entered the confluence region. There many settled, becoming the *habitants* in several new farming villages. Initially, the unauthorized—and unorthodox, compared with prior established French communities in North America—settlements existed in what the French referred to as the Illinois Country. That remained a designation for the confluence region, although after 1717, the Illinois was formally attached to the administrative apparatus in the lower Mississippi valley. Thus it was also mapped as Upper Louisiana. Yet connecting a few small communities to a weak colonial structure hardly guaranteed French claims over the vast Mississippi valley.[34]

First and foremost, the viability of those settlements and of the crown's claims required that various Indians acquiesce to the French presence. In the lower Missouri valley, that especially meant cultivating understandings with the Osages. Complicating this goal were the enmities that existed between Indian nations. As in the western Great Lakes, such conflicts opened up opportunities for French mediation. But unlike Indians in the western Great Lakes, the Osages were not in a weakened or disoriented condition. Also unlike the *pays d'en haut* where the French faced as yet no serious imperial competitors, the Mississippi and Missouri valleys had attracted the attention of Spanish authorities. Moreover, even as French officials grappled with borderland complications, they confronted internal differences pitting imperial concerns against individual and local interests.

That internal conflict dated to the 1690s, from the first moment that French colonists moved into the confluence region. Newcomers, most of whom previously resided in the St. Lawrence valley, had come against the wishes of Canadian officials. Indeed, their relocation into *le pays des Illinois* defied a royal edict prohibiting settlement west of Montreal. From the perspective of Versailles, letting colonists wander further into the interior served no interest for the crown. Furs were already available in abundance, and migration threatened to spread an already thin colonial population. Adding pressure for restraint on settlement in the Mississippi valley were the pleas of missionaries, who claimed that contact with brandy-bearing traders contaminated Indians. But issuing decrees and enforcing them were not the same, as Louis XIV and rival monarchs repeatedly discovered.[35]

In the early eighteenth century, a few hundred Canadian colonists moved into the Illinois Country. They clustered not in Indian villages, as had traders in the *pays d'en haut*, but in new communities of their own. True, these settlements were often built alongside native towns, and the frequency of intermarriage and other forms of intercourse blurred the borders between French and Indian villages. Established in 1699, the first of the "French" towns took its name from the greatest of Indian North America's urban centers, Cahokia. In fact, the new village was located several miles from the site of the giant mounds, and its handful of humble homes bore no resemblance to the grandeur of the original. Three years after the second Cahokia came Kaskaskia, and these communities were joined in the 1720s and

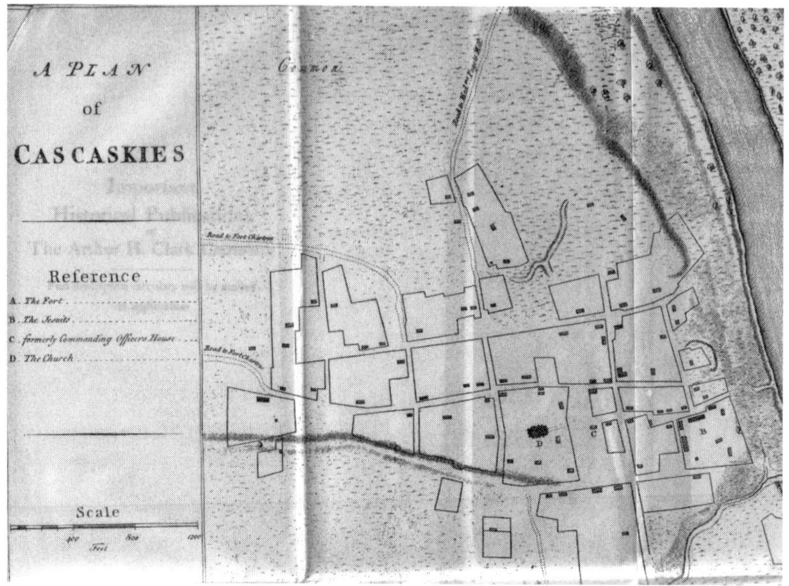

Figure 1. 1770 map of the village of Kaskaskia from Captain Philip Pittman, *The Present State of the European Settlements on the Mississippi* (London, 1770).

early 1730s by three more new villages (Chartres, St. Philippe, and Prairie du Rocher), all strung out along a fifty-mile stretch of bottomland on the east bank of the Mississippi, opposite from and south of the mouth of the Missouri.[36]

In common, these Illinois communities were settled primarily by Canadians. The roots of colonists were evident in the styles of their homes, which, following French Canadian customs (and contrasting with English American vernacular architecture), were distinguished by vertical logs, wraparound porches, and steep sloped roofs. So did the pattern of individually tended long lots, extending in narrow strips back from the river, resemble Canadian precedents.[37]

But architectural and cadastral similarities masked profound ecological, political, and social differences between Canada and the confluence region. Most immediately apparent, winters in the Illinois Country were not nearly as severe as in the St.

Lawrence valley. "The climate is almost the same as in France," contended a French military officer who spent two years in the confluence region. In addition, the extensive grasslands in the Illinois Country contrasted with the thick forests to the north and east. Indeed, French colonists showed their fondness for prairie by locating each of their new villages in the confluence region amidst expanses of grassy meadows. Lacking heavy axes to clear timber, it made good sense to save hard labor and instead take advantage of the ready-made pasturage and the grain-growing fertility offered by grasslands.[38]

The communities that early colonists established also looked more like French villages than Canadian settlements. Instead of dispersing their dwellings along the riverfront as had occurred along the St. Lawrence, the *habitants* who moved into the Mississippi valley resided in compact villages whose layout hearkened back to a remembered French blueprint. In the Illinois Country, colonists usually occupied square town lots that contained residence, garden, stable, barn, and barnyard animals. Adjacent to the village was a large commonly fenced field, which was itself divided but not fenced, into long, narrow strips owned by individual *habitants*. In addition, another field upon which stock grazed and residents gathered wood was held in common by all villagers. Thus did Illinois colonists replicate traditional arrangements—or at least what they assumed to be customary patterns of settlement.[39]

On closer inspection, Illinois villages departed from both medieval and colonial French models. In France and Canada, several layers of government officials watched carefully over the lives of subjects. Among other duties, these authorities enforced the dues and obligations that peasants and *habitants* owed seigneurs. In Canada, the seigneur was often the Catholic Church, which controlled much of the land in the St. Lawrence and which gave Canada the highest ratio of priests to European population outside of Rome. By contrast, the settlement of the Illinois Country was unauthorized, and in the first decades of the eighteenth century it remained a land over which the hand of imperial government lacked a firm grasp. The "resulting society," observed historian Winstanley Briggs, "was very much what northern French villagers thought the early modern village *ought* to be, in the same way that the early New England town was an English version of the same idea."[40]

Illinois *habitants* exercised considerable control over local governance in the early eighteenth century. As in colonial New England, household heads in Illinois came together for periodic town meetings. To be sure, French officials put in place a chain of authority that formally subordinated these household heads (and their dependents) to an appointed local commandant, who reported to the military commander at Ft. Chartres, who answered to the governor general in New Orleans, who took orders from the royal minister of the marine, who was the king's man. But the shallow reach of formal lines of authority left plenty of room for more informal community control over local matters—so much so that an aristocratic French visitor decried how common colonists presented themselves as "lords and masters" of their local worlds.[41]

Like New Englanders as well, Illinois *habitants* escaped semi-feudal land tenure and obtained fee simple titles. Compared with the old world and older colonial settlements, the distribution of land among Illinois *habitants* was also strikingly equitable. By no means was this an egalitarian society. Hierarchies within and between households were too deeply embedded in the prior histories of *habitants* to be dislodged. Still, the differences in landholding and the deferences expected to wealthier residents were far less pronounced than in other French realms. Typically, the better off owned only 50 or 100 percent more land than average holders, and the possibility of acquiring additional holdings further diminished the social distance between elite and common folk. The availability of land allowed many newcomers to move quickly from working for others as *engagés* to working their own lands. Moreover, the average holding was generally two to three times the size of Canadian lots. That, too, eased a concern shared by colonists in New England and New France: how to provide farmland for future generations.[42]

The parallels between the new hamlets in the Illinois Country and the older communities in New England should not be pushed too far. First, and what would have been most obvious to the residents of both, was the difference in the established churches. In French Illinois, that meant the supremacy of Catholicism. New Englanders, for their part, adhered to a militant Protestantism. Less conspicuous, but of considerable significance, were economic and material divergences. A survey of eighteenth-century household inventories in the Illinois Country showed that spinning wheels and sheep, two prominent features of colonial New England life, were absent from French villages. In this respect at least, the mercantilist precepts of the French state were effectively imposed on settlers in the most peripheral of French colonies. Instead of woolen garments and homespun garb, Illinois *habitants* wore animal skins or relied on imported cloth. Perhaps the greatest difference between New England and the Illinois Country was not what they wore but where they came from. Although the population of New England's towns was much larger, it was also less diverse than those living in Illinois communities. A 1732 census of the Illinois County tallied only 471 people. Yet this number included an assortment that was far more heterogeneous than in New England. In addition to Canadian-born *habitants*, the total counted a number of Indian men and women. Some of these were slaves, taken as captives by other Indians and then traded to the French; more of the resident Indians, however, were related, often by marriage, to colonists. The census also registered 164 individuals of African descent. Unlike most colonists, who came to Illinois towns from the north by their own choice, these were slaves who had no choice about their relocation. The numbers of involuntary migrants heading upriver grew significantly during the 1730s; a 1737 census listed 314 slaves, nearly doubling the figure from five years earlier and approaching one-third of the population of "French" villages in the Illinois Country.[43]

Together French *habitants*, Indian relations and exchanged captives, and African slaves accounted for Upper Louisiana's increasing, if still relatively small, colonial census, and their joint labors also produced impressive surpluses of grains and meat. In contrast to the thin soils and short growing seasons that characterized French settlements in the St. Lawrence valley and Great Lakes, the confluence region boasted far better conditions for the cultivation of wheat, oats, and maize. The last item was initially an Indian crop, but French *habitants* in the Illinois Country adapted it. That adaptation had limits, however, for colonists retained their prejudices against eating Indian corn, even as they recognized its value as fodder for stock and slaves. In the second quarter of the eighteenth century, the surpluses that farmers in the confluence region harvested found a solid market in New Orleans and other lower Mississippi settlements. Indeed, the volume was sufficient to keep Lower Louisiana's colonists fed and to induce Mississippi shippers to abandon the canoes favored by Great Lakes traders in favor of larger, flat-bottomed boats, or *bateaux*. Measuring thirty feet from bow to stern and eight feet across, these *bateaux* made it feasible for Upper Louisiana farmers to help provision Lower Louisiana's colonists.[44]

French officials in the confluence region did not welcome the independence and innovations of Illinois *habitants*, but beyond the enforcement of certain mercantilist regulations, they could do little to rein in local "traditions." Just as those officials accommodated Indian expectations about gifts, so they recognized that the nodes of imperial authority were too distant and too weak to prevent migration into the Illinois Country. In general, the few officials who were in place in the early eighteenth century tolerated what *habitants* almost immediately claimed were customary arrangements of holding and transferring real property and of governing local affairs. That was a wise course, for when an official tried to impose his own rule, he learned the limits of his authority. Such a humbling lesson was imparted to Sieur de Pradel, the commander at Fort de Chartres, in 1725. After arresting a *habitant* for alleged insolence, the commander found himself besieged by unruly locals, and he soon fled to New Orleans. Not wishing to upset farmers, whose food production was essential to the maintenance of plantations in Lower Louisiana, Sieur de Pradel's successors took note of his fate and left intact a system of unprecedented self-governance, at least when it came to purely local matters.[45]

Although the defiance of Illinois *habitants* undoubtedly disturbed the crown's vision of colonial order, his agents in North America were more preoccupied with intercultural and interimperial affairs. Even before the Illinois had been settled by Europeans, the king's men directed their fire at unlicensed traders working west from the confluence region. As early as 1683, La Salle wrote of a rumor that two French traders had, without any official blessing, gone to Missouri and Osage towns to initiate exchanges. La Salle's report was not confirmed, but a decade later, it was certain that a handful of *coureurs de bois* had come from Canada into the confluence region and then advanced up the Missouri as far as the Osage River. That handful became at least twenty Canadian traders in 1703 and more than one hundred the following year. Alarmed by these increases, colonial officials based in Quebec and New Orleans sought to gain control over commerce with Indians by limiting it to *voyageurs.* Accusing unlicensed traders of unsettling intercultural relations by perpetrating frauds against native partners and trafficking in Indian slaves, imperial authorities called for suppression of the *coureurs de bois.* As troubling, several of these itinerant traders were said to be seeking a kind of southwest passage that would take them not to the Pacific but to Santa Fe. That disturbed colonial authorities who feared that a passage to Spanish New Mexico would divert the trade and allegiances of the people of the confluence region away from France. Yet, despite many official condemnations, the numbers of *coureurs de bois* continued to grow and, in the process, further exposed the limits of colonial authority.[46]

For Spanish authorities, not the reality of their French counterparts' weakness but a misperception of their strength caused anxiety and provoked a new round of Spanish expansion. Fearing that French posts along the Gulf Coast and near the mouth of the Mississippi would serve as a base for attacking Spanish mines in Mexico and ships in the Caribbean, Spain established towns and missions of its own in what is now Texas. To the north, French connections with Missouri valley nations also prompted Spain into a defensive expansion. Here, one concern was the circulation of French goods, especially firearms. Through trading and raiding, guns passed across the plains and into the hands of Apache and Comanche Indians, who turned them on Spanish communities in northern Mexico and New Mexico. Another matter was the movement of *coureurs de bois* toward Santa Fe, which Spanish authorities mistakenly interpreted as the first stage of an officially sanctioned French invasion. In 1720, to counter French influence in the Missouri valley and other western tributaries of the Mississippi, the Spanish governor in New Mexico sent an expedition to the north and east. This party, which consisted of about fifty Spanish colonists and a like number of friendly Indians, made it to the Platte River. There they massacred a group of Pawnees, an action that did nothing for Indian–Spanish relations, but the expedition did get the attention of French officials in the Mississippi valley and beyond.[47]

That attention translated into further efforts to cement French foundations in the Mississippi and Missouri valleys and led colonial officials to shift from reluctant acceptance to genuine encouragement of settlement. Although French *habitants* from Canada had by 1720 established several towns on the east bank of the confluence region, they had planted no permanent settlements on the west side of the Mississippi. Two decades earlier in 1702, Father Gabriel Marest had established a mission on the west bank of the Mississippi at the mouth of the Des Peres River. Following the established practices of French missionaries, the site was shared with an Indian village—in this case, one occupied by Kaskaskia Indians who had relocated their town from across the Mississippi River. The construction of a few cabins and a log chapel marked the Des Peres mission as the first French settlement in present-day Missouri. The following year a number of French traders also took up residence. In 1703, however, the Kaskaskias abandoned the low-lying site, finding it unhealthy, prone to flooding, and not easily defended. With the departure of the Kaskaskias back across the Mississippi, the mission and surrounding French community collapsed. That left the French presence on the west side of the river resting on the unauthorized and intermittent occupation of scores of *coureurs de bois.*[48]

So matters stood until the fall of 1723, when, in response to recent Spanish forays, a French army officer, Étienne Veniard, Sieur de Bourgmond, led a party up the Missouri River. His orders were to construct a fort, which would attest to French claims and attract trade from Missouri River Indians. The site de Bourgmond chose for what was named Fort Orleans lay at the confluence of the Missouri and Grand rivers. This was close to a Missouri Indian village, but its chief purpose was to solidify bonds with the Osages and other Indians who might otherwise turn to the Spanish. For a few years, the fort was a hive of activity and a center of intercultural dealings. By the end of the 1720s, however, Fort Orleans had been evacuated, leaving the west bank of the confluence region and the entire Missouri valley without any firm French footings.[49]

Although French settlements were as yet confined to the east bank of the Mississippi, residents crossed the river regularly to pursue opportunities. Trading for skins with Indians up the Missouri River was one lure. So were the salt springs at a site near the west bank of the Mississippi, which French visitors called simply La Saline.[50]

In addition to skins and salt, the other side of the Mississippi contained deposits of lead that attracted colonists from across the river. Although not the precious metals that Europeans most coveted, lead was a vital and valuable resource. Efforts to profit from mining, however, ran into difficulties from the start. First, Indians on both sides of the Mississippi objected to and interfered with mining operations. Second, French enterprisers lacked the capital and the technical expertise to extract and smelt lead with the required efficiency. Third, the labor force proved unreliable. One observer described the *habitants* doubling as miners as "wastrels," who stopped working as soon as they had "extracted enough of the ore to supply" themselves "with a living for the rest of the year." Putting African slaves to work in lead mining was a solution, but the "expense of negroes" limited this option and kept operations on a small scale.[51]

From these footings, primarily on the eastern side of the Mississippi, but extending to the west bank as well, the French presumed to secure their claims to a vast territory whose unknown borders followed the course of all of the rivers that came together in the confluence region. Of course, the lands that the French now mapped as "Upper Louisiana" were not recognized by imperial rivals. From the south and west, the Spanish asserted their own presumptions and launched their own forays. By the 1740s, a potentially greater threat emerged from the east, where English traders and colonists were poised to penetrate the Ohio valley and push their own claims to the confluence region. Such maneuverings inflated the importance of the Illinois Country to the French empire. Only by securing control of the confluence region could France knit together its holdings in Canada and Lower Louisiana and keep British colonists and traders from marching across French claims in the Ohio valley. In the 1750s, the policy of containment led to war between Britain and France, with control over the confluence region hanging on the outcome. Through the first half of the eighteenth century, however, what most stood in the way of French, or for that matter Spanish and British, control of the confluence region was the might of its diverse Indian occupants.

In the lower Missouri valley during the first half of the eighteenth century, this balance of power favored the Osages. True, the Osages' position was hardly certain and heartily contested. The presence of the French, the interest of imperial competitors, and the designs of Indian rivals challenged the Osages' regional hegemony. But from their place in between, the Osages reigned.

Indian rivals posed the most immediate threat to Osage hegemony over the lower Missouri and adjacent lands. Neighboring groups up the Missouri and on the eastern plains resented the Osages' control over the flow of trade goods from the French into the area. Osage raids, in which horses were stolen and people were killed or captured, added to the grievances of targeted groups. Banding together, Wichita and Comanche warriors attacked an Osage village in 1750. With most of the town's inhabitants away hunting, the attackers took revenge on those—mostly young and old—left behind. But this victory was the exception. For the most part, the Osages' enemies made no lasting alliances, and on their own, each lacked the numbers to overcome the Osages' advantages.[52]

In addition to numbers, the Osages' chief advantage was their access to French firearms. Because the Spanish prohibited trade in flintlock muskets, Indians in the middle of the North American continent had only French traders as a source for what the Osage called *wa-ho-ton-the* ("thing that causes things to cry out"). In hunting, these imported weapons were too noisy and unreliable to displace bows and arrows. In warfare, by contrast, French-supplied muskets were more effective, and they gave the Osages a decisive edge over neighboring groups, whom the Osages blocked from acquiring guns and ammunition.[53]

Although not primarily for hunting, firearms dramatically altered the ways in which Osages hunted and lived. Most obvious, to obtain weapons of war, the Osages hunted more. As hunting seasons lengthened, skilled hunters enjoyed enhanced prestige and sought to translate that status into greater authority in village politics. This sometimes led younger men to defy elders and to vie with headmen whose claims to leadership rested only on their kinship. It also resulted in an increase in polygyny, as successful hunters often married several women.[54]

The distorting effects of colonialism and commercialism should not be exaggerated, however—at least not in the first decades of the eighteenth century. If the Osages came to value some imported items and to rely on French firearms, this dependence never approached dependency. That is, the Osages retained the ability to feed, clothe, and shelter themselves without outside assistance. Moreover, as in the past, the adoption of new practices did not entail the abandonment of traditional ways.

For the Osages and their increasingly diverse neighbors, prior histories mattered. Indians in the region included longer established groups and those, like the Osages, who had relocated more recently. For both longer and more lately settled, previous expectations and experiences shaped how they lived and how they dealt with one another and with the newest arrivals from Europe and Africa. For European colonists as well, the weight of prior arrangements and understandings configured subsistence schedules, interpersonal attachments, and their relations with the various Indians with whom they mated and traded.

Prior histories alone did not determine the history of the confluence region, however. The adaptability of the Osages, as they adjusted to new homelands and new opportunities, demonstrated the ability of Indians for creative, though not destabilizing, change. Such adaptations enabled the Osages to dominate a good portion of the lower Missouri valley and to make themselves the most powerful group across the confluence region. Canadian colonists also developed unusual communities in the Illinois Country. In many respects, these were idealized versions of traditional French villages. But in developing those ideals—especially about property holding and local governance—and in incorporating Indians and Africans, the Illinois settlements became quite untraditional.

2.

Traditions

During the 1740s, land grants enticed *habitants* to cross the Mississippi and, around 1750, to establish the village of Ste. Genevieve. Initially, this crossing made no difference. Life in and around the new village resembled the older towns on the other side of the Mississippi. On both sides of the Mississippi, French villagers drew on and departed from colonial histories. In their system of local governance, their elimination of feudal lords, and their broad and relatively equitable distribution of landholdings, Ste. Genevieve and sister communities in the mid-eighteenth century looked more like mid-seventeenth-century New England than like older parts of New France. The prevalence of slavery in the Illinois Country and the imbalanced demography of Ste. Genevieve, however, were more reminiscent of another English colonial region: the Chesapeake. More like the Chesapeake than New England, Illinois settlements also directed much of their agricultural production to distant markets.

A different set of commercial considerations inspired the founding of a second settlement on the west bank of the Mississippi. This was St. Louis, which was established in 1764 near the confluence of the Missouri and Mississippi rivers. In contrast with Ste. Genevieve, the founders of St. Louis reverted to the

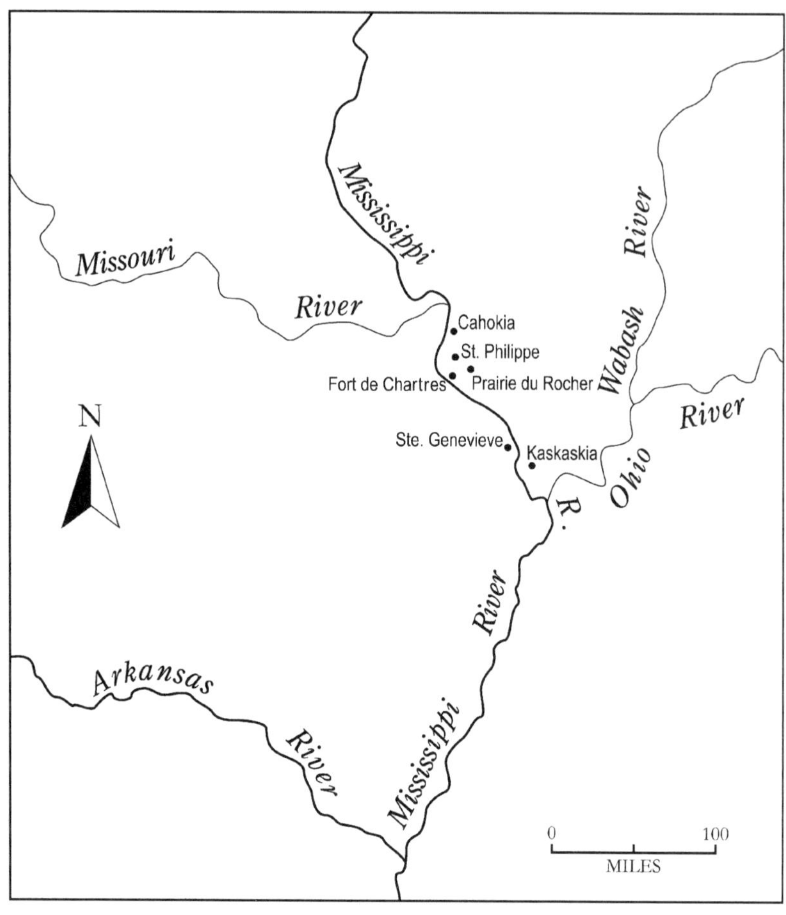

Map 3. French Settlements in the Confluence Region, c. 1750s.

former French emphasis on trade between cultures rather than export of agriculture.

Even as French traders from New Orleans laid out St. Louis, imperial shifts altered its situation and remapped the confluence region. Defeated in its war against Great Britain, France ceded St. Louis, Ste. Genevieve, and all its claims west of the Mississippi to Spain. Canada, the Great Lakes, and all lands on the east side of the confluence region became British territory. With the stroke of very distant pens, New France disappeared from North America and the Mississippi turned into a border between

Spanish and British colonial possessions. Thereafter, the peoples of the confluence region had to adjust to life in a divided and contested borderland. More surprising were the adjustments made by Spanish and British authorities. Partially abandoning prior colonial habits, the new players learned that, in dealing with Indians and colonists in the confluence region, it made sense to follow what had become the traditions of the French.

The Customs of Ste. Genevieve

In histories of the state of Missouri, the establishment and initial development of the village of Ste. Genevieve has merited much attention and generated some controversy. The attention owes to Ste. Genevieve's place as the first enduring European settlement in what would one day become the state of Missouri. The controversy traces to the date of its origins, with some histories giving 1735 as the year of Ste. Genevieve's founding, and others delaying it until the 1740s or even as late as 1751. That uncertainty reflects the insignificance of the event at the time, for in the beginning the customs of Ste. Genevieve mirrored those of existing villages in the Illinois Country.[1]

Only in retrospect did the settling of Ste. Genevieve take on much significance; the establishment of the village garnered little notice—so little, in fact, that none of its pioneer inhabitants documented the day they crossed the Mississippi to erect a new town or work in adjacent fields. True, many of these first settlers were illiterate, but then even if they could write, they had little reason to mark the occasion. At the time of Ste Genevieve's founding, neither *habitants* nor French officials viewed the Mississippi River as a border. Traversing the Mississippi—to trade with Indians, to gather salt, to mine lead—was not unusual. In fact, in an era of poor roads and rickety wagons, it was far easier to cross the river than to transport goods overland between villages on the eastern side of the Mississippi. That the French initially colonized the east bank owed primarily to topographical, not political, considerations. On the east side of the river, an alluvial plain, stretching back as much as three miles from the Mississippi, provided invitingly fertile, if flood-prone, fields for farmers. By contrast, much of the opposite bank contained little bottomland, and the higher ground near the river was not only less fertile but also less easily broken by the primitive plows used by French farmers.

A small stretch of bottomland did exist on the west bank, and it was there that *habitants* took up lands and built homes. This was the site for Ste. Genevieve, a village named for the patron saint of Paris but whose founders had no grand cosmopolitan ambitions. Theirs was to be an agricultural settlement in which life replicated that of the Illinois communities from which its first residents hailed.

For the most part, the earliest inhabitants migrated from nearby Kaskaskia. As fields around Kaskaskia lost some of their fertility, residents looked to cultivate convenient and as yet unbroken bottomland on the west bank. During the 1740s, a number of *habitants* obtained land cessions from colonial authorities at Fort de Chartres. These required grantees to move across the river for a minimum of one year and provide some logs for the new village's chapel. Although royal edicts specified that failure to fulfill these obligations for individual occupancy and communal improvement would result in forfeiture of the lands, grantees do not seem to have relocated immediately. By the early 1750s, however, a few houses had been constructed, with a 1752 census recording nine property owners and twenty-three residents. Still the village, while permanently occupied, lacked its own administrative apparatus. Throughout the 1750s, civil and religious matters continued to be handled in Kaskaskia or Fort de Chartres. That the new village was called Ste. Genevieve *des* Cascaskias attested to its satellite status.[2]

During the 1750s, the new village developed along lines familiar to the Illinois Country. Residents clustered in a village along the river. Town lots typically measured about one arpent square. Initially, homes tended to be small, about six hundred square feet in a single room with a dirt floor. Over time, more prosperous families added rooms, walnut floors, and whitewashed walls. Outbuildings appeared, including barns, stables, henhouses, kitchens, and slave quarters. Town lots also found space for orchards and vegetable gardens, which generally were tended by women. The focus of male agricultural activity was the "big field commons," which ran back from the village and away from the river. Surrounded by a single fence, the big field was, in spite of its name, not a true common. As in towns across the Mississippi, the fence was built and maintained as a common enterprise, but the land inside was divided into strips of individually owned plowland. The true commons, where privately owned livestock grazed on communally held land, lay outside the enclosed big field.[3]

Like their cousins across the Mississippi, the *habitants* of Ste. Genevieve fell back on customary beliefs and time-tested ways. Long-standing practices set the schedule and character of agricultural life and labor. Oblivious to the agricultural reforms of the eighteenth century, *habitants* made no move to rotate crops, replenish soils with nitrogen-fixing clover, or exchange heavy medieval plows for more up-to-date models. Such innovations made little sense where lands were abundant, soils still fresh, and labor, both free and slave, usually scarce. The worldviews of *habitants*, both of this world and the next, showed no sign of Enlightenment influences. As historian Carl Ekberg concluded, "The overwhelming majority of townspeople thought that the sun revolved around the earth and that the Mississippi River flowed to the Gulf of Mexico because the waters of the river had an irresistible desire to join with those of the ocean." Although a Jesuit mission was located in nearby Kaskaskia, the people of Ste. Genevieve subscribed to a faith untouched by the turbulent debates among Catholics of which the Jesuit order was a product. Indeed, Jesuit priests who crossed over to Ste. Genevieve encountered some hostility. This was not a sign of popular irreligiosity. To the contrary, the people firmly believed in a life guided by mysterious, supernatural forces, and in spite of the ribald reception they occasionally gave clerics, they considered themselves good Catholics. Their Roman Catholicism, like their daily lives, "was earthy and robust," in Ekberg's judgment, more "medieval" than what eighteenth-century Jesuits and Enlightenment *philosophes* considered modern.[4]

In their expectations of life and their life expectancies, the people of early Ste. Genevieve adhered as well to premodern patterns. At around forty per thousand residents, annual birth rates were high, though not as high as in Canada. As elsewhere, infant mortality took a heavy toll; perhaps one-third of children perished before their first birthday. That helped account for an annual death rate nearing thirty per thousand and for life expectancies under thirty years at birth. Those who survived their first year had better chances for a longer life; men averaged well into their forties, but women averaged several years less owing to the frequency of deaths during or soon after childbirth. As in other communities across the river with a similar demographic profile, the high rates of birth, death, and remarriage gave Ste. Genevieve's households a jumbled character with various mixtures of parents, stepparents, children, and stepchildren often congregated under one roof.[5]

The hold of custom, then, was immense, but what passed for traditional was not always of long standing. For example, the heads of Ste. Genevieve households maintained the innovative system of local governance that had emerged in villages to the east. Together assembled *habitants* agreed to a set of eighteen rules to regulate the big field and its fence. They also elected a syndic and six arbiters to oversee village affairs. All this was done in the name of custom, though such traditions had no standing in Canada. In fact, the elections and communal regulations were relative novelties, which in effective practice had originated in the Illinois Country.

A blend of the truly traditional with more novel arrangements also characterized relations between the sexes. In keeping with long established practices, men in Ste. Genevieve and other Illinois towns exercised control over agriculture in the big field, while women worked primarily in the home and surrounding gardens. But the wholesale replication of familiar divisions of labor and household responsibilities ran up against a demographic profile quite unlike that of France. In the early 1750s, Ste. Genevieve had three times as many French men as French women; two decades later, such men still outnumbered women of European descent by a three to two margin. That situation paralleled not New England but the first English settlements in the Chesapeake. As in seventeenth-century Virginia, Creole women in eighteenth-century Ste. Genevieve gained certain opportunities from their scarcity. In both places, females married at younger ages than did males and, if widowed, had a choice of partners for remarriage. True, intermarriages with Indian women were far more common in the Illinois Country than in the Chesapeake. Yet even more than in the Chesapeake, women in Ste. Genevieve acquired unprecedented economic and social power. In part, this owed to the imbalance between men and women, but just as important were laws and customs regulating marital property and inheritance. Unlike women in British America, French colonial women did not forfeit all of their property upon marriage. Inheritance practices also gave Ste. Genevieve's widows half of their husbands' estate, whereas British American wives could expect only one-third. "The almost exclusive right, which the women have to the property," observed a visitor to Ste. Genevieve, gave wives "more influence over their husbands than is common in most other countries." That influence over household matters expanded when husbands were absent. For those who combined farming with extended leaves for fur trading, such absences were common. In these cases, temporary abandonment brought empowerment, as women assumed responsibilities for farm management and commercial transactions that were hardly customary.[6]

By no means did the enhanced position of wives elevate them to equality with their husbands. For "traditionalists" like the colonists of Ste. Genevieve, such a fundamental rearrangement of gender hierarchies was unthinkable. If widows and wives with absent husbands often acquired more authority than was customary, women seldom controlled the circumstances by which they were left without spouses. Divorce was unknown, and only in the most exceptional cases were women's petitions for legal separation granted. Customary double standards also governed premarital and extramarital intercourse. Premarital sex was not uncommon among young couples in Ste. Genevieve, and it seems to have carried no stigma for women, except in rare instances where pregnancies ensued and marriages did not. Even more damaging was the loss of reputation suffered by wives who engaged in exposed adulterous liaisons. In these cases, the double standard asserted itself with particular force, for usually only women in Ste. Genevieve and sister French communities across the river faced judicial penalties for their illicit affairs.[7]

Inequalities remained an unquestioned fact of life between the sexes as well as within the ranks of men and women, but the disparities were untraditional. The availability of land made Ste. Genevieve and other villages in the Illinois Country a land of opportunity for many of its early colonists. As in other traditional societies, which in the middle of the eighteenth century still included all of the colonial societies of the Americas, wealth had its privileges. Richer men expected and received deference from poorer persons. Still, if the distribution of land and other property was not equal among households, the differences were far less pronounced than in Canada or France. Moreover, the social structure was a fluid one, enabling some enterprising and fortunate men to rise to the top of the economic pyramid. Thus did Francois Vallé, an impoverished immigrant from Canada to the Illinois Country, quickly transform himself into the wealthiest man in Ste. Genevieve. Like many other newcomers, Vallé did not immediately settle into the life of a full-time farmer. Initially he worked as a trader and a lead miner. By the mid-1760s Vallé had become the largest landholder in Ste. Genevieve. He also invested heavily in slaves. With sixty-three, he owned more than one-quarter of all of the slaves in Ste. Genevieve's census.[8]

If fluid opportunities challenged customary notions about rankings fixed by birth, no doubt existed about who occupied the bottom rung of Ste. Genevieve society. These were slaves, who in the 1750s and 1760s were found in 40 percent of the households in the French towns of the confluence region and who made up about the same percentage of the population of Ste. Genevieve. After Vallé, the next largest slaveholder owned twenty. But such sizeable holdings were the exceptions. Most slaveholders owned only one or two slaves. The vast majority of *habitants* could not afford to invest more in human property, especially since the price of slaves had nearly doubled during the second quarter of the eighteenth century, making a single adult African male more expensive than the cost of a house and town lot. Nonetheless, despite rising prices and attempts by officials in Lower Louisiana to curb the export of slaves upriver, the slave population in Upper Louisiana continued to grow. The 1752 census counted almost six hundred slaves, or approximately four out of nine persons in the French towns of the Illinois Country. Of these unfree laborers, approximately three-quarters were of African descent; the rest were Indians, usually taken as captives on the Plains, then traded to the French. Because most captives were women and children, females made up three-fifths of the Indian slaves. By contrast, the sex ratio was reversed among African slaves, with men outnumbering women three to two.[9]

The customs of slavery in Ste. Genevieve and other French towns in Upper Louisiana were nominally regulated by the *Code Noir*. Originally issued in 1685 to govern the treatment of slaves in the West Indies, the code became the law of Louisiana in 1724. Its fifty-five articles defined slaves as chattel and authorized whippings for disobedience. More serious crimes merited more severe punishments. Runaways, for example, faced brandings and mutilations. Free blacks, too, came under the code's provisions, with restrictions placed on their choice of occupations and harsher penalties stipulated than for whites convicted of the same crime. At the same time, the *Code Noir* recognized that, although slaves were property, they were also human beings with souls to be saved. In addition to allowing for religious instruction and baptism, the code limited working hours to from sunrise to sunset, called for proper housing, clothing, and feeding, and forbade the rape of female slaves. In striking contrast to British America, the French laws proscribed the sale of children away from their parents. Under Article XX, slaves even gained the right to take masters to court for violating the provisions of the code.[10]

As with other impressive imperial documents, the *Code Noir* did not live up to its billing. In the Caribbean, sugar planters paid little heed to the planks that safeguarded the slaves' well-being. In Upper Louisiana, slave owners knew imperial authority was not sufficient to enforce the code. Other factors, however, combined to offer a measure of protection to slaves in the Illinois

Country. Not least was economics. In the West Indies, slaves died in droves from the killing regime that sugar planters imposed. But planters in the West Indies replaced their dying slaves with fresh imports from Africa. In Upper Louisiana, *habitants* could not reasonably follow that strategy. The cost of importing slaves to the confluence region was much greater than to the Caribbean, and the market for wheat was not nearly as profitable as that for sugar.[11]

The presence of Indian slaves further complicated the regulation and customs of slavery in Upper Louisiana. Rather than lumping all chattel together, Illinois slaveholders drew distinctions between their African and Indian property. Although the possession of Indian slaves was not new to French colonists, those in the confluence region were in a sensitive position. Most of the Indians held as slaves came via trade from captives taken in the Missouri valley. Enough came from the "Panis" (Pawnees) that it became a designation for all Indian slaves. But if Panis in Canada lost hope of returning to the Missouri valley, Indian slaves in the Illinois Country were not so distant from their former homes—or at least from peoples with relations to their kin. In addition, the colonists in Ste. Genevieve and sister villages knew they survived at the mercy of neighboring Indian groups, which had the power to overwhelm any and all of the French settlements. Better, then, to treat Indian slaves as neighboring Indians did. In practice, this meant *habitants* rarely put Indian slaves to work in the big field; most toiled instead as domestic servants.[12]

The accommodations accomplished their chief purpose: in the 1750s and early 1760s, French villagers and Indian neighbors maintained good relations. By conforming the customs of slavery and trade toward Indian understandings and by the continuance of intermarriages between French men and Indian women, Ste. Genevieve followed in the generally peaceful intercultural footsteps that prevailed in communities across the Mississippi.

Keeping intercultural affairs quiet, the Osages, who presented the greatest potential threat to Ste. Genevieve, steered clear in these years. At the time of Ste. Genevieve's founding, internal splits and external challenges preoccupied the Osage nation. The northern band of the Osages, often referred to as the Little Osage, moved their villages north of the Missouri River during the 1740s. That put more distance between the Little and Big Osages, and as the northern band extended their hunting into what is now Iowa, they came into conflict with rival Indian claimants. Meanwhile, the Big Osages continued the strategy of being between that had served them so well. But although the Osages tried to choke off trade between the French and Plains Indians, the Pawnees had by 1750 acquired enough French guns to challenge the Osages' dominance. Joining with Comanches and Wichitas, the Pawnees attacked Osage hunters, killing twenty-two, in the summer of 1751. Rebuffed in a bid for French aid, the Osage launched their own raids to the west. By the end of the 1750s, these succeeded in pushing the villages of the Wichitas south from the Arkansas to the Red River.[13]

With the Osages' attentions diverted westward, Ste. Genevieve got off to a smooth start. To be sure, not all was wonderful, as the village's nickname, Misère (French for misery), attested. The sobriquet owed to the floods that repeatedly struck Ste. Genevieve. Still, if the town was often damp and muddy, its pioneers, unlike those in many other new settlements, suffered no "starving times." In fact, life compared favorably with most other mid-eighteenth-century situations in which residents might have found themselves. For African slaves, being in the Illinois Country was clearly better and their life expectancies were certainly longer than in the killing fields of the Caribbean. For French women, the advantages that came from unbalanced sex ratios *and* beneficial property laws were undeniable. For their husbands, there was freedom from too oppressive authority, greater say over local affairs, and more than adequate sustenance. If not prosperity, there was peace with the Indians of the confluence region and with fellow villagers. Indeed, one of the striking features of town records was the absence of physical violence. Of course, disputes occurred, as did unreported incidents of domestic violence. But the courts of early Ste. Genevieve heard no case in which a *habitant* physically attacked his neighbor. Ste. Genevieve was no paradise, but for the few hundred people who called it home in the mid-1760s, its often recently invented traditions generally made life a lot better than miserable.[14]

The Strange Birth of St. Louis

In the mid-1760s, the west bank of the Mississippi became home to a second colonial settlement. From above, the cluster of houses, the adjacent big field with individual long lots, and the common pastures looked much like Ste. Genevieve. But St. Louis was a different kind of community. Its nickname, "*pain-court*" (short of bread), reflected its shortcomings as an agricultural center. Its founders and most of its first residents were too devoted to commerce to take care of cultivation. St. Louis was also born under strange circumstances because its establishment coincided with the departure of New France and the transfer of the western side of the confluence region to the Spanish.[15]

The imperial maneuverings that resulted in the division of the confluence region along the Mississippi played out far from the scene. Although the latest, and to that point greatest, conflict between France and Britain started with skirmishes in the upper Ohio valley, the battle zone, which extended across both sides of the Atlantic, never traveled down the Ohio to its mouth. During the war, Fort de Chartres housed British prisoners. It also served as a supply center for French troops and Indian allies in the upper Ohio valley. Some of the grain that Illinois *habitants* previously shipped down the Mississippi was diverted up the Ohio to feed Fort Duquesne. But the war itself remained at a distance. Fort de Chartres and surrounding villages escaped the devastation suffered by soldiers and civilians in combat theaters to the east. News of the war did filter into Upper Louisiana, making inhabitants aware of France's initial victories and subsequent defeats. No one in the Illinois Country, however, knew of the secret talks begun shortly after the fall of Quebec between France and Spain.[16]

Suspending their rivalry over the borders and peoples in between Louisiana and Spanish provinces, the Catholic monarchs of France and Spain, who were second cousins, made common cause against Protestant Britain. In the early 1760s, the allies commenced negotiations to hand over French territory west of the Mississippi to Spain. For France, the proposed cession prevented Britain from gaining possession of Upper and Lower Louisiana, and it held the possibility of a retrocession from one cousin to another at some future date. Initially, Spanish diplomats resisted the deal, fearing the cost of administering what had not been a profitable colony for France. Fear of further British expansion to the borders of Texas and New Mexico, however, was more powerful. On November 3, 1762, France and Spain signed the Treaty of Fontainebleau, although its contents were not immediately divulged. The following year, the Treaty of Paris closed the Seven Years' War and revealed the various border realignments that made England and Spain new neighbors in the Mississippi valley.[17]

Not until 1764 did word of these arrangements reach French officials in Louisiana, who, in the meantime, had hatched their own plans for the postwar reconstruction of the Mississippi valley. Although the war had not come to Louisiana, the disruption of transatlantic shipping had drastically reduced its exports. Upon his arrival in New Orleans in June 1763, the new French governor, as yet unaware of impending territorial transfers, looked to stimulate the colony's moribund economy. To reinvigorate the fur trade of Upper Louisiana, the governor granted the mercantile firm of Maxent, Laclède, and Company a six-year license to conduct trade with Indians along the Missouri and upper Mississippi rivers. For this exclusive privilege, the firm, headed by the prominent New Orleans merchant Antoine Maxent, was expected to build a post, which would draw trade in and keep foreign traffickers out.

Responsibility for selecting the site and managing the company's affairs in Upper Louisiana fell to Maxent's partner, Pierre Laclède Liguest, assisted by Auguste Chouteau, the fourteen-year-old son of Laclède's longtime female companion. In the fall of 1763, Laclède and Chouteau headed up the Mississippi in a company of approximately thirty men. Just south of the mouth of the Missouri, Laclède identified what he considered an ideal spot. Although the site had no bottomland between the river and the limestone bluffs that rose close by the west bank, Laclède's concerns were not agricultural. For his designs, the site was perfect, holding the promise of becoming "one of the finest cities in America."[18]

While wintering across the Mississippi at Fort de Chartres, Laclède learned of the colonial reshuffling and quickly reshaped his plans to reflect the changed situation. Ascertaining that many of the French *habitants* on what was now British territory preferred to live under a Catholic monarch, Laclède decided to build a town around his trading post. As Chouteau recalled, his superior then "cordially invited all those dissatisfied Frenchmen" to relocate to the new town. In February 1764, Laclède dispatched his assistant to oversee the construction of temporary shelters in the town, which he designated St. Louis. In the spring, Laclède came across the river and took charge of laying out the first streets of St. Louis.[19]

Progress moved smoothly until October, when several hundred Missouri Indians appeared, with the object of residing next to the trading post. The Missouris' "fear of the Great Osage," reported a French official, motivated the decision "to take refuge here." Likening themselves to "the ducks and the geese, who traveled until they found a fine country, where there was beautiful, open water" on which to "obtain an easy living," the Missouris, according to Chouteau, declared their desire to "live together in the greatest friendship." Yet despite the profession of peaceful purposes and the fact that the Missouris who reached St. Louis were mostly women and children, their presence unsettled many of the recently settled French colonists. The departure of *habitants* stalled the development of the town. More troubling in Laclède's view, the proximity of the Missouris threatened to bring trade-ruining intertribal warfare to the vicinity of St. Louis. Meeting with Missouri headmen, Laclède cleverly employed the Indians' waterfowl metaphor to persuade them to abandon plans to settle near St. Louis. In open water, pointed out Laclède, ducks and geese were easy prey for eagles and other birds of prey. But upriver, in a "woody place covered with brush," they would be safer, if not from the Big Osages, then at least from warriors across the Mississippi. The metaphorical twist worked: the Missouris abandoned their settlement plans, although they did extract some presents from Laclède before taking leave.[20]

Having defused one potential crisis, Maxent, Laclède, and Company faced new challenges in building the town and its trade. With the removal of the Missouris, *habitants* returned, and in the following years, a stream of French immigrants from now British Illinois swelled the population of St. Louis to about five hundred. As was typical in French villages in the Illinois Country, one-third of the residents of St. Louis were slaves. These were primarily of African descent, although a few Indians were also held in bondage in early St. Louis. But while slaves helped produce agricultural surpluses in Ste. Genevieve and older villages across the Mississippi, St. Louis knew no such abundance. To the contrary, as its nickname acknowledged, the residents of St. Louis grew too little grain to feed themselves. Only imports from Ste. Genevieve sustained the town's inhabitants, the vast majority of whom were involved in one or another aspect of the trade with Indians. Often that meant waiting for Indians to come to St. Louis to barter. By 1770, dozens of Indian groups made annual visits (and sometimes several visits each year) to St. Louis.[21]

For Maxent, Laclède, and Company, the political situation of St. Louis was both a blessing and a curse. The withdrawal of the Missouris left the site free of competing occupants. That spared St. Louis from becoming a target of war parties. Instead, the post emerged as a neutral ground to which all Indians could come to trade. Extending the reach of their St. Louis–based nexus, Maxent, Laclède, and Company also sent agents to Indian villages up the Mississippi and Missouri rivers. At the same time, the political situation undermined the firm's hopes for a monopoly on trade with Indians. In April 1765, in an effort to assert the enterprise's exclusive rights, Laclède demanded the confiscation of a boatload of goods as it entered the Missouri River. The goods belonged to Jean Datchurut, a Ste. Genevieve merchant, and were destined for trade with Indians upriver. Officials in St. Louis complied with Laclède's request. This action, however, was subsequently overturned by New Orleans' authorities, who cited the French king's cancellation of the governor of

Louisiana's grant to Maxent, Laclède, and Company and ordered the firm to pay compensation plus damages to Datchurut. By this time, of course, the decrees of the French king and his officials had no standing. But the Spanish were slow to replace French authorities. Instead, a political vacuum allowed traders to work the western side of the Mississippi valley without fear of imperial restrictions.[22]

In this free trade environment, Maxent, Laclède, and Company were forced to compete in a town where commerce was king. Indeed, not since Cahokia's demise several centuries earlier had the confluence region seen a commercial center with the reach of St. Louis. But for St. Louis to achieve Laclède's promise of becoming "one of the finest cities in America," it would have to adjust to new colonial rulers. Born free of imperial restrictions, the traders of St. Louis and their Indian partners would have to accommodate Spanish authority—much as the diverse inhabitants across the Mississippi would have to serve British masters. As it turned out, though, the more significant adjustments and accommodations were made not by inhabitants but by Spanish and British authorities.

Adjustments and Accommodations

Adjustments and accommodations were not what the successors of the French had in mind when they formulated plans for ruling the Mississippi valley. Quite the opposite, monarchs and ministers in London and Madrid contemplated establishing colonial regimes along familiar lines. They expected colonists to conform with new imperial edicts and presumed to treat Indians as conquered peoples. But the recalcitrance of colonists, the resistance of Indians, and the rivalry of imperial neighbors impelled administrators to change course. Modifying their prior colonialisms, British and Spanish authorities learned that getting along in the confluence region required emulating the practices (or at least appearing to emulate the practices) of French predecessors.

For the British, this bending came only after hundreds of departing colonists made their break from the east bank and thousands of rebelling Indians broke imperial administrators of their arrogant pretenses. Even before the British arrived on the scene, dread of what they *might* do prompted a substantial exodus from Illinois villages—both Indian and French, with St. Louis being a chief beneficiary of the out-migration. The flight left houses unoccupied and fields untended in Cahokia, Kaskaskia, Prairie du Rocher, and Chartres. In the past, seasonal trips by *habitants* to trade with Indians or to transport goods to New Orleans reduced the population of these villages by 30 percent. Such mixing of occupations and temporary departures from villages had become part of the customs of the country. But the flow across the Mississippi and across the new border was of a far greater and apparently more permanent order. In St. Philippe, the crossing reduced the population to a single *habitant.* Arriving in the partially depopulated territory, a British captain acknowledged that "fear of the English" inspired the flight of French Creoles to the Spanish side. Still, sure of the superiority of their system, British officials could only attribute the mass departure to the former inhabitants' "ignoran[ce] of our Constitution."[23]

What the British, in their arrogance, *did* do prompted a widespread uprising that engaged Indian peoples up and down the Ohio valley and around the Great Lakes. Chiefly responsible for setting off this unrest was a decisive alteration of policy toward Indians. As one official put it, "The Indians must be Taught to Fear Us and then they'l act Like Fr[ien]ds." Such was the opinion of Lord Jeffrey Amherst, the British military commander in North America. After conquering New France, Amherst was not inclined to conciliate Indians with expensive presents or sit through the time-consuming rituals of Indian diplomacy. In Amherst's view, gifts discouraged Indian labor, while participation, for example, in the calumet ceremony misled Indians about their relationship with British authority. Ignoring the counsel of more experienced advisors and eschewing negotiations with native leaders, Amherst dictated an end to gift giving. Henceforth, he ordered that trade be carried out on a strictly commercial basis. Indian hunters would be paid for the skins they exchanged and not encouraged in their indolence and insolence.[24]

Incensed by such unilateral impositions, Indians rose up in the spring of 1763. Beginning in May, war parties from dozens of villages around the Great Lakes and Ohio valley attacked British posts in the western country and extended their raids to settlements on the eastern side of the Appalachians. Where the previous war was fought at a distance from the confluence region, this uprising drew in Illinois Indians and included an assault on Fort Ouiatonon on the Wabash River. British authorities linked the participation of Illinois and other Indians to a vast conspiracy, which they traced to Pontiac, an Ottawa headman. Pontiac, who journeyed across Illinois, was especially vocal in his disdain for the arrogant ways of the British and in his rejection of the British presumption that their victory over the French translated into a conquest of Indian occupants. Indians, Pontiac repeatedly reminded Indian audiences and British officers, too, "had never sold any part of their country to the French," so the French had no right to sell it to the British (or the Spanish). No doubt, Pontiac's orations played a part in inciting opposition to British presumptions, but the Indians' uprising was as much the product of a number of prophets. Offering similar visions of Indian renaissance through rituals of cultural purification, native prophets urged a return to ancient customs and a cleansing of European influences.[25]

The message of Indian revitalization resonated with tremendous force throughout the Ohio Country and Great Lakes Region, but the effort to dislodge the British and restore a precolonial world ran against a desire to retain the benefits of intercultural exchange. Despite prophetic inspiration, insurrectionaries did not, for the most part, long for a complete elimination of all persons and things European. Instead, many, including Pontiac, supported a return of the French. Comparing the French to the English, a Kaskaskia headman explained that the latter "is filled with wickedness and has not the white heart like our [French] father." Unfortunately, this rejection alone would not bring back the French as Pontiac learned when the French commander, who continued at Fort de Chartres, refused to lend assistance.[26]

The failure to bring back the French king or to make common cause with remaining French colonists damaged the long-term prospects of Indian insurrectionists. If Indians could chase British colonists from backcountry settlements and British troops from outlying posts, they needed trade goods and weapons to make these victories enduring. But deprived of imperial backing to counter British power, the Indian confederacy soon saw its gains overturned.

Although the British by 1765 had quelled the insurrection, their triumph was ambiguous. The experience and expense of fighting Indians chastened officials, who rethought policies and practices. Repealing Amherst's vindictive program, British authorities agreed on the need to accommodate Indian expectations about the character of exchange. When British traders reentered the western country, they carried presents and they allowed Indians to set the protocol for conducting intercultural negotiations. In addition to these symbolic shows of generosity and esteem, British policymakers also tried to offer a substantive assurance of their respect for Indian lands. By royal proclamation, George III drew an internal border at the crest of the Appalachians. Beyond this line, colonists were not to go. The Ohio valley down to its confluence with the Mississippi was reserved for Indian occupants, licensed traders, and previously settled *habitants.*

Issuing edicts and enforcing them, however, were not the same, making further accommodations essential. Almost immediately, hunters from the British American backcountry breached the proclamation line and intruded on Indian lands. Ostensibly hunting for skins, these men also acted as hunters for lands, for themselves and for monied speculators. Having only a limited number of soldiers to patrol a vast territory, British officials had no way to curb these incursions into the upper Ohio valley. Down the Ohio, the British had as yet no presence at all. Not until October 1765, two and a half years after the Treaty of Paris, did a British contingent under the command of Captain Thomas Stirling arrive at Fort de Chartres to take formal control from the French. With only one hundred men and with the memory of the recent sacking of British forts fresh in mind, Stirling wisely sought to assuage, not antagonize, local Indians.

He adopted a similarly conciliatory stance toward French *habitants.* At one point, British officials had considered a plan to relocate French villagers in the Illinois Country to lands near

Detroit, where the British military could more easily keep a closer eye on them. Coming a few years after the removal of the Acadian population, the British had experience in the expulsion and dispersal of French colonists. But in this instance, French *habitants* in the confluence region beat British administrators to the punch. In the face of French migration west, the British scrapped plans to force them east. Instead, to stem the flow *out* of British territory, a declaration granting "the liberty of the Catholic religion" was circulated. Further guarantees about freedom of movement and the right to buy and sell property were offered as well. These adjustments succeeded in slowing the exodus to the Spanish side of the Mississippi and in enticing a few earlier emigrants to return to homes on the eastern bank.[27]

Across the Mississippi, the Spanish also accommodated French colonists and Indian inhabitants, though this, too, was not the original intention. First, the Spanish had to be convinced that Louisiana was worth ruling at all. When initially presented with the French offer of the western side of the Mississippi valley plus New Orleans, Spanish negotiators balked. Rather quickly, however, old defensive considerations prompted a turnaround. The same logic that had pushed Spanish colonization northward into Texas a half-century earlier backed the takeover of a portion of French Louisiana: if Texas served as a buffer protecting the valuable mines of northern Mexico, then holding the western side of the Mississippi valley would thicken the protective barrier.

Having accepted the French cession, Spanish authorities had still to establish their control over a vast province whose boundaries were not really known and whose inhabitants were not reconciled to new rulers. For several years, those inhabitants did not have to submit to any Spanish standard-bearer. Its treasury depleted, the Spanish crown had no money to expend on expanded colonial possessions. Between November 1762, when the transfer took place, and March 1766, when the first Spanish governor landed in New Orleans, more than three years elapsed in which Spain had no official presence in Spanish Louisiana. During those years, French officials stayed in place, which maintained a minimal veneer of colonial authority. The arrival of Governor Antonio de Ulloa belatedly brought a Spanish head to

Louisiana's governance and finally forced Spain to pay for the colony's defense and administration. But only ninety soldiers accompanied the new governor, a number hardly sufficient to make Spanish claims meaningful much beyond New Orleans. Pending reinforcements, Ulloa chose to make imperial authority, such as it was, a two-headed creature. He continued to administer Lower Louisiana in partnership with the acting French commandant. Away from New Orleans, the Spanish remained dependent on French subordinates to oversee Upper Louisiana (or what the Spanish more often referred to as the Illinois, though the present boundaries of the state of Illinois lay across the river in British territory).

To lessen that dependence and create at least a token Spanish presence, Ulloa sent a contingent of soldiers under the command of Captain Francisco Ríu up the Mississippi in April 1769. Ignoring warnings about "scattering" his small force, Ulloa allocated forty-five men for the expedition. Their first mission was to build and man two forts near the mouth of the Missouri River, one on the north side and one on its south side. These, Ulloa hoped, would keep "the savages in harmony with the Colony" and "prevent the British neighbors from intruding in the lands and dominions which belong to His [Spanish] Majesty."[28]

Recognizing the weakness of the Spanish position, Ulloa's instructions to the expedition's commander urged "politeness" in dealing with British neighbors, Indian inhabitants, and French colonists. In particular, Ulloa, along with his superiors, understood that the Spanish had to adopt a new set of policies regarding Indians—not only in Louisiana but throughout Spain's American empire. Instead of the conquest, tribute taking, labor expropriation, and missionization that had previously prevailed in Spanish colonies to the south and west, advocates of reform insisted that cultivating alliances and trading ties in the manner of the French offered a cheaper and more profitable way to run an empire. In keeping with the new directions pushed by his superiors, Governor Ulloa advised his subordinates to "exercise a great deal of tact and care with the Savages. . . . We must make them believe that we go into their lands without any claim of right, but because they want us to go." Essential to maintaining good relations, wrote Ulloa, was to follow the French lead and distribute presents. By doing this, the Indians "will understand that we want to do everything they have been accustomed to, and we do not wish to introduce any novelty among them." The key, in short, was to make the Indians believe that the Spanish and French were one and the same.[29]

Yet Ulloa did not propose to do exactly as the French. Like Amherst, Ulloa considered the Indians "people who like to have lots of things given to them" and who "will sell their friendship for anything that is offered for it." Because they were "never satisfied," care had to be taken not to give too much too soon. Moreover, the governor of Louisiana knew that his superiors were not prepared to underwrite the expenditures for gifts allowed by his French predecessors. Thus the "distribution of presents must be done in a different way and under different formalities from those exercised by the French," with careful accounting to ensure the utmost frugality. Ulloa further advocated that Indians in "the interior" of the Missouri valley be made "as far as possible . . . to forget the use of muskets," meaning that Spanish authorities should stop traders from supplying guns.[30]

Such economy in gifting and restriction on trading did not sit well with Indians in the confluence region. Having learned to expect more from French officials and having taught British representatives that presents were an essential part of intercultural trade and diplomacy, Indian leaders voiced disappointment with Spanish proposals. At the first meeting between Spanish emissaries and visiting Indian leaders in St. Louis, the limited offering of gifts became a source of contention. More disturbing to the Spanish representatives, the Indian headmen let it be known that they found the British more generous with presents.

That not so subtle threat caught the attention of the Spanish, who got additional instruction in balance of power politics in dealings with the Osages. As in the French era, the Osages continued to play their position between to great advantage. In the 1770s, the Osages moved their villages south and west, putting more distance between themselves and the seats of colonial authority. Yet the new locations remained within the reach of British traders, preventing the Spanish from monopolizing trade or dictating terms of intercourse. The Osages also had the numbers to back up their own demands. In the early 1770s, the Little

Osages fielded approximately four hundred warriors, the Great Osages perhaps twice that number. That made the Osages a potent foe, which the Spanish learned about in 1772. Angry about Spain's tight-fisted trading policies, groups of Little Osage and Missouri Indians attacked traders traveling up the Missouri River. In response, the lieutenant governor ordered a cutoff of trade with those nations. In turn, the Little Osages and Missouris went on the offensive, attacking one of the Spanish forts along the Missouri. The fort's small force quickly fled, leaving the Indians free to plunder the post's munitions and provisions. The raiding party then moved on St. Louis. There, in a striking display of defiance and of borderland balance of power politics, the invading Indians raised a British flag.[31]

By no means did the scope of this incident equal the widespread uprising that had occurred where the British had supplanted the French. No prophetic visions seem to have inspired those who made the attack on the Spanish fort or raised the British flag at St. Louis. The number of Indians involved in this raid was also much smaller than had participated in the attacks against dozens of British posts and backcountry settlements. Consequently, Spanish soldiers with assistance from French colonists were, in short order, able to remove the British flag and run the Indians off.

Still, just as shows of Indian strength had forced the British to amend policies and practices in the Ohio valley and Great Lakes, so, too, the Spanish adopted a more conciliatory line in the wake of the raid. Military action required more money and manpower than Spanish officials could readily muster. With direct force not yet a viable option, lieutenant governors in St. Louis thought they might coerce "good behavior" by threatening trade sanctions. But these threats had little meaning in the early years of Spanish rule, for the Osages had the power and the location to trade with whom they pleased. Realizing that they could not stop traders from British territory from engaging the Osages, the Spanish, at least temporarily, dropped their efforts to discipline the Osages. Instead, they tried to control more of the Osages' trade by being more generous with presents. By and large, that strategy succeeded. In 1775, the Osages were supplying traders licensed by Spain with more than twenty-two

Figure 3. Color lithograph, copied from an 1805 painting of the Osage chief Le Soldat du Chene, from one of the original folios of McKenney and Hall's *History of the Indian Tribes of North America* (1837–1844). Courtesy of the Autry National Center.

thousand pounds of pelts. This amounted to nearly half the volume of trade between Spain and Indians in Spanish Illinois.[32]

By bending their practices toward Indian expectations, the Spanish secured peace and continued trade with the Osages; Spanish practices, however, remained at odds with the expectations of many colonists in the confluence region. In Ste. Genevieve, for the most part, the onset of the Spanish regime had little impact on the lives of *habitants.* As farmers, their primary livelihoods were not tied to Spanish trade policies with Indians. It did not matter much whether they were ruled by Louis XV or his Bourbon cousin Carlos III, as long as they could still send their agricultural surpluses to markets in New Orleans. In St. Louis, by contrast, Spanish rule and new mercantilist impositions provoked more immediate discord. That was no surprise given that these policies aimed first to establish closer imperial control over the fur trade, a business in which most of the residents of St. Louis were involved. Consequently, opposition was widespread when Captain Ríu, under orders from Governor Ulloa, banned traders from going to Indian villages until licenses were issued in New Orleans. Such restrictions threatened the freewheeling system that had characterized the first years of St. Louis. In the face of local hostility, Ríu reconsidered the order, but Ulloa, after getting reports of turmoil in Upper Louisiana, sent Captain Don Pedro Piernas to replace Ríu in August 1768.[33]

To quiet Upper Louisiana, Ulloa contemplated bringing more governable settlers to the region. Acadian families, lately expelled from their homelands and now headed for Louisiana, seemed good candidates. According to Ulloa, the Acadians were "a quiet people, of excellent habits," who were "docile and pious in their religion." The governor also corresponded with Catholics in Maryland about relocating to Louisiana.[34]

Before Ulloa could implement these colonization ideas, he was himself sacked. Unlike Ríu, however, his removal was orchestrated not by his superiors but by his subjects. In New Orleans, as in St. Louis, merchants reacted angrily to efforts to impose mercantilist trade policies. Conspiring together, New Orleans traders sponsored a boisterous demonstration against Ulloa's governance in the fall of 1768. This was followed by calls for the withdrawal of the Spanish and a return to French rule. Nothing demonstrated the fragility of Spanish control more than the success of what came to be known as the "Revolution of 1768." Within a matter of days, Ulloa had taken flight.[35]

The departure of Ulloa did not, however, bring the hoped for departure of the Spanish. Instead, Carlos III dispatched Lieutenant General Alejandro O'Reilly, with twenty-one ships and two thousand troops, to reassert Spanish control over the rebellious province. Arriving in August 1769, O'Reilly quickly cracked down. The leaders of the previous year's "revolution" were arrested and charged with treason. Five of the convicted rebels were executed by firing squad, and six more were given long prison sentences. All colonists were made to swear allegiance to the Spanish monarch. Such repression earned its instigator, now installed as the governor of Louisiana, the nickname "Bloody O'Reilly."[36]

In spite of the show of force and the sobriquet, O'Reilly did not—and could not—rule Louisiana by terror alone. Even with additional troops, Spain could not prevent the incursions of British traders into parts of the neighboring Louisiana colony. That, in turn, further diminished the control that the Spanish exercised over Indian nations within the boundaries of the colony. Unable to subjugate Indians, O'Reilly, like Ulloa before him, recognized the need for accommodations. Indeed, the new governor advised his underlings to take on the role of the French and act as mediators in disputes between rival Indians.[37]

The accommodations of the Spanish involved the adoption not only of French practices but also of French people. In Louisiana, the Spanish crown relied heavily on non-Spanish officials, starting at the top with the Irishman O'Reilly as the colony's governor. In Upper Louisiana, the Spanish had little choice but to employ French subordinates, for the Spanish presence was very thin. Captain Piernas, appointed by O'Reilly as lieutenant governor for Upper Louisiana, commanded a force that was reduced to thirty-three soldiers—and these were divided between nine at Ste. Genevieve, seven at Fort Don Carlos, and seventeen in St. Louis. With no reinforcements forthcoming, the lieutenant governor left French holdovers in charge of the administration of most local affairs and also of local militias in St. Louis and Ste. Genevieve. Thus when residents of St. Louis and Ste. Genevieve took the required oath to Carlos III, they did so under the direction of officials who had until recently been in the service of his cousin, Louis XV. Almost all government business continued to be conducted in French because, as a frustrated successor of Piernas acknowledged, "there is not at this post anyone who can write Spanish even moderately well."[38]

Trade with Indians also remained the preserve of French men turned Spanish subjects, though Governor O'Reilly did make some important changes. If many in St. Louis's trading community initially objected to licensing, most acquiesced to a policy that eliminated the monopoly granted to Maxent, Laclède, and Company. To obtain these licenses, traders had first to profess their loyalty to the Spanish crown. That was simple enough. The harder part was adhering to Spanish bans on established products of exchange. Firearms were not to be dealt to Indians, nor was livestock (which was assumed to have been stolen from Spanish New Mexico and Texas) to be acquired from them. Licensed traders also had to cease trafficking in Indian slaves.[39]

This prohibition came along with modifications in the ethnic composition and legal regulation of Louisiana's slaves. In addition to ending trade in Indian captives, O'Reilly ordered the emancipation of all Indian slaves held by Spanish subjects. With regard to African slaves, the Spanish governor faced several conflicts between previous French practices and the rules that prevailed in other Spanish colonies. The French *Code Noir*, for example, prohibited miscegenation and sought to prevent slaves from purchasing their freedom; Spanish laws did neither. Of course, the French ban on interracial sex between masters and slaves was widely ignored throughout Louisiana, and free blacks already represented a small but growing segment of the colony's population. Consequently, confronted with differences in slave codes, O'Reilly moved slowly to substitute Spanish for French statutes.[40]

In the administration of laws and the adjudication of disputes, the Spanish deferred as well to inherited conventions. In theory, the Spanish did establish a judicial system of their own.

Under this regime in Upper Louisiana, a local official handled minor civil suits and criminal cases, while the lieutenant governor sat in judgment on more serious matters. Final disposition of the most serious matters, including capital cases, fell on the shoulders of the governor general in New Orleans. In practice, however, many disputes never reached formal courts. French colonists preferred to rely on arbitrators to resolve most conflicts between neighbors, and Spanish officials left this custom intact. As one Spanish governor in New Orleans informed his subordinate, the lieutenant governor, in St. Louis, "In all disputes between interested parties or claims between residents when they are not matters that might be injurious to the government or to the general public, it is best for the parties concerned to leave such cases to the decision of the arbitral Judges or friendly arbitrators." Most important from the point of view of imperial officialdom was "to prevent the residents from becoming entangled in lawsuits." Even when disputes did come before local officials or the lieutenant governor, decisions usually followed the custom of arbitrators, who typically based their rulings on what they determined to be unwritten community norms. Traditions—some old, some new—remained the most important facts of life, regardless of which empire's flag flew over the colonial settlements of the confluence region.[41]

The third quarter of the eighteenth century witnessed significant alterations to the maps that colonizers plotted of the confluence region. Around midcentury, the establishment of Ste. Genevieve brought the customs of French villages in the Illinois Country to the west bank of the Mississippi. As in communities across the "father of waters," the *habitants* of Ste. Genevieve were creatures of tradition; yet in many cases, the conventions to which they adhered were as much inventions of the Illinois Country as they were long-standing colonial precedents or even longer-standing medieval practices. The addition of St. Louis to colonial maps denoted the further development of the west bank. Conceived by New Orleans merchants as a trading outpost, its founders hoped that St. Louis would be a center for intercultural commerce in the confluence region. From its inception, St. Louis fulfilled that expectation, but its birth occurred at the very moment when France relinquished its colonies in North America. In the wake of the Seven Years' War, the Mississippi became a boundary between English and Spanish claims.

This remapping presented the peoples of the confluence region with perils and possibilities. On the British side, new imperial impositions jeopardized the arrangements worked out among and between French and Indians. Against this peril, Indians fought, while *habitants*, in a quieter show of defiance, sought refuge in Spanish lands west of the Mississippi River. The actions of both Indians and colonists reflected a desire to restore the status quo ante. Contrary to the hopes of Indian rebels and colonial refugees, however, the French king (and his subordinates) did not then return to the Mississippi valley. But all was hardly lost, for resistance compelled British officials to behave more like the French. Similarly, Spanish administrations sparked unrest when they presumed to dictate rules to occupants on their side of the river. They, too, came quickly to understand that neither colonists nor Indians could be reconciled to a new regime by force alone. Rather, the governance of this borderland required a bending of policies and a blending of practices. And here again, adjustments and accommodations eased the transition from one colonial regime to another.

During the eighteenth century, colonial promoters, particularly in British America, touted various North American territories as a good, or even as the best, "poor man's country." But it was Upper Louisiana in the third quarter of the century, first under the French and later divided between Spanish and British rule, that perhaps most deserved the title. In the villages of the confluence region, colonists got by more easily and got ahead more readily than in the places from which they had come. Whether formally administered by French, Spanish, or British officials, Upper Louisiana's colonists generally escaped the burdens that imperial rule imposed in other parts of North America. Instead, they were able to follow and invent their own traditions. Left to an unprecedented extent to govern themselves, pioneering *habitants* took advantage of available land, excellent soil, and the strong market for wheat in Lower Louisiana. To these attractions for farmers were added the possibilities for profiting from trade with Indians. That this activity took men away from their villages for extended periods contributed to the confluence region's unique status: not only was it a good poor man's country but it also may have been the best poor woman's country.[42]

3.

Newcomers

The American Revolution resulted in another remapping of the confluence region. For the most part, however, the intercultural accommodations that had developed in previous decades persisted through the last quarter of the eighteenth century. Taking over the eastern side of the confluence region, Americans initially repeated the mistakes of British officials after the Seven Years' War. But the strength displayed by a confederation of Indians in the Great Lakes and Ohio valley—and the support the confederation received from the British—forced American leaders to temper their arrogance, at least temporarily. More remarkable than any shifts in official stance were the reconciliations that occurred on the ground. On the western side of the confluence region during the 1780s and 1790s, the Spanish wrestled with how to secure their rule in the face of imperial rivals and unsettled relations with Indians and colonists. Concluding that a significant increase in population was essential, Spanish authorities lured a few thousand migrants from the Ohio valley into Upper Louisiana. The newcomers included both Indians, primarily Shawnees and Delawares, and Americans. For decades, these peoples had battled one another for control of the Ohio valley. But in the confluence region, at least initially, they resided to-

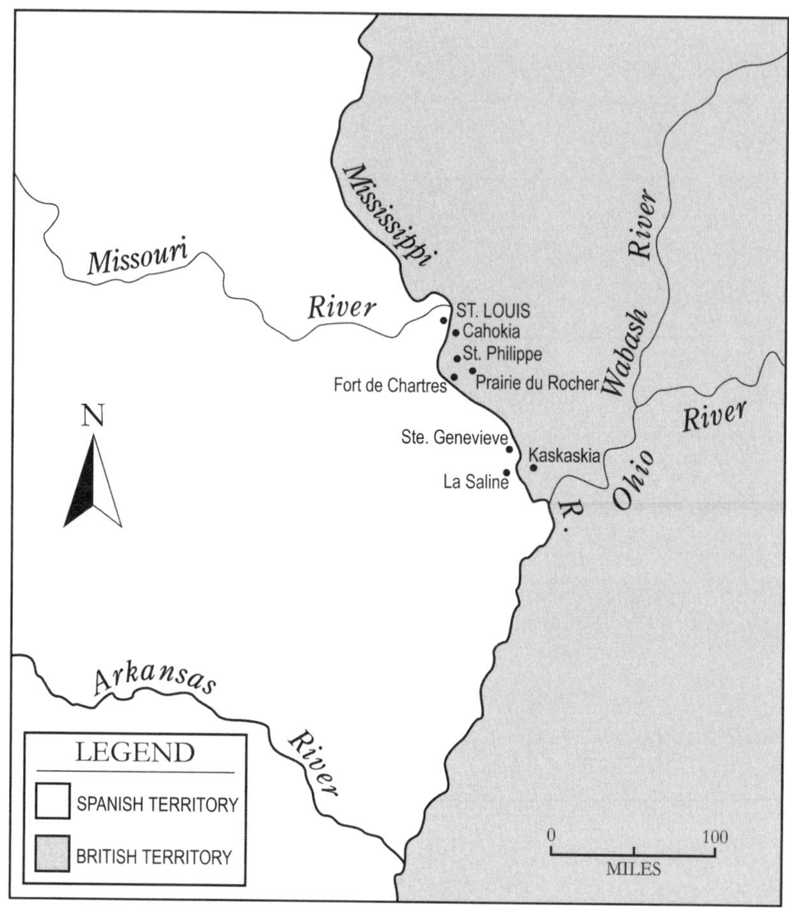

Map 4. Colonial Settlements in the Confluence Region, c. 1770s.

gether on unexpectedly friendly terms. Their presence exacerbated tensions with previously established colonists and Indians, however. In addition, the newcomers did not eliminate the threat to Spanish rule posed by imperial rivals and by the Osages, who remained the most powerful nation in the confluence region to century's end.

Revolution and Repetition

Unlike the Seven Years' War, the American Revolution brought combat directly into the confluence region. These local battles were admittedly minor engagements in a much broader war that was both an unprecedented struggle for independence and one more chapter in the long competition between European empires for control of North America. As a result of the Revolution, a new contender emerged in the confluence region; the eastern side of the Mississippi valley became the western border of the United States. Still, even as the ambitions of American pioneers and the expansionism of the American republic forced Indians, established colonists, and imperial rivals to rethink their strategies, much about intercultural and interimperial relations continued to follow familiar scripts.

Before the Treaty of Paris (1783) formalized the independence of the United States and the redrawing of regional maps, Americans staked claims to a vast "western country." In the 1760s in defiance of British imperial dictates, a few thousand settlers moved across the Appalachians to take up residence in the upper Ohio valley. The number of colonists in the Ohio valley surged ahead in the mid-1770s. Nearly coincident with the outbreak of fighting between British soldiers and Massachusetts minutemen, Daniel Boone led a party of thirty men to the Kentucky River, where they established Boonesborough as an outpost of a new colony. By July 1776, when the Continental Congress issued a Declaration of Independence, several other settlements had also been founded in what is now central Kentucky. True, the cause of American nationhood was not a major concern for those who moved into Kentucky or Tennessee. The independence that mattered most to them came to men who owned real estate. It was for individual land claims that they risked their lives and the lives of their dependents.[1]

And quite a risk it was, for the lands to which newcomers sought exclusive rights were claimed as well by a variety of Indian nations, especially Cherokees, Delawares, and Shawnees. Not all chose to fight for possession. Some preferred to reach a peaceful understanding with the newcomers. The Shawnees and Delawares were themselves relatively new to the Ohio valley, having migrated west from Pennsylvania earlier in the eighteenth century. But within Shawnee, Delaware, and Cherokee villages were many, especially younger men, who rejected further attempts at conciliation with land-mad pioneers. In the

British, these advocates of war found a source of support, for the ministers of George III were now more determined to roll back the illegal settlements that had been made beyond the Appalachians. With British supplies, Indian warriors launched attacks against pioneer enclaves south of the Ohio River. In turn, pioneers in Kentucky and Tennessee struck back, though in seeking vengeance, they often failed to discriminate between friendly or neutral Indians and those who had aligned with the British.[2]

The most daring of these "retaliations," led by George Rogers Clark, supplanted the British from their posts in the confluence region. Shortly after setting off from the Falls of the Ohio River (present-day Louisville) in June 1778, Clark's force surprised British troops at Fort Massac (opposite the mouth of the Tennessee River). After taking that fort, Clark marched his army of less than two hundred men to Kaskaskia, where another British station surrendered on July 4. From there, Clark planned to move on to Detroit, the principal base from which the British supplied Great Lakes and Ohio valley Indians. But Clark had lost the element of secrecy so crucial to his initial successes in the confluence region. Defections, too, had diminished the size of his force. Although Clark captured Vincennes in February 1779, Detroit remained beyond his reach. Disappointed, he returned to Kentucky. A small contingent of American troops, however, stayed behind on the east bank of the Mississippi.[3]

The appearance of American soldiers presented a problem for Spanish officials across the river. In Madrid, Havana, and New Orleans, authorities celebrated any defeat of the British, old enemies from whom the Spanish had lost territories to regain. In St. Louis, the newly arrived Spanish lieutenant governor, Fernando de Leyba, also welcomed the disappearance of the British, whose traders had continuously trespassed across the Mississippi and lured Indians in the upper Mississippi and Missouri valleys with cheaper and better goods. By offering an alternative source for European manufactures, these encroachments subverted the efforts of Leyba and his predecessors to control trade and Indians in Upper Louisiana. Yet the appearance of Americans caused equal concern. Troublesome as traders were, there were few of them. The westering movement of settlers, by contrast, had already brought several thousand newcomers into the Ohio valley and its tributaries. Should the success of Clark's force open up the confluence region to American pioneers, their numbers threatened to spill across the Mississippi and undermine Spanish possession of Upper Louisiana.

Neutral during the Revolution's early years, Spain ultimately declared war on Britain in July 1779. But the Spanish crown did not enter into a military alliance with rebellious American colonists and refused even to recognize the independence of the United States before 1783. Within the confluence region, though, Spanish officials more readily assisted Americans across the Mississippi. Almost immediately, Leyba and Clark forged a solid friendship, and the lieutenant governor permitted Clark to purchase desperately needed supplies from St. Louis merchants. Absent this infusion, the American garrison could not have retained its position in the confluence region.[4]

After Spain declared war against Britain, Upper Louisiana braced for a British invasion of its principal settlements. To bolster defenses, Leyba ordered construction of a road between St. Louis and Ste. Genevieve and the improvement of fortifications around the former town. The hurried preparations were only partially completed when in May 1780 close to one thousand British-supplied Indians (primarily Menominees, Winnebagos, Sacs, and Foxes) came down the Mississippi and advanced on St. Louis. Although the invaders were repulsed, the defenders reported seventy-nine killed, wounded, or captured, a significant loss for a village whose population totaled only about seven hundred. Directing much of their grief and anger at Leyba, the irritation of locals intensified when the lieutenant governor failed to secure a return of captives from a visiting Sac and Fox delegation.[5]

Leyba's death in June 1780 left the task of rebuilding the trust of colonists, restoring peaceful relations with Indians, and securing Spanish claims in Upper Louisiana to his successors. These responsibilities fell first to Francisco Cruzat, who had also occupied the post of lieutenant governor in Upper Louisiana before Leyba. In Cruzat's favor, he made fewer demands on the time and taxes of locals. He also displayed more skill in his negotiations with Indians, using gifts and diplomacy to win several groups of British-supplied Indians into (or sometimes back into) the Spanish trading fold. In 1782, he delightedly reported that "four principal chiefs" of the Shawnees, Delawares, Chickasaws, and Cherokees had come to St. Louis "with the intention . . . of establishing a firm and sincere peace with the Spaniards." Yet Cruzat overstated when he claimed to have detached these nations "completely from the affiliations they had previously had with the English." Likewise, his report misled the governor of Louisiana, who mistakenly informed his superior that Cruzat had made peace with some 140 tribes living east of the Mississippi. In fact, the achievement was far more limited and far less permanent. Like his predecessors—and his successors—Cruzat lacked the resources to erase the competitive advantages that traders operating under the British umbrella enjoyed. With fewer gifts to dispense and with licensed Spanish traders hampered by higher priced goods, Upper Louisiana's lieutenant governors found it impossible to gain or keep the commerce and affections of Indians in the Ohio, Mississippi, and Missouri valleys. By 1782, and continuing throughout the decade, British traders dominated intercultural commerce on both sides of the upper Mississippi valley. Pulled away from peaceful exchanges with the Spanish, numerous Indians turned to raids on colonial settlements in Upper Louisiana. Ste. Genevieve's villagers, in particular, complained about the "barbaric madness of the Indians," who stormed their village "from all sides."[6]

Here, the rhetoric of petitioners exaggerated their "critical position." Raids were frequent and were impossible to contain, so long as inter-Indian and interimperial politics were so confused. But while the incursions cost *habitants* many horses, they resulted in very few deaths. Compared with the bloody warfare being conducted by Indians and Americans in the Ohio valley, the thievery that beset the Spanish part of the confluence region hardly measured up as "barbaric madness."

In the Ohio valley, bloodshed and barbarism had reached much higher levels and did not abate at the end of the Revolution. Under the terms of the Treaty of Paris, the United States acquired the lands between the Appalachians and the Mississippi (south of the Great Lakes and north of Florida, which was ceded to Spain). That these were the lands which Great Britain had just twenty years earlier permanently guaranteed to Indian occupants deepened the Indians' sense of betrayal. So, too, the haughtiness of American officials intensified the anger of Indians. Just as British officers had pretended in the early 1760s that western Indians had surrendered along with the French, so Americans presumed to dictate, not negotiate, with those whom they dismissed as defeated. Typical was George Rogers Clark's statement that "inviting" Indians to negotiate treaties was "considered by them" a sign of "fear" and that "giving them great presents confirmed it." Needless to say, Clark's echoing of Lord Jeffrey Amherst did not accord with Indian understandings about the conduct of intercultural diplomacy and the meaning of presents. No more than in the 1760s did Ohio valley Indians in the 1780s see themselves as having been conquered.[7]

Again, however, Ohio valley Indians divided over how to respond to British betrayal and American arrogance. Many concluded that it was better to move than fight and looked to relocate to lands west of the Mississippi. Others held out hope that an accommodation, which would protect the integrity of Indian claims, might be reached with Americans. But these hopes dimmed when American squatters pushed their farmsteads north of the Ohio River. They died when American militias attacked "friendly" Indian villages and murdered conciliatory Indian leaders. In the face of such aggression, Ohio valley Indians launched their own strikes against American settlements, and more than ever before, they joined together across village and ethnic lines to unite in resistance.[8]

Various factors contributed to the good fortunes of the confederation of Indians in the decade after the Treaty of Paris. First, the British desertion was not as complete as the Treaty of Paris suggested. Making peace did not mean that King George III and his ministers had reconciled themselves to the loss of American colonies. Because the crown's agents viewed western

Indians as crucial to recovering his majesty's possessions, they rushed to reassure their wartime partners that the alliance continued. Reneging on the treaty provision that stipulated the evacuation of British posts south of the Great Lakes, British officials promised Indians that these forts would be maintained and would dispense the gifts, trade goods, and arms that natives needed to defend their homelands. The arrogance, incompetence, and divisions among American adversaries stiffened the resolve of the Indian confederacy, too. By repeating the earlier errors of the British—that is, by treating natives as conquered peoples, by allowing murderers of Indians to go unpunished, and by failing to keep squatters from trespassing across the Ohio—Americans left Indians with little choice but to unite and fight. By contrast, the new nation lacked such common purpose or concerted power. Its own confederation of states assigned the national government too few resources to quell Indian resistance or assert control over the settlement of western lands. The ratification of a national constitution strengthened the federal government, but the army of the United States initially proved unable to quash Indian defiance. First in 1790 and again in 1791, the federal government mustered its troops to attack Ohio Indians, and both times the armies were routed. In the second confrontation, an American force, under the inept command of General Arthur St. Clair, lost 630 soldiers. In terms of casualties, the battle ranked—and still ranks—as the greatest victory North American Indians ever won against the United States.[9]

The triumphs of the British-backed Indian confederation heartened those who wished to see the Revolution reversed. For the British, the victories of Ohio valley Indians validated the wisdom of postrevolutionary policies in North America. By holding on to forts south of the Great Lakes and by arming and encouraging Indian warriors, the British seemed well positioned to reclaim a good portion of territory. For Indians, who had the most to gain, reversing the Revolution meant that American settlements would be rolled back. Ideally, this required the removal of all American colonists to lands east of the Appalachians. More realistically, Indian leaders called for the designation of the Ohio River as a boundary between the United States and Indian country, with American settlements confined to isolated pockets in central Kentucky and eastern Tennessee. To this end, Indians welcomed British supplies; few, however, wanted to return to the situation immediately before the Revolution. Instead, most dreamed of a more distant time, if not prior to the arrival of Europeans, then at least to the borderland that existed before the Seven Years' War when Anglo-French rivalry placed Ohio valley Indians in the enviable position of being between and not beneath any colonial power.[10]

On the Ohio River side of the Mississippi valley, the decade after the American Revolution evoked a sense of déjà vu. Supplanting the British, Americans repeated the error of their predecessor's intercultural ways. As in the 1760s, so again in the 1780s, outsiders claimed to have conquered occupants. Indians disputed these assertions, never more effectively than in victories over American armies in 1790 and 1791. Although these triumphs did not reverse the American Revolution, they did leave the borders of the Ohio valley uncertain. Ten years after the Treaty of Paris had written Indian countries out of the Ohio valley, the headmen of a rising Indian confederation insisted that the Ohio River, not the Mississippi, marked the boundary of the United States.

Immigration and Integration

On the western side of the Mississippi, the decade after the American Revolution was not so violent, but it was also characterized by borders of dubious solidity. Like the United States, Spain asserted its claim to a vast North American territory with a border on the Mississippi. And like the United States, the border had only a limited impact on the ground. Indeed, in Upper Louisiana in the wake of the American Revolution, Spanish officials confronted a situation that made it almost impossible to defend the colony, much less effectively administer it. As before the Revolution, lieutenant governors in Upper Louisiana depended on French subjects, whose loyalties they sometimes questioned. Moreover, these colonists were too few in number to make Spain's extensive claims meaningful. West of St. Louis and

Ste. Genevieve, the Osages retained their predominance. From the east, British traders continued to trespass, stealing trade, siphoning revenue from the colony's economy, and sabotaging Spanish control over Indians within and beyond the borders of Louisiana. Compounding this mix of concerns were tensions generated by the intentions of Americans, who were still few in number directly across the Mississippi but who were seen as a growing threat as their settlements expanded across the Ohio valley. These Americans, cautioned Governor Francisco Luis Hector de Carondelet in 1793, were "a vast and restless people" whose territorial "ambition" would not be limited to their side of the Mississippi.[11]

After the Revolution, Spanish officials issued frequent alarms along these lines. Seeking to counter the expansionism of American pioneers, the Spanish closed the mouth of the Mississippi River to American shipping in 1784. In an age when overland transportation across the Appalachians was prohibitively expensive, the closing of the Mississippi deprived settlers in Kentucky and Tennessee of their only viable outlet for long-distance commerce. This economic choking, it was hoped, would diminish the appeal of the trans-Appalachian region to American settlers. It certainly stirred discontent among western Americans, which the Spanish sought to harness by entering into secret talks with leaders in Kentucky and Tennessee. The most prominent of these leaders was James Wilkinson, a general in the Continental army now engaged in local politics and land speculation. The details of the negotiations remain cloudy, but the basic deal offered to Americans in the Ohio valley was clear: sever ties to the United States, accept some connection to the Spanish empire, and regain the right to navigate the Mississippi.[12]

Weighing policy options, Spanish officials determined that the future of Louisiana as a profitable and defensible colony hinged first on attracting more people and then converting those immigrants into faithful subjects of the Spanish empire. Already before the Revolution, this conclusion inspired efforts to resettle displaced Acadians in Louisiana. These refugees located in Lower Louisiana; schemes to bring immigrants to Upper Louisiana received a boost during the Revolution. In 1778, Governor Bernardo de Galvez directed his subordinate in Upper Louisiana "to employ such means as prudence may dictate" to "increase the population of the settlements committed to his charge, especially with French Canadian families living among the English." Suffering oppression first as Catholics and then in "being forced [by the British] to bear arms against the *Bostoneses*," French Canadians seemed ripe for a move. Going beyond simply tendering words of encouragement, Galvez recognized that few could afford to migrate without financial support. Accordingly, his directive called for the royal treasury to provide each family with a tract of land, a ration of maize, an assortment of domesticated animals, and a set of tools "with which they may easily found and establish a household" in Upper Louisiana.[13]

Generous as these inducements appeared, they generated little immigration from Canada, forcing Spanish officials to look far and near for potential newcomers. Far entailed enticing Catholics from various parts of Europe, yet these invitations also yielded few new colonists. Near meant focusing on *habitants* across the Mississippi, and this appeal proved more successful. Just as the British takeover after the Seven Years' War had prompted a small number to move to the Spanish side of the Mississippi, so the American conquest reawakened the unease of Catholic residents. Not many crossed over, however, until later in the 1780s. Here, the chief cause of unsettlement was not fear of religious persecution but insecurity about slaveholdings, a result of the Northwest Ordinance's inclusion of an antislavery plank.[14]

Along with more *habitants*, then, came more slaves, whose presence unsettled Spanish officials. In Upper Louisiana, slaves accounted for close to 40 percent of the colonial census in the early 1770s. In the mid-1780s, this proportion had declined to about 20 percent. But the influx of slaveholders following the Northwest Ordinance raised the percentage of slaves back to about 30 percent by the early 1790s. Even before this influx, Spanish officials tightened restrictions on slaves. In 1781, in response to a supposed outbreak of "unruly conduct," Lieutenant Governor Cruzat "prohibit[ed] the slaves, under the penalty of fifty lashes of the whip, to hold any assembly at night." In addition to confining slaves to their cabins after dark, Cruzat extended his regulation of slave movement by forbidding them to dance, "either by day or night, . . . without an express permission from their masters and the consent of the government." Clearly, Cruzat believed that slave dances, like similar Indian rites, were not mere diversions. Indeed, the possibility of an Indian–African connection was much on Cruzat's mind and lurked behind the lieutenant governor's ban on slaves adorning themselves in the manner of Indians. Because some slaves were Indians, this provision, designed to prevent slaves from passing themselves off as Indians, presumably applied only to those of African descent.[15]

The presence of Indian slaves compounded the problems facing Spanish officials. Although rumors of a slave insurrection occasionally spread in Spanish Louisiana, no significant revolt occurred in the upper portions of the colony. Yet the fears of Spanish authorities persisted, not so much about the African slaves in their midst as about the Indian ones. A holdover from the French era, the trade in and enslavement of Indian captives placed colonial settlements in the middle of intertribal rivalries. In this case, however, being between offered no advantage. Seeking to eliminate a persistent irritant in the colony's intercultural relations, Cruzat's successor, Manuel Perez, ordered all subjects in 1787 not to "acquire, buy, or appropriate any savage slave." But while the practice of holding and dealing Indian slaves diminished under the Spanish regime in Louisiana, the edicts of imperial officials could not end it.[16]

Intercultural concerns and interimperial considerations played a critical part in what turned out to be Spain's most successful immigration policy in the decade after the American Revolution: the decision to open Upper Louisiana to Indians from the Ohio valley. Already in the mid-1770s scores of Shawnees had relocated west of the Mississippi. The numbers of Shawnees and neighboring Ohio valley Indians who traversed the Mississippi leapt ahead after the Revolution, pushed west by changes in imperial geography. "From the moment that we had the misfortune of losing our French father and learned that the

Spaniards were to be our neighbors, we had a great desire . . . to establish a sincere friendship" with the Spanish, reported a delegation of Ohio valley Indians. In the telling of Spanish officials in St. Louis, the independence of the United States was "the greatest blow" to Ohio valley Indians, short of their "total destruction." Seeking refuge from Americans who had extended "themselves like a plague of locusts in the territories of the Ohio River," Shawnees and Delawares appealed to the Spanish lieutenant governor to shelter them from their "cruelest enemies."[17]

If not the loyal Catholic subjects upon which colonial officials had initially pinned their immigration and integration plans, the Spanish nonetheless welcomed the Shawnees and Delawares as a buffer against mutual enemies to the east and west. To encourage their relocation, the Spanish set aside an approximately 750 square mile tract south and west of Ste. Genevieve for these refugees from the Ohio valley. By the 1790s, at least six new villages, inhabited by around 1,200 Shawnees and 600 Delawares, had been established. Most of the new towns were situated along or near Apple Creek, though, in contrast with French *habitants*, the Shawnees and Delawares eschewed the alluvial bottomland adjacent to the Mississippi in favor of locations set back several miles from the river. This position pleased Spanish authorities, because it placed the Shawnees and Delawares between colonial settlements and the Osages villages. In addition, the relocation further south of several hundred Cherokees added to the protective buffer that the Spanish hoped immigrating Indians might provide against the Osages.[18]

In their dealings with immigrant Indians, Spanish authorities once more relied on a French mediator. In this instance, the intermediary, Louis Lorimier, was himself an immigrant from the Ohio valley. As a trader, Lorimier had lived among Ohio Indians for several years, gaining fluency in several Indian languages and marrying a Shawnee. Aligned with the British during the Revolution, Lorimier's storehouse in present-day Ohio was sacked by Kentucky troops under the command of George Rogers Clark in 1782. Financially ruined, Lorimier joined the Shawnee-Delaware exodus to Spanish Louisiana. There his influence and kinship connections with the immigrant Indians made him a valuable broker between Spanish authorities and the newcomers. So "true and faithful" were his services that in 1792 Lieutenant Governor Zenon Trudeau granted Lorimier exclusive rights to the trade with the Shawnees and Delawares. Trudeau charged Lorimier with "bringing as many [Shawnees and Delawares] as possible over to this side" and "posting them as conveniently as may be to our settlements."[19]

That Spanish authorities wished to encourage the relocation of more Indians and to have them establish villages close to existing colonial settlements attested to the success of this immigration policy. More than Catholics from Europe, Canada, or the eastern side of the confluence region, Indian refugees from the Ohio valley proved the most reliable source of newcomers to Upper Louisiana. Moreover, in the view of Spanish officials, the Shawnees and Delawares had integrated well and stood ready to render "aid in case of war with the whites [Americans] as well as with the Osages."[20]

Even as the Spanish welcomed the added numbers and security that immigrant Indians brought to Upper Louisiana, their imperial policy took a paradoxical turn. Although the Spanish regarded the expansion of the United States and its citizens as a (if not the) major threat, they decided in 1787 to open the Mississippi to American shipping, albeit with significant duties applied. More surprising and still more paradoxical was the decision to open the borders of Louisiana to American immigrants. Working first through a French intermediary in Kentucky, Pierre Wouves d'Arges, Spanish authorities found a more potent agent and advocate in James Wilkinson. From Wilkinson and independent of him, Spanish officials received a variety of proposals, including one from George Rogers Clark, to facilitate the resettlement of Americans in Louisiana. After his conquest of British posts in the confluence region, Clark had fashioned a good relationship with Lieutenant Governor Leyba, but by 1787 Leyba was long gone. Instead, George Morgan, a former trader in the Illinois Country and colonel in the American army, gained influential backers, including Diego de Gardoqui, the Spanish minister to the United States, for his colonization scheme. In Philadelphia, Gardoqui and Morgan struck a deal that gave the

American colonizer an enormous land grant, some fifteen million acres across from the mouth of the Ohio River and extending back two degrees of longitude from the Mississippi. In addition to land and a salary, Morgan came away with the right to establish a semi-autonomous colony in which he appointed local officials, a representative assembly passed laws, and Protestant worship was protected. Without waiting for royal confirmation, Morgan circulated handbills promoting the new colony, which he named "New Madrid."[21]

Word of the opening of Louisiana to American emigration pleased American officials. "I wish a hundred thousand of our inhabitants would accept the invitation," wrote Secretary of State Thomas Jefferson to President George Washington in 1789. To Jefferson, the immigration of Americans into Louisiana promised to deliver "to us peaceably what may otherwise cost a war." The trick for American diplomats was to "complain of this seduction of our inhabitants just enough to make the [Spanish] believe it a very wise policy for them, and confirm them in it."[22]

By contrast, Spanish officials in Louisiana reacted far less enthusiastically, especially about the terms under which Morgan's colony was to be populated and administered. Though a supporter in principle of American immigration, Governor Estéban Miró partially rebuffed Morgan. Miró considered the grant excessive and the independence that it afforded Morgan's colony antithetical to the transformation of newcomers into loyal Catholic subjects. "Great concessions to one single individual have never produced the desired effect of populating it," wrote Miró to his superiors. Were Morgan's grant to be confirmed, "the greater part of it would remain uncultivated forever." Still, while Miró refused to allow Morgan his "little republic," he sent the American aspirant off with a reduced grant and an appointment as vice commandant of the district of New Madrid.[23]

Others, in and out of Spain's colonial administration, thought even this too generous and argued that the entire American initiative was misguided. Among the outsiders who expressed opposition was the French trader Barthélemi Tardiveau. Acknowledging admiration for the "inventive genius" displayed by Americans, Tardiveau conceded that a few Americans would be a useful addition to Spanish Louisiana. But "let them form a body," he warned, "and no great time elapses before they aspire to take over the reins of government." As an alternative, Tardiveau urged Spanish officials to permit him to recruit in France, where "a great number of persons respectable by their birth . . . cannot endure the change which the [French] revolution has introduced." Tardiveau's recommendations intrigued Miró's successor, Governor Francisco Luis Hector, Baron de Carondelet, who shared Tardiveau's doubts about the assimilability of Americans. Carondelet, however, was also suspicious of Tardiveau's loyalties—and with good reason, since Tardiveau had earlier sought to persuade the French to retake Louisiana.[24]

After taking office in 1792, Carondelet pushed for repeal of Spain's conciliatory overtures toward the United States and its citizens. This reversal involved tightening restrictions on American shipping on the Mississippi, removing Americans who had crossed into Spanish territory without official permission, and discouraging further immigration from the United States. Carondelet also negotiated alliances with Indians on the eastern side of the Mississippi, in hopes of stiffening their resistance to additional American expansion.[25]

Despite the concerns of Carondelet and others, the American presence was not as yet too daunting. By 1790, fewer than three hundred Americans (including more than one hundred slaves) had moved to Upper Louisiana. Morgan's colony, as Miró predicted, had foundered. Most of the seventy colonists who had initially accompanied Morgan had, in the wake of flooding and sickness, departed New Madrid for points east. So, too, had Morgan returned to the United States. Of more immediate concern to the Spanish in the early 1790s was not the threat posed by Americans from the east but that raised by the escalating conflict with the Osages to the west.[26]

Escalation and Accommodation

In opening Louisiana to westering Indians and Americans, colonial officials calculated that the incorporation of newcomers would secure Spanish rule west of the Mississippi River. But in the decade after the American Revolution, immigration and attempted integration offered no answer to major problems of colonial administration and exacerbated existing tensions. In particular, the presence of newcomers did not resolve the conflicts that arose from Spanish regulations on trade with Indians. And because newcomers occupied lands claimed by the Osages, their advent heightened intercultural strife in the confluence region.

Even before the arrival of immigrant Indians and Americans, Spanish policies governing intercultural trade provoked discord. Under this system, the lieutenant governor of Upper Louisiana assigned exclusive rights to the trade of particular tribes to individuals. Such privileges came at a price; typically, lieutenant governors awarded licenses to the highest bidder, often, in the words of a disappointed would-be trader, "*pour une somme considerable.*" As representatives of the crown, the dealings of traders, almost all of whom were French Creoles, were supposed to uphold the interests of the Spanish empire. On occasion, when rumors circulated that the French wished to reclaim their North American empire or when alarms arose that the French Revolution's insurrectionary spirit was infecting Louisiana's population, Spanish officials wondered about the allegiances of licensed traders (as well as other colonial subjects). But those closest to the scene were quick to dispute "reports that the majority of the inhabitants of St. Louis were disloyal." To the contrary, after conducting a tour of St. Louis and attending a ball at the home of Auguste Chouteau, the town's most prominent merchant, a Spanish official reassured his superiors that "all manifest their great affection toward the [Spanish] King." Not "a single tricolored ribbon" was in evidence, and although the wife of one licensed trader wore a tricolored dress, this reflected "the poor taste of the lady" rather than her political sentiments. Had the Spanish listened more carefully to French conversations, however, they would have picked up some rumblings. Favored traders frequently grumbled that the high cost of obtaining licenses together with mercantilist restrictions eliminated profits. They complained, too, that interlopers frequently trespassed on their exclusive rights. Some of these were fellow Creoles, who refused to accede to a policy that gave all commerce with Missouri valley Indians to a handful of wealthy and well-connected men. In St. Louis in particular, where much of the male Creole population aspired to engage in intercultural commerce, the system encouraged transgressions.[27]

Along with internal violations, external competition undermined the integrity and profitability of the Spanish trading system. After the American Revolution, British traders had not removed themselves from posts and exchange networks south of the Great Lakes. Quite the opposite, they maintained their ties with Ohio valley Indians and increased their presence on both sides of the upper Mississippi valley. Offering better deals, British traders trespassed promiscuously across Spanish territory and successfully diverted much of the commerce with Indians north of the Missouri River to posts in Canada. Even on the Missouri and south of it where Spanish-licensed traders held their own, the competition cut severely into profits. In the 1770s, St. Louis–based merchants enjoyed margins of between 100 and 300 percent. By contrast, in the early 1790s, these had dwindled to 25 percent. Add to this the many risks involved in exchanging goods and getting them to and from St. Louis and New Orleans, and those with Spanish licenses seemed in an unenviable position. Yet it was not just foreign interlopers who diverted the products of intercultural commerce away from New Orleans. Many St. Louis traders, including the firm of Auguste Chouteau and other licensees, took advantage of the higher prices paid for pelts at British posts on the Great Lakes. Increasingly, they shipped buffalo robes and deerskins to New Orleans, while sending higher valued beaver and otter pelts to Michilimackinac (located at North America's other great confluence, where Lakes Huron, Michigan, and Superior come together).[28]

In the face of widespread breaches of mercantilist principles, lieutenant governors in Upper Louisiana talked tough—then looked the other way. Beyond issuing stern warnings, the officials could do little but reconcile themselves to the illicit commerce. In the 1780s and early 1790s, they had neither the manpower to police the borders of Upper Louisiana against British intrusions nor the willpower to alienate their own subjects by punishing them for dealing with foreign elements. Lacking the economic means to offset British advantages, Upper Louisiana's lieutenant governors were further hampered by the pressure to reduce official expenditures. Again and again, superiors in New Orleans and Havana urged subordinates in St. Louis to become less generous in making gifts to the scores of Indian delegations that visited St. Louis every spring. Yet officials in Upper Louisiana could not curb the flow of presents without causing disaffection among Indians in the confluence region and creating more defections to British trading networks. Accordingly, lieutenant governors continued to host lavish feasts for visiting Indians, during which they dispensed a broad inventory of gifts. This distribution sometimes included brandy, despite an official ban on the use of alcohol in intercourse with Indians. Here, too, lieutenant governors concluded that they had no choice but to contravene their own edicts, lest additional commerce be expropriated by imperial competitors.[29]

Throughout the 1780s, Spanish authorities also backed away from plans to retaliate against Indians who plundered traders and pillaged colonial settlements. That some of these raiders hailed from villages across the Mississippi in the territory of the United States inhibited Spanish actions. But colonial settlers and Spanish officials complained repeatedly as well about thefts committed by Indians within the boundaries of Upper Louisiana, identifying the Missouris and the Little and Big Osages as the culprits. Still, so long as little violence was done in the act of robbing traders and stealing horses, the Spanish were reluctant to upset the status quo. As was so often the case, this accommodation was born of weakness. With less than one hundred soldiers in Upper Louisiana, the Spanish were outnumbered several times by the Little and Big Osages. With military options deemed too costly and too uncertain of success, economic coercion seemed the next best option. But prohibitions on trade, reasoned Spanish authorities, punished an entire nation of Indians for the depredations of a few. More to the point, those officials understood that cutting off trade would hurt Spanish subjects and imperial balance sheets more than Indians. Governor Miró feared that the Osages would merely turn to foreign traders and that the exposure of Spanish impotence would "bring about worse consequences."[30]

During the late 1780s, conflicts involving the Osages climbed to higher levels. For decades, the Osages, like the Spanish, had struggled to defend the borders of their domain against interlopers. In general, these were inter-Indian conflicts. To the west, the Osages' expansionism and their position between peoples like the Pawnees and Wichitas and St. Louis traders created ongoing tensions and outbreaks of violence. From the southeast, Chickasaws, Choctaws, and Cherokees, and from the northeast, Potawatomi, Kickapoo, and particularly Sac and Fox were among the Indian peoples who, under heightened pressure from American expansionism, crossed the Mississippi to hunt in what the Osages claimed was their country. Again and again, confrontations with trespassers set off rounds of assaults and retaliations. On occasion, the traditional diplomacy of "covering the dead," whereby the aggrieved party accepted a gift as compensation for the loss of a loved one, put a halt to the cycle of violence. But this lasted only until the next trespassing sparked a new wave of raids and revenge seeking.

The entrance of Indians who came not only to hunt but also to occupy villages on the western side of the confluence region compounded the Osages' grievances. "Scarcely" had Shawnees and Delawares "encamped" in Upper Louisiana before "they were harassed by the Osages," reported Lieutenant Governor Zenon Trudeau. Stepping up their efforts to intimidate newcomers and their colonial allies, the Osages, in the late 1780s and early 1790s, intercepted more traders and launched more strikes against both recent immigrants and longer established villagers. In response, a delegation of immigrant Indians, including Delawares, Miamis, Ottawas, Potawatomis, Peorias, and Shawnees, appealed to Trudeau for assistance to "prevent [the Osages] from killing us and stealing our horses."[31]

In their correspondence, Spanish leaders demonstrated little empathy for or understanding of the Osages' situation. Never did a governor or lieutenant governor take note of the similarities between the Spanish and the Osages, both of whom, after all, were trying to defend territory (most of which was technically unoccupied) against invaders. Instead, especially in the late 1780s and early 1790s, Spanish authorities dismissed claims from Osage leaders that their nation was innocent of thefts from European traders and colonists or justified in attacking Indian trespassers. According to the conventional wisdom among Europeans, the Osages were inveterate thieves and liars, who "never spot a loose horse without feeling a passionate desire to steal it," in spite of "the fact that they have repeatedly promised most solemnly to respect the property of whites." Nor did Spanish officials ever truly accept the logic of Osage and neighboring Indians' ideas about intercultural exchange. Ever pressed to economize, a succession of lieutenant governors never overcame the conviction that bestowing presents amounted to anything more than bribes to encourage good behavior. Like the Indians' ways of war, including the practice of covering the dead, the meaning behind the rituals of gifting remained alien to the Spanish. So, too, colonial administrators apprehended almost nothing about the internal politics of the Osages. Beyond the recognition that the Osages were split between "Big" and "Little" bands, Spanish leaders knew very little about the organization of Osage society or about the exacting challenges with which their Osage counterparts were coping.[32]

Largely unnoticed by the Spanish, a century of direct contact with various Europeans had produced far-reaching changes in Osage culture. The inequalities that had opened with the spread of horses deepened with the inauguration of intercultural trade. In pursuit of European goods, the Osages extended and expanded their hunting. This doubling and even tripling of time spent hunting put more pressure on local populations of deer and buffalo, and it triggered more fighting between tribes. Within the Osages' villages, the distribution of exotic items became a source of contention. Those who had greater access to European goods, and thus controlled their redistribution among fellow villagers, gained stature. Sometimes this status translated into more wives, with polygyny becoming more widespread during the eighteenth century. The burdens of preparing ever more

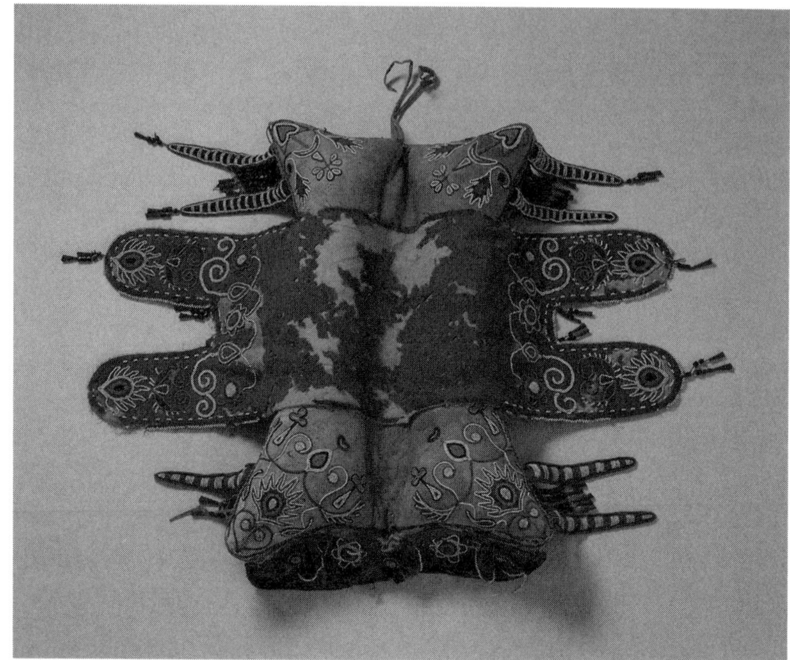

Figure 4. This Métis pad saddle from the mid-nineteenth century reflects the influence of European styles among the Indians of the Missouri valley. Its floral beadwork and embroidery can be traced to French Ursuline nuns who introduced the artistic motifs and techniques to the Huron and Iroquois in the seventeenth century. These then spread west into the Great Lakes and Missouri valley during the eighteenth century. Courtesy of the Autry National Center.

skins fell entirely on Osage women. To flesh, dry, dress, and de-hair thousands of raw hides and pelts consumed more and more of women's time.[33]

Contact and cross-cultural exchange with Europeans inspired political changes in Osage society as well. Where village and clan headmen were traditionally chosen on a hereditary basis, leadership was increasingly a contested affair. Skilled hunters and warriors demanded more say, and younger men (who were often the most skilled hunters and warriors) defied the wishes of elders. Twice in the eighteenth century, internal fracturing led to the splintering of the Osages and the formation of separate independent bands. The first of these schisms occurred in 1700 and resulted in the division between the Little and Big Osages. The second split in 1785 involved the breaking away of two more bands from parent communities.

Not that Europeans were wholly unaware of the changes they had set in motion. In fact, Spanish colonial authorities, like the French and British, manipulated the flow of gifts to foment strife within and between Indian nations. By channeling gifts and offering medals to particular chiefs, Europeans elevated some Indian leaders at the expense of others. By diverting these presents to other individuals, colonial administrators undermined the position of out-of-favor leaders. More than sowing jealousies, colonial authorities hoped that commerce would contribute to Indian dependence and cause Indian trading partners to conform more with European expectations. In addition to shifting the basis of exchange away from gifts and toward more straightforward commercial dealings, Europeans wished to redesign the political systems of Indians. In the case of the Osages, this entailed the breakdown of the traditional division between peace and war leaders and the establishment of centralized authority in a single chief.

Momentous as the changes of the previous century were, they had not as of the 1780s reduced the Osages to a subordinate position. The Osages had grown steadily more dependent on European imports, but they had not succumbed to dependency. That is, they remained more than able to feed and clothe themselves without support from outsiders. Nor were Europeans able to dictate the terms of trade. So long as more than one colonial power vied for the Osages' affections and skins, the Osages maintained their control over the protocols of exchange. Despite internal fractures and the lack of a centralized political structure, the Osages retained sufficient numbers and unity to threaten those who threatened them.

By the early 1790s, however, the challenges to the Osages' regional supremacy had clearly increased. The Missouris, who generally allied with the Osages, suffered heavy casualties at the hands of raiding parties from across the Mississippi. A smallpox outbreak further depleted the tribe's ranks. During the 1790s, surviving Missouris dispersed among the Otos, Kansas, and Osages. By no means was the Osages' plight so desperate. But with the addition of immigrant Indians to their ranks, Spanish authorities felt more confident about taking on the Osages. As a first step in 1790, the Spanish called back traders from Osage villages and suspended all exchange. Once again, this punishment had limited impact on the Osages, who turned to American and British suppliers and plundered Spanish-licensed traders heading up the Missouri. Pulling back, Lieutenant Governor Trudeau opted to reopen trade with the Osages, a decision that St. Louis merchants welcomed. Immigrant Indians and colonists in Ste. Genevieve, however, protested the reversal and demanded a declaration of war against the Osages. Still reluctant to wage a war that he felt could not be won and thus would only damage the reputation of the Spanish, Trudeau wavered. But his superior, Governor Carondelet, pushed for a test with the Osages. Because "white men" in Upper Louisiana were "scarcely sufficient in number to protect" their own settlements, much less successfully invade Osage villages, Trudeau concluded that the assistance of immigrant Indians was essential. If the newcomers "act in concert, they will be able to strike a terrible blow, which may drive the Osage Indians far away." Turning to Louis Lorimier for assistance in recruiting Shawnees and Delawares, Trudeau promised the victors the fruits of conquest. To Shawnees, Delawares, and other Indians who defeated the Osages would come "a territory more abundant in animals than they have ever seen."[34]

Finally, in June 1793, the escalation of conflict peaked with a declaration of war against the Osages. Residents of Ste. Genevieve celebrated the news with "great acclamations of joy." Neighboring Indians were also pleased, relishing the prospect of the Osages being belatedly disciplined for their depredations and deterred from committing future offenses.[35]

Yet the war did not come. Once more, the edicts of colonial authorities carried no real force. No declaration of words alone could give the Spanish in Louisiana an army capable of conquering the Osages. Despite their jubilation about the declaration of war, Ste. Genevieve's *habitants* did not rush to enlist in the planned military campaign. Shawnees and Delawares also refused to launch an offensive. The promises of Trudeau were not enough; what immigrant Indians required were weapons and other war-making materiel. When Spanish authorities failed to provide necessary supplies, the newcomers suspended their preparations for war. The Spanish bid to bring Indians on the plains into an alliance against the Osages failed for similar reasons.[36]

In a matter of months, the clamor for escalation gave way to renewed appeals for accommodation with the Osages. Emboldened by the impotence of their adversaries, Osage bands continued their attacks against the property and persons of colonists and immigrant Indians. In January 1794, an Osage party raided Ste. Genevieve, stealing twenty horses, killing one *habitant*, and leaving villagers shaken. In the wake of this foray, sentiment in Ste. Genevieve switched from war to peace. At the same time, Spanish authorities were rethinking their policy of confrontation, which had, after all, produced no gains. Moreover, imperial rivalries again intruded on the calculations of Spanish policy-makers. In early 1794, rumors reached Spanish officials that Edmond Genet, an emissary to the United States from revolutionary France, was conspiring with Americans to raise an army to invade Upper Louisiana. That the invading force was supposedly to be commanded by George Rogers Clark heightened the anxieties of Spanish authorities. Worried that the Osages might combine with Franco-American invaders, Governor Carondelet abruptly called off the war against them in April 1794. At a conference with Osage headmen, Trudeau made a show of force, arranging "that various exercises by the artillery and troops should be performed . . . to give them a great idea of our strength." Yet instead of following this ritualized display with an attack on Osage villages, the lieutenant governor resorted to a customary ceremony of conciliation, offering the Osage chiefs an assortment of presents.[37]

In May 1794, in a further sign of the return to previous patterns of intercultural accommodation, the Spanish put relations with the Osages back in the seasoned hands of Auguste Chouteau and his family. Having been engaged in trade with Indians in the confluence region for several decades, Chouteau and his relatives understood the traditions that had long governed intercourse between French traders and the Osages. Indeed, like many French traders, Auguste and his brother Pierre had lived for a time among the Osages, marrying Indian women, fathering *métis* offspring, and earning the confidence of their extended trading families. Auguste Chouteau also understood how to cultivate Spanish authorities, often entertaining lieutenant governors at his St. Louis home and sending various gifts to governors in New Orleans. Such hospitality endeared Chouteau to Spanish officials, who reciprocated by repeatedly granting exclusive trading licenses to the Chouteaus. These connections served the family again in 1794. In the wake of the near war, the Chouteaus received from Governor Carondelet a six-year monopoly on trade with the Osages. In exchange, Auguste promised to have a fort built on the Osage River and to maintain a garrison of twenty men there under the supervision of his brother Pierre (as part of the deal, the Spanish agreed to pay the salaries of the men stationed at the post).[38]

Named Fort Carondelet, the stockade theoretically gave the Spanish a military presence in the heart of Osage Country, but the fort promoted accommodation via gifts and trade rather than via confrontation between peoples. Although the Chouteaus had promised to construct an impressive two-story edifice with brick or stone walls, the actual structure, completed in 1795, looked more like the typical wood-framed trading post that French *voyageurs* had established at various points in the interior of North America. Indeed, that is how the Chouteaus viewed it, which is why they manned the fort not with soldiers but with traders in their employ (while also on the Spanish payroll). Fort Carondelet, as operated by the Chouteaus, was principally a site at which to dispense gifts and goods and obtain pelts from the Osages. Only on this basis, experience taught the Chouteaus, could peoples from so many different places get along in the confluence region.

Not that the Chouteaus were above manipulating the Osages for their own advantage. Like various imperial officials, the Chouteaus tried to insert themselves into the internal affairs of the Osages. Most daring were the Chouteaus' efforts to alter the hereditary selection of village leaders and instead install chiefs of their own choosing. The opportunity for such interference presented itself after a 1794 Chickasaw raid killed three Osage chiefs. Seizing the moment, the Chouteaus managed to have Pawhiuskah (White Hair) selected as the principal peace chief of the northern band of Big Osages. That selection did not sit well with the hereditary claimant, Gratomohse (Clermont II or "Iron Hawk"), whose objections caused yet another split in the Osages' ranks.[39]

Still, the influence of the Chouteaus, like the impact of commerce with Europeans, was not simply divisive or immediately destructive to the Osages. During the eighteenth century, the Osages' demand for European goods was genuine. At century's end, the Chouteaus kept their clients well stocked with various wares. As important, the Chouteaus provided the Osages with ample supplies of muskets, gunpowder, and lead, which insured that the Osages would remain a formidable contender in the increasingly complicated competition for occupancy and opportunity within the confluence region.

Conflict and Confluence

In the confluence region, the last years of the eighteenth century continued the mix of intercultural conflict and comity that had marked the previous several decades. With the Chouteaus in charge of trade with the Osages, disturbances from that quarter quieted after 1794. Still, the Osages remained a source of trouble to neighboring Indians, colonists, and Spanish officials. Juggling a familiar set of problems, Spanish authorities launched an audacious new initiative in the late 1790s. This involved a renewed and expanded bid to bring Americans into Upper Louisiana. The ways of these newcomers, so different from those of longer-settled French colonists, generated friction. Surprisingly, however, the Americans who arrived in Spanish territory in the 1790s got along fairly well with an earlier set of newcomers, Shawnee and Delaware Indians, with whom it turned out they had much in common.

Having averted war with the Osages, Spanish authorities turned their attentions back to other threats. One continuing source of unease was the loyalty of the Francophone population, concerns that grew following the visit of French agent Georges Henri Victor Collot to Louisiana in 1796. Collot's mission tied to covert French designs of regaining control not only of Louisiana from Spain but also of the Ohio valley from the United States. The agent's activities in and around St. Louis, however, betrayed the supposed secrecy of the mission and generated pro-French demonstrations—"little orgies and indecent scenes" was how a Spanish official described them—among the local populace.[40]

Worrisome as these internal threats were, Spanish authorities expressed shriller alarms about various external challengers. These included adversarial Indians, interloping British traders, and "intrepid, indomitable" Americans. At times, Spanish governors and lieutenant governors identified the first group as the most immediately dangerous. More often, British traders and the empire they represented figured as the greatest short-term menace. In the long run, though, Spanish officials agreed that the "tranquility" of Louisiana was hostage to "the ambitious designs and projects of our turbulent neighbors the Americans." Against this menace, the Spanish hoped to make common cause with Indians who occupied the lands between Louisiana and American settlements. Yet by 1795, Spanish authorities conceded that support for strategically positioned Indian groups offered only a temporary shield. In a few years, these allies would be overwhelmed, and at that point "nothing will be sufficient to obstruct" the spread of Americans, first into the valleys of the Mississippi and Missouri and then southward through the Spanish empire's rich internal provinces. Nothing, that is, unless Spain employed "this precious time . . . in acquiring a population capable of disputing with them the borders of both rivers" and making Louisiana an "invincible barrier."[41]

But here the Spanish ran up against a persistent problem: where would this population come from? In 1795, in spite of frequently voiced fears about American intentions, the decision was taken to lift the ban on American immigration. This strategy seemed to contradict conventional wisdom. After all, it meant that the Spanish were paradoxically entrusting the defense of Louisiana *against* Americans into the hands *of* Americans.

This shift in policy came only after colonial officials determined they had no realistic alternative. Other sources for increasing the population of Louisiana had not fulfilled expectations. Indian newcomers were thought too few in number and too unreliable as loyal colonial subjects; Catholic immigration totals from Canada and Europe were even more disappointing. The United States alone could "supply a great number of families," concluded Lieutenant Governor Trudeau. International developments contributed as well to the change in course. Rumors of France's interest in retaking Louisiana renewed concerns about an invasion from that quarter or of an insurrection by French colonists. More worrisome were the persistent intrusions of British traders, particularly in light of Spain's break with England in what had been an alliance against revolutionary France. To this was added the alarming news of a *rapprochement* between Great Britain and the United States. Looking to forge more cordial relations with the American republic, the Spanish empire acceded to the 1795 Treaty of San Lorenzo, which resolved the disputed boundary between the United States and Spanish Florida and guaranteed Americans the right to navigate the Mississippi to its mouth. That same year, against the advice of Governor Carondelet, Spain reopened Louisiana to American immigration.[42]

In retrospect, the wisdom of Carondelet's warning is apparent; at the time, however, the policy did not appear quite so strange. As Trudeau correctly gauged, many Americans in the Ohio valley were "disgusted with their [federal] Government," which had not in their view protected them from Indians or provided them with secure land titles. By offering a more peaceful situation and a better deal on land, the more optimistic among Spanish officials believed they could pull Americans to Louisiana and away from their still tenuous national attachments. In this hope, they were not alone. The British, too, had undertaken a similar program to lure disgruntled Americans to Upper Canada (now Ontario). The Spanish appeal, then, began with ample land grants. In addition, promotional tracts that were circulated in Kentucky and Tennessee touted the blessings of Upper Louisiana while skillfully playing on the sources of western American discontent. Thus, Kentuckians and Tennesseans learned that the country on the Spanish side of the confluence region boasted soils similar to the best lands in the Ohio valley. Its "very healthy" climate was remarkably temperate, with autumn reportedly lasting until the fifteenth of January! More plausible and more attractive to Kentuckians and Tennesseans, whose lands were endlessly entangled in overlapping claims and expensive litigations, was the assertion that Upper Louisiana was "exempt from chicanery & lawyers." Instead, the few disputes that had arisen were "terminated, either amicably, . . . or else by arbitration, and always without expense." The pamphlet also promised a respite for the war-weary; in Louisiana, the Indians were "all friendly to Spain" and happy to assist colonists.[43]

How much of this was believed we do not know, but in contrast with previous recruitment efforts, the invitation to Americans spurred an influx that exceeded Spanish expectations. Numerous newcomers attested to the pull of the advertisements. John Dodson headed west in the spring of 1798 after seeing an announcement in the *Kentucky Gazette.* That same year, William James, "in consequence of the encouragements, announced in Kentucky, . . . determined . . . to come and settle" on the Spanish side of the confluence region. For immigrant Moses Austin, the rush required little promotion, for a country that has "everything to make its settlers Rich and Happy" could hardly "remain Unnoticed by the American people." In Austin's case, the lure was especially strong, thanks to a generous grant of more than 7,000 arpents (about 6,000 acres) from the Spanish government. On this land, Austin planned to make his fortune by setting up a lead mining operation. Other newcomers, like Daniel Boone and his sons Daniel Morgan and Nathan, came with lesser ambitions. Having lost most of his land claims in Kentucky and having tired of defending his surveys in one lawsuit after another, Daniel Boone found the Spanish offer of 1,000 arpents (about 850 acres) for himself and an additional 1,400 arpents for his sons a sufficient inducement to relocate in

Upper Louisiana. By 1800, so many other Americans had accepted the Spanish invitation that these newcomers already outnumbered the approximately two thousand French colonists on the western side of the confluence region.[44]

The newcomers' settlements soon dotted the west bank of the Mississippi from New Madrid to St. Louis and in places extended inland from the river. The strongest concentration of American immigrants was at Cape Girardeau, near the post of Louis Lorimier and close to the principal village of the Shawnees. Unlike this earlier group of immigrants from the Ohio valley to the confluence region, the newer newcomers did not cluster in villages. Instead, the Americans tended to disperse their habitations across the countryside. This pattern contrasted as well with that of longer-established French *habitants*, as did the Americans' willingness to move into upland areas at some distance from the water's edge. For his lead mining enterprise, Moses Austin chose a site (Mine à Breton or Potosi) forty miles west of Ste. Genevieve. The Boones took up lands at Femme Osage, thirty miles west of St. Louis. For Austin, the presence of lead dictated his selection. For the Boones and other Americans, the quality of lands was a key criteria, as was their belief that riparian areas were less healthy. The benefits of American locations impressed at least one Frenchman, Nicholas de Finiels, who observed that the latest newcomers could be counted on "to pick an advantageous spot," while his countrymen, "who had occupied these shores for sixty years, never thought of building there." What is more, added Trudeau, the Americans' settlements were "already better than those of the Creoles and Canadians."[45]

During the late 1790s (and for many decades afterward), the cultural differences between long settled French and recently arrived Americans spurred considerable commentary. Sometimes these were relatively neutral descriptions of French versus American ways, highlighting, for example, distinctions in architectural forms (French vertical log construction against American horizontal style) or agricultural and dietary preferences (French wheat as opposed to American corn). More often, though, cross-cultural commentaries came down in favor of one people's ways over the other. Typically, such comparisons set the traditionalism of Creoles against the inventiveness of Americans. Even as he credited the "industry" of Americans, de Finiels wrote a lengthy "homage" to Creole customs. Their easy ways and communal spirit, he observed, allowed the residents of Ste. Genevieve to "maintain the mark of friendliness and simplicity that characterized their forefathers." The villagers were like "an extended family, bound together more by camaraderie than by blood." But in almost the next breath, de Finiels shifted into a drawn-out condemnation of the "sloth and indolence" of *habitants.* Some critics went further. The harshest insisted that French colonists must forsake their customs, especially their system of common-fenced open-field cultivation. So, too, the French connection with Indians, from whom they had "contract[ed] their manners" and with whom they lived in the "grossest ignorance," came under fire from the advocates of what were seen as American ways.[46]

Beneath the rhetoric of oppositions lay some significant differences in worldview. As geographer Walter Schroeder has detailed, French colonists lived in compact villages and farmed narrow strips. Their properties often "fronted" on the Mississippi River, making theirs "a linear, riverine conception of spatial organization." By contrast, Americans "thought in areas." On the dispersed farmsteads that Americans occupied further from the river, "no one side of a property was intended to be more important than other sides." What mattered was the total area, which "extended in all directions from the farmstead."[47]

Although French and American zones of occupation did not often intersect, in places the conflict between French and American practices and worldviews heated up. One such flashpoint was around Moses Austin's lead mine. There, *habitants* spent a portion of each year skimming lead from the top three to four feet of soil. This, they held, was not trespassing. Appropriating unused lead from the surface, they insisted, was analogous to gleaning after the harvest or to taking wood from forests that Creoles considered common property. But this assertion of customary common rights flew in the face of Austin's more exclusive understanding of private property. At century's end, the issue remained unresolved, with angry words frequently exchanged and resentments still simmering.[48]

Simmering, but not boiling over. If tensions between French and Americans ran high at times and in places, Upper Louisiana saw no eruptions of violence between Creoles and newcomers in the late 1790s. According to Lieutenant Governor Trudeau, the vast majority of Americans had "behaved very well," not imposing on others, but instead quietly acclimating to life in a cultural crossroads. Like others before them, all of whom had once been newcomers to the confluence region, the Americans adapted, adjusted, and accommodated.[49]

Defying all expectations, peaceful relations generally prevailed between American newcomers and the Indian peoples they had driven from the Ohio valley. After more than a generation of warfare between American pioneers and Ohio valley Indians, these former adversaries coexisted amicably in the confluence region. Moses Austin's son Stephen remembered that hundreds of Shawnees and Delawares visited his father's store at Mine à Breton "to do business" and to socialize. Indeed, young Stephen recalled that as a boy he "often played with the Shawnee children." Similarly amicable intercourse occurred at the Boone homestead. Not only did Daniel Boone occasionally entertain Shawnees at his Femme Osage home, but he also joined with them on hunting excursions. Back in 1778, some of these same Indians had taken Boone prisoner, and after his escape they had fought against him in a number of bloody encounters. Reunited two decades later, captors and former captive developed a warm camaraderie, reminiscing about times when "we were all glad," while seeming to forget all the nastiness that had come between them. To be sure, the closeness of Daniel Boone's engagement with the Shawnees was exceptional, yet other transplanted Americans also overcame prior histories to participate in hunting, horse racing, gambling, drinking, and dancing with transplanted Indians.[50]

What underlay this unexpected collaboration was the evolution of syncretic cultural elements among Ohio valley transplants. For several generations, first in Pennsylvania, then in the

Ohio valley, and now on the west bank of the Mississippi, the Shawnees and Delawares had lived in close proximity to American colonists. If these frontiers had often turned into dark and bloody grounds, they also served as training grounds. Borrowing from—and in fear of—one another, frontier peoples had developed increasingly similar subsistence systems and material cultures. In the confluence region, the process of cultural convergence had gone far enough that several observers commented on a blurring of boundaries between the ways of westering Indians and westering Americans. As evidence, these commentators usually pointed to the adoption by Americans (and other European colonists) of Indian modes of dress (the use of animal skins or the preference for leather britches and moccasins as opposed to knee britches and European footwear), Indian crops (especially corn, but also squash, pumpkins, and beans), and increased reliance on hunting.[51]

Of equal significance were borrowings that ran the other way. The Shawnees, in particular, had made considerable adjustments, which white observers almost always characterized as "progress." Although the Shawnees resided in compact villages that more closely resembled French towns than American-style "open country neighborhoods," their mixed modes of subsistence and land use patterns were difficult to distinguish from those of Americans nearby. Perhaps the most far-reaching of these adaptations was the Shawnees' embrace of stock raising. At their village near Cape Girardeau, which like American settlements was located on high ground beyond the Mississippi's flood plain, the Shawnees possessed large herds of cattle and pigs. Like European colonists in general, the Shawnees allowed their livestock to roam free in adjacent forests. But it was from Americans in particular that the Shawnees learned to raise stock. This was most visible around their fields, which, Nicholas de Finiels recognized, were "securely fenced . . . in the American-style." Adding to the resemblance between Shawnee and American settlements was their shared practice of laying logs horizontally for their structures. Only on close inspection did observers notice a subtle difference in cabin architecture: Indians notched their logs on the top, while Americans did so on the bottom. But this small variation in material cultures was lost on many contemporaries, who emphasized instead the apparent confluence of cultures. And it has also not helped later archaeologists, who, despite considerable excavations, have been unable to distinguish immigrant Indian from pioneer American sites near Apple Creek.[52]

To be sure, the baggage of bloody prior histories and deep-seated cultural differences was not simply left behind in the Ohio valley. West of the Mississippi, the similarities in the material cultures of Indian and American newcomers masked enduring gaps in underlying understandings and cultural values. If, for example, hunting exemplified a confluence of Indian and American practices, it also exhibited their abiding apartness. Although Indians and Americans occasionally hunted together in Spanish Louisiana, they continued to view their prey in oppositional ways. Shawnees and Delawares maintained the elaborate rites by which they expressed their gratitude to animal "kin." In taking up stock raising, immigrant Indians integrated domesticated animals into existing rituals; ceremonies once exclusively connected with hunting became means of paying respect to slaughtered cattle and pigs. Such ceremonialism had no analog among Americans, whose worldview acknowledged no spiritual powers or special obligations to animals. So, too, the powers and obligations of men and women marked a persistent divide between Indian and American newcomers. For Americans, farming was thought to be the responsibility of men; for Indians, the fields were the domain of women. Control over this and other life-giving and life-sustaining activities gave Shawnee and Delaware women sway within their villages that also had no parallel among patriarchal American counterparts.[53]

Divergent constructions of property rights also stood in the way of a deeper cultural confluence. The Americans' ideal of eternal, individuated ownership of a specific tract contradicted the understandings of Shawnees and Delawares, whose villagers held their land collectively, assigning only a temporary usufruct right to the farmers of smaller parcels. Moreover, the Americans' notion that unimproved lands were "vacant" led to squatting within the territory assigned by Spanish authorities to immigrant Indians. These incursions elicited protests, but to the end of the eighteenth century they did not much disturb the peace between Indian and American newcomers. In fact, many of the Americans who settled near Shawnee and Delaware villages performed useful services, acting as gunsmiths and blacksmiths, for neighboring Indians. Some men went further in attaching themselves to Indian communities by marrying Indian women.[54]

Contributing as well to the concord between erstwhile enemies was the presence of a common foe, the Osages. Under the management of the Chouteaus, relations with the Osages did not deteriorate into all-out war, but matters were hardly harmonious. First, rival traders in St. Louis remained unreconciled to an agreement that guaranteed the Chouteaus exclusive rights to the commerce with the Osages. This was understandable, since the monopoly handed the Chouteaus approximately forty percent of all of the Indian trade through St. Louis. Whenever bands of Osages were accused of committing depredations, competing traders were quick to denounce the Chouteaus' ineffectiveness and to demand a change in the system. Neighboring Indians, too, expressed continuing resentments about the lenient treatment given the Osages. As one immigrant Indian chief complained, the Osages "get nothing but caresses and are supplied with everything," in spite of their long record of misdeeds. Yet in the late 1790s, the most frequent targets of Osage raids were Indian and American immigrants from the Ohio valley, which had the effect of tightening the bonds between these newcomers.[55]

By the end of the eighteenth century, the western side of the confluence region had been part of Spain's empire for nearly four decades. By no means had the Spanish established uncontested control over the colony that they had inherited from the French. To the contrary, away from the confluence of the Missouri and Mississippi, Spanish power steadily diminished. Indeed, not too far up the Missouri, the might of the Osages subordinated the pretensions of the Spanish. Even at the mouth of the Missouri and near the western banks of the Mississippi, the Spanish empire could claim only a tenuous hold. The loyalties of French colonists were too uncertain; the customs, manners, and language of Creoles were no more Hispanicized at the end of the 1790s than they had been at the beginning of the 1760s. From the 1780s, the emergence of the United States, with its borders if not too many of its citizens just across the Mississippi, added to Spanish concerns.

Against imperial rivals and Indian adversaries, the Spanish initiated various schemes to solidify their control over Upper Louisiana by bringing in newcomers. When hopes for a sizeable immigration of European Catholics did not materialize, the Spanish turned to Indians from the Ohio valley. This policy succeeded, though these newcomers alone did not secure Spanish authority. In a seemingly counterintuitive move, the Spanish then opened Upper Louisiana to Americans. To the amazement of everyone familiar with their past hatreds and hostilities, westering Indians and westering Americans peaceably coexisted. Their amicable relations demonstrated that in the confluence region not only rivers but also peoples came together.

Cultural confluence augmented Upper Louisiana's standing as a good poor man's country. In the late eighteenth century, peoples in the confluence region still got by more easily and some got ahead more readily than in the places from which they had come. But what made the Spanish side of the confluence region an extraordinary poor man's country was how former foes now got along so famously.

4.

Transfers

In the first decade of the nineteenth century, the western side of the confluence region changed colonial hands not once but twice. First, Spain sold Louisiana back to France, then the United States acquired the territory from France. With the Louisiana Purchase, the Mississippi again ceased to be a border—at least not a border between Euro-American empires and republics. The United States now claimed all the lands from the confluence region to the sources of the Ohio, Missouri, and Mississippi rivers. Along these corridors, American ambitions spread across North America, led first to the far West by a party commanded by Meriwether Lewis and William Clark.

Consequential as this remapping proved to be, not all changed immediately. In many respects, the final years before the American purchase and the first years afterward mirrored one another and seemed to reprise the borderland-frontier history of preceding decades. On the western side of the confluence region, the agents of American exploration and expansion recognized that in dealings with French colonists and Indian peoples adjustments and accommodations were essential, at least in the short run.

In the latter part of the decade, however, assertions and impositions gained the upper hand when Americans interacted with

Indians of the confluence region. No longer sharing a border with another colonial power, American pioneers, and to a lesser extent American officials, were less constrained in their pursuit of happiness. In the lower Missouri valley, Shawnees and Delawares, despite their demonstrated friendship with earlier American settlers in the region, found their hold on the country slipping. Under pressure, the Osages surrendered a good portion of their country to the American republic, a cession that signaled the transfer of regional supremacy to the United States.

Retrocession and Repetition

In a deal that augured a return to the past, representatives of Spain and France signed the Treaty of San Ildefonso on October 1, 1800. The treaty provided for the transfer of the Louisiana Territory from Spain to France. For Spain, the loss of Louisiana promised to relieve the royal treasury of the expenses of administering what had never been a profitable colony. For France, the reacquisition brought back control (or at least the presumption of control) over a vast North American territory. More than a mere restoration, Napoleon envisioned Louisiana as the foundation for an enlarged North American empire, one that might regain Canada and appropriate all or at least part of the United States as well. Rumors of such designs—and they were just rumors, for Spain and France had struck their deal in secret—alarmed American officials, beginning with the newly elected president, Thomas Jefferson. "There is on the globe one single spot, the possessor of which is our natural and habitual enemy," wrote Jefferson in the spring of 1802 of the reported French takeover of New Orleans. "The day that France takes New Orleans," Jefferson worried, the United States "must marry" itself to "the British fleet and nation." These fears about the future independence of the United States prodded Jefferson to initiate the negotiations that aimed to secure New Orleans for the United States. Surprisingly, the talks led to the purchase of all of the Louisiana Territory. In March 1804, little more than three years after the territory had reverted to France, the American flag was raised at St. Louis.[1]

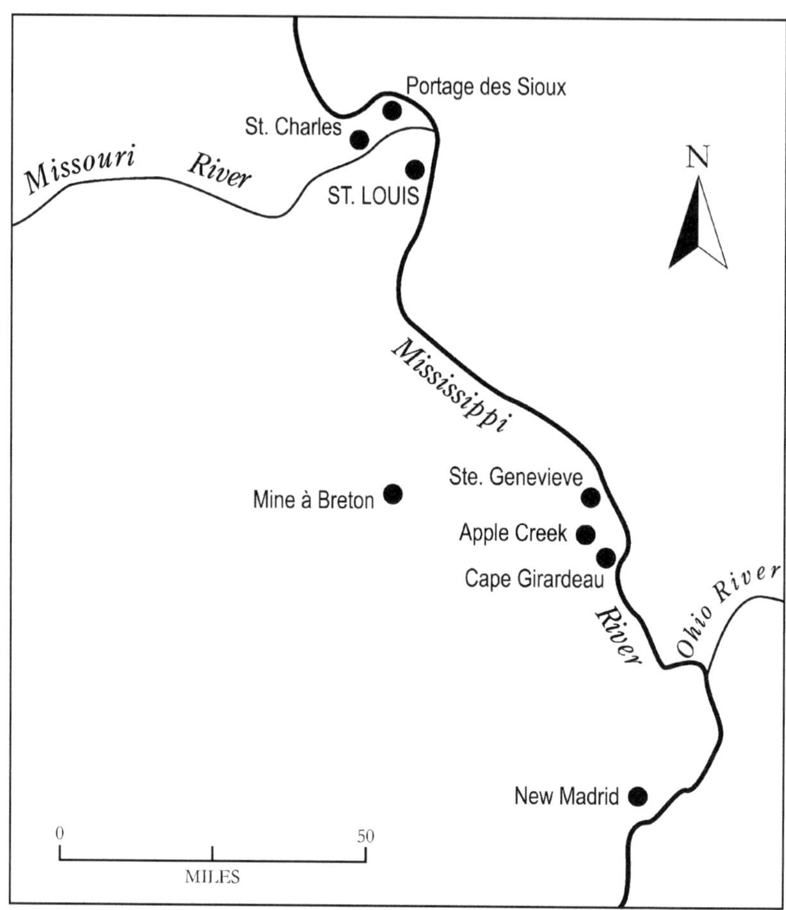

Map 5. The Western Side of the Confluence Region, c. 1810.

This transfer occurred less than a year after inhabitants of the confluence region learned about the retrocession from Spain to France. Not until the spring of 1803 did residents of Upper Louisiana's villages hear officially that they resided again in a French colony. Yet just as the previous cession brought no initial change in governing personnel, so the retrocession left Spanish officials in place. Whereas four decades earlier Spain had assumed responsibility for the payment of French officials, now France did the same for Spanish soldiers and administrators (many of whom were French).

Rather than retreat into inactivity, Spanish officials introduced some significant policy changes in the months and years after October 1, 1800. In Indian affairs, the most pressing matter remained the Osages. If a quasi-peace prevailed through the second half of the 1790s, raids against colonial settlements and inter-Indian violence continued, threatening to escalate into a broader war. Spanish officials also grappled with the problem of intercultural trade. The exclusive rights to the Osage trade that had been granted to the Chouteaus in 1794 had expired in 1799, but Spanish officials had renewed the agreement and then granted a subsequent four-year extension in 1800. This did not sit well with the Chouteaus' competitors in St. Louis, several of whom banded together under the leadership of Manuel Lisa to contest the Chouteaus' continuing monopoly. At a meeting in New Orleans in June 1802 with the new governor, Juan Manuel de Salcedo, Lisa proposed that his partners would assume responsibility for paying the troops stationed at Fort Carondelet, would forgo the two thousand peso annuity guaranteed to the Chouteaus, and would also build a grist mill near St. Louis. The governor accepted this offer, canceling the Chouteaus' contract and assigning the Osage trade to Manuel Lisa's concern.[2]

Upon closer inspection, Lisa's compact contained a loophole that allowed the Chouteaus to maintain a portion of the Osage trade. Lisa's license applied only to Osages within the Missouri valley; the bands who had moved south and west to take up villages in the Arkansas River watershed were not covered. Earlier, the Chouteaus had tried to persuade the Osages in Arkansas to return to their former homes; now they used their influence to convince Missouri-basin Osages to make the Arkansas valley their place of residence. The Chouteaus' entreaties induced a substantial migration from north to south—to the dismay of White Hair, a headman among the northern Big Osages.

The Osages who stayed with White Hair faced heightening pressure from newcomers to the Missouri valley. From east of the Mississippi, more and more Indians crossed over to the western side of the confluence region. Many came only to hunt, but their encroachments into what the Osages considered their country led to violent encounters. North of the Missouri River,

Potawatomi, Kickapoo, and Sac and Fox bands clashed repeatedly with Osages. To the south, Cherokees, Choctaws, and Chickasaws extended their hunting into Osage territory in the Ozarks, which also provoked bloody run-ins. In addition, the Osages confronted rising numbers of permanent settlers on lands between the Mississippi and the south bank of the Missouri River. Between 1800 and 1804, the population of Upper Louisiana jumped by more than 50 percent, with the vast majority of this increase attributable to the continuing surge of Anglo-Americans and their African American slaves.[3]

Like Indian interlopers, Americans found themselves unwelcome in Osage country. Daniel Boone's son Nathan learned this in the fall of 1803 and again in the winter of 1804. While trapping on the Niango and Grand rivers, Nathan and several accomplices were twice intercepted by Osage parties and twice forced to surrender their store of skins, as well as their horses and other property. Nathan remembered that his father had suffered a similar expropriation in the late 1760s on one of his first hunts in Kentucky. Like his father, Nathan might have considered himself lucky to have escaped a bloodier punishment. Not everyone was so fortunate. Just as a number of the long hunters who accompanied the elder Boone into the Ohio valley were killed when caught poaching, so the next generation of American pioneers found themselves the targets of the Osages of the Missouri valley. In the early nineteenth century, the Osages mostly took property, but they also occasionally killed people. In particular, the Osages targeted the more exposed American positions. One such raid in 1802 struck Moses Austin's mining operation. In this instance, the local Creole population, resentful of Austin's rejection of their customary skimming rights, refused to join the defense against the Osages. But with a cannon and other arms, Austin and fellow Americans repulsed the assault.[4]

In mounting a spirited defense, the Osages in the Missouri valley sought to avoid the fate of those Indians in the confluence region who could no longer fend for themselves. Such was the unfortunate lot of the Peorias. Decimated by warfare, disease, and liquor, the surviving remnants of this nation had taken up residence on the outskirts of Ste. Genevieve. In 1801, their colonial neighbors complained that the Peorias had become a nuisance, generally intoxicated and frequently guilty of "thefts of grain and fruits" from Ste. Genevieve's Big Field. Accordingly, *habitants* petitioned Spanish authorities "to order the Peoria Indians not to settle within two or three miles of their town." In this case, removal was limited to a short distance, but the Peorias' descent into dependency was a path that White Hair and his followers were determined not to follow.[5]

Yet the Osages could do little to slow the flow of newcomers, at least not as long as Spanish authorities in Upper Louisiana were so generous with land grants. After the Treaty of San Ildefonso, the lieutenant governor and post commandants found themselves in an imperial vacuum; the lines of authority were uncertain and so was the payment of their salaries. Faced with mounting debts and no longer truly answerable to superiors, Lieutenant Governor Charles de Hault Delassus felt free to ignore an order to desist from transferring lands out of the royal (now French as opposed to Spanish) domain. Instead, after 1800, Delassus rewarded himself and his friends with huge gifts of land. He also bestowed smaller, though still substantial, awards on humbler folks, primarily emigrating Americans from whom officials skimmed a significant fee off the top of all land deals. By 1804, Spanish grants made primarily after Spain had ceded any claim within the confluence region totaled over 1.4 million acres. These covered much of the land (and certainly most of the best lands) along the Mississippi from New Madrid to well above the Missouri River and stretched in places more than one hundred miles inland.[6]

Some of these grants stipulated the size and location of lands, but other concessions specified only the amount of arpents. In theory, holders of these "naked" or "floating" concessions were supposed to locate and survey their chosen real estate. Grantees were then to submit their claims to the governor in New Orleans, who had exclusive authority to validate titles. In practice, few moved quickly to have surveys done. In 1804, an American official estimated that only half of the grants had been located.

Even where locations had been plotted, boundaries were not sharply demarcated. The phrase "more or less" frequently substituted for precise property lines. Rarely had these boundaries been validated by the governor. As of 1804, 95 percent of grants in Upper Louisiana reportedly remained incomplete.[7]

For those who emigrated to Upper Louisiana from Kentucky, the Spanish land system likely seemed disturbingly familiar, yet not so disturbing as to cut off the flow of Americans across the Mississippi. In the initial American settlement of the Bluegrass region of central Kentucky in the 1770s and 1780s, pioneers also acquired grants with vague or no locations, and sloppy surveying compounded the ensuing confusion among claimants. Most land seekers in Kentucky failed to turn their claims into uncontested titles. Instead, lawsuits entangled nearly every tract, prompting tens of thousands of Kentucky pioneers to look elsewhere for fertile and abundant lands where clear titles could be had. During the 1790s, the lands immediately north of the Ohio River lured many ex-Kentuckians, especially as Indian resistance diminished in the second half of the decade. Adding to the attractions of lands in the Northwest Territory was the orderly system for surveying and distribution put in place by the U.S. government. But throughout the 1790s, the administrations of George Washington and John Adams diminished immigration into the territory north of the Ohio River by keeping land prices relatively expensive and refusing to offer generous terms of credit. Moreover, the ban on slavery in the Northwest Territory discouraged slaveholders from relocating there. For those with slaves, the "Green River Country," south and west of the Bluegrass region, emerged in the 1790s as an enticing destination, thanks to liberal homesteading terms offered by the state of Kentucky. For the same reasons, so did Upper Louisiana, whose non-Indian population increased from approximately six thousand in 1800 to over ten thousand in 1804. Much of this rise owed to the continuing influx of white Americans, who along with their black slaves accounted for about 60 percent of the territory's census in 1804.[8]

That year brought the transfer of sovereignty over the Louisiana Territory from France to the United States. Initially

President Jefferson had fastened only on securing New Orleans, negotiations, which he entrusted to Robert Livingston, the American ambassador to France, and James Monroe, the minister plenipotentiary. But the American diplomats got an unexpected surprise when French resolve not to part with New Orleans shifted to an offer to sell all of Louisiana. Behind this unexpected turn was the inability of a French army to subdue the revolt of slaves in Haiti, cooling Emperor Napoleon's dream of restoring the French empire on the North American mainland. The negotiators soon settled on a purchase price of fifteen million dollars (which with interest payments spread over eighteen years would cost the United States about twice that amount). All this, the American emissaries conceded in a letter to Secretary of State James Madison, went well beyond what was "contemplated in our appointment; but we are persuaded that the Circumstances and Considerations which induced us to make it, will justify us."[9]

The treaty was signed in Paris on April 30, 1803, but formal approval still required Senate approval. Before submitting the treaty, Jefferson had to overcome his own uncertainties about the constitutionality of the purchase. But the difficulties and delays involved in ratifying an amendment to the U.S. Constitution persuaded Jefferson to accept the simpler procedure of confirming a treaty. Trying to rally opposition to the acquisition, members of the Federalist Party contended that the price was too high, especially for a government whose annual revenue of around ten million dollars was already largely consumed by a substantial national debt. These opponents argued as well that taking over so much territory would lead to the dissolution of the union, for no republic could be sustained across such enormous distances. Supporters countered that the price was a fantastic bargain, obtaining for the United States a vast and valuable territory without the cost of a war. Rather than threatening the republic, territorial expansion would safeguard the virtue of its citizens by providing farmsteads for future generations of Americans. With a solid majority in Congress embracing these "Jeffersonian" principles, the treaty gained approval, and Louisiana became part of the United States.[10]

While politicians wrangled over the treaty in the nation's capital, moneyed men angled to acquire more land in Upper Louisiana. Confident that land prices would rise substantially after the territory was joined to the United States, speculators took advantage of the interlude between treaty signing and formal transfer to obtain vast new holdings. In the last months of 1803 and the first weeks of 1804, tens of thousands of additional acres passed into the hands of Auguste Chouteau and other leading merchants in St. Louis. Like Spanish grants issued after October 1, 1800, these required backdating to protect the appearance of legitimacy. Ideally, that meant a date of issue prior to the Treaty of San Ildefonso. That, however, demanded a double forgery, both of the date and of the lieutenant governor (Trudeau rather than Delassus). Simpler, if less secure, was to date documents prior to December 20, 1803, the day on which the United States formally assumed control over New Orleans and Lower Louisiana.[11]

Several weeks passed before American officials got to St. Louis and announced control over Upper Louisiana. At ceremonies in St. Louis on March 9 and 10, 1804, Captain Amos Stoddard, appointed as the first American commandant of Upper Louisiana, represented the United States. Because France had no official in place, Stoddard also acted as the agent for Napoleon's regime. On the first day, Stoddard received documents from Delassus turning Upper Louisiana over from Spain to France. The next day, Stoddard took control on behalf of the United States. Filled with optimism, Stoddard wrote enthusiastically about Upper Louisiana and its inhabitants. Although Jefferson had deemed New Orleans the essential acquisition, Stoddard foresaw a great future for St. Louis. "This place will stand in the same relation to New Orleans, as Albany to New York," wrote Stoddard shortly after his arrival in St. Louis. In fact, St. Louis would eclipse Albany, for its location would bring to it "all the produce transported by the great rivers which meet near this point, after traversing such fine and fertile countries." The attitude of the populace also pleased Stoddard. "I have not been able to discover any aversion to the new order of things; on the contrary, a cordial acquiescence seems to prevail among all ranks of people." Less sanguine about the district's prospects was the departing Spanish lieutenant governor. Despite his windfall from land grants, his last entry in a journal cataloguing the licensing of Indian traders in Upper Louisiana captured four decades of Spanish frustration with a colony whose promise had never translated into imperial profits: "The devil may take all!"[12]

First Years of American Rule

In Upper Louisiana and across the confluence region, the transition to American rule occurred quietly, although anyone with an ear to the ground would have picked up some rumblings just beneath the surface. The "cordial acquiescence" noted by Stoddard masked a deep unease among the territory's inhabitants. In the first seasons of American sovereignty, many in Louisiana were unreconciled to the new order. According to one resident, some believed—or at least spread the rumor—that "the transfer of the Country by the FIRST CONSUL [Napoleon] is only a temporary thing & that he will ere long take them under his wing again." Nor did Stoddard hear about how Osages on the Arkansas River reacted to word of the Louisiana Purchase. That information reached the Osages in a note carried by an emissary of the Chouteaus, but that letter, William Clark reported, "was Committed to the flaims, the Indians not believing" or not accepting "that the Americans had possession of the Countrey." Despite this apparent deafness, Stoddard demonstrated considerable flexibility in his new assignment. His accommodations helped to keep peace among a diverse populace and win over a number of influential French colonists. His successors continued to woo (and be wooed) by the Chouteaus and other wealthy merchants in St. Louis. But James Wilkinson, the first governor of the Louisiana Territory, displayed less of Stoddard's talents for accommodation and found himself entangled in controversies left over from French and Spanish regimes, as well as in new ones of his own making.[13]

Article III of the treaty between the United States and France stipulated that "the inhabitants of the ceded territory shall be incorporated in the union of the United States, and admitted as soon as possible, according to the principles of the federal constitution, to the enjoyment of all the rights, advantages, and immunities of citizens of the United States." Here the United States promised a speedy transition for Louisiana from territory to statehood. The article also pledged that "in the meantime" Louisiana's colonists "shall be maintained and protected in the free enjoyment of their liberty, property, and the religion which they profess." This guarantee of religious freedom was supposed to comfort the territory's Catholic inhabitants, while the security offered to property was intended to relieve the concerns of French and American colonists holding Spanish land grants.[14]

Americans on the scene expressed varying views about the prospects for the speedy assimilation of the French population into the American republic. The most disapproving denigrated the laziness and stupidity of French colonists and proclaimed *habitants* hopelessly unfit for incorporation into the citizenry of the United States. Kinder, though still critical, was the judgment of territorial official Frederick Bates: "They are blameless and inoffensive for the most part, but they know nothing of the duties of a soldier." In addition to lacking martial spirit, the French in the confluence region were also supposedly distinguished by their communal orientation. Where Americans happily scattered their farmsteads across the countryside, Bates opined that the French "cannot bear the idea of separation." For French men "to live in a country without a neighbour in less than half a mile is worse than death." Somewhat more favorable was Bates's slant on French women, who "dance with inimitable grace," if "rather too much in the style of actresses."[15]

As the first American commander in Upper Louisiana, Stoddard's assessment of French colonists carried special weight. Like Bates, Stoddard was taken by French women, although his gaze fastened less on their dancing than on their "influence over their husbands." This was greater than that exercised by American wives, a difference Stoddard attributed to the property rights that French women, in contrast to Americans, retained during marriage. Of French husbands, Stoddard deemed them "indolent but honest" and living proof of the adage that "ignorance tends to happiness," for "of all the people on the globe," they "appear to be the happiest." That, at least, made them governable and, with proper education in the English language and in republican ways, made them candidates for the incorporation envisioned by Article III.[16]

Jefferson had contemplated a very different future for Upper Louisiana. Instead of rapidly incorporating the territory into the United States, Jefferson planned to discourage additional white settlement in that portion of Louisiana lying north of the thirty-first parallel. Below that line, the United States would establish the Territory of Orleans, which would follow the usual track to statehood. North of the thirty-first parallel, however, Jefferson suggested that a constitutional amendment be required before lands could be reopened to individual purchasers. Taking this logic a step further, Jefferson floated a proposal to drain Upper Louisiana of its French and American colonists. Under this scheme, whites on the western side of the confluence region would trade their lands for equal holdings in the Ohio valley. At the same time, Indians living east of the Mississippi would relocate to the Missouri side. In Jefferson's view, separating Indians from white Americans would end warfare between them. Moreover, it would allow American expansion to occur in an orderly fashion, with colonists occupying contiguous squares. Only when lands east of the Mississippi were filled up, a process that Jefferson envisioned would take fifty years, would American settlers recolonize Upper Louisiana. By that distant day, Jefferson hoped that Indians would be properly civilized and readily assimilated into American society. Eventual white settlement west of the Mississippi River would, however, still be carefully managed to ensure that farmsteads were not strewn about in a haphazard manner and that litigation over land titles did not once more clog American courts.[17]

If Jefferson sought to avoid the confusion that had accompanied American advance into Kentucky and Tennessee, his plan, like earlier proclamations that presumed to restrict the westward spread of American pioneers, did not spell out how the edict would be enforced. As Massachusetts senator Rufus King discerned, "Nothing but a cordon of troops will restrain our people from going over the [Mississippi] River and settling themselves down upon the western bank." But no more than George III or a series of Spanish governors in Louisiana did Jefferson have the money or the manpower to keep American pioneers out.[18]

Nor did Jefferson have much support in Congress or the confluence region for this plan. Not surprisingly, Federalists, many of whom opposed the purchase itself, were sharply critical of Jefferson's designs for administering the newly acquired territory. Even members of Jefferson's party were unenthusiastic about his proposal. Hostility greeted the plan in the confluence region, where few if any individuals indicated a willingness to relocate. Indians on the eastern side of the Mississippi did not welcome removal, and colonists in Upper Louisiana did not want more Indians living among them. Moreover, if populations were transferred and Upper Louisiana left entirely to Indians, colonists claimed that commerce up and down the Mississippi would be ever endangered. Instead of a borderless corridor, the Mississippi would revert to a contested borderland, thus sabotaging the political and economic advantages that had been won when the United States gained possession of both sides of the Mississippi. As Moses Austin warned, the Mississippi "would become a Nest of Robbers . . . more dangerous" to navigate than "the wilds of Arabia."[19]

What Austin and fellow colonists did want was to secure their property claims. For that reason, news or simply rumors that the United States government was closing the territory to further American emigration, pushing for the desettlement of existing colonists, refusing to validate land titles, and limiting approval to grants issued before October 1, 1800, generated considerable anxiety among both French and American residents. So did word that Congress was debating bringing both sides of the confluence region under the unified governance of the Indiana Territory. By Amos Stoddard's estimate, four-fifths of Upper Louisiana's French and American settlers objected to this incorporation, which they feared would deprive them of local autonomy and leave them at the mercy of distant officials.[20]

Of greatest concern, however, was the threat that consolidation posed to slaveholdings in Upper Louisiana. Slavery, after all, was banned in Indiana (and other territories north of the Ohio River). Masters feared that this provision would be extended across the Mississippi. At the very least, they warned that the uncertainty about slavery's future encouraged rebelliousness among Upper Louisiana's slave laborers. To forestall an insurrection, a committee of prominent French slave owners in St. Louis petitioned Captain Stoddard to reinstate the "Black Code" that "under the old French Government and Spanish . . . was our Guide" and that guaranteed "tranquility" of the colony prior to the American era.[21]

In the face of widespread opposition, the Jefferson administration retreated from its more controversial schemes and sought to mollify the darkest fears of Upper Louisiana's colonists. Meriwether Lewis, who was instructed by Jefferson to investigate the receptivity of the residents of St. Louis to the idea of population transfers, reported that, though he had given the matter his "best attention," he did not think colonists could be persuaded to withdraw. Jefferson bowed to reality, and talk died down in Washington about moving peoples. On the administrative front, Jefferson and congressional lawmakers also arrived at a compromise that diminished concerns in Upper Louisiana. Although Congress did vote to attach Upper Louisiana to the Indiana Territory, it allowed for the retention of two sets of laws. Thus was the question of slavery resolved—for the moment.[22]

The consolidation of the two territories, effective October 1, 1804, marked the end of Amos Stoddard's tenure as the chief American official in Upper Louisiana. During his seven months in command, Stoddard had striven to put a conciliatory face on American rule. Stoddard learned a little French and considered it "a duty as well as a pleasure" to make French colonists "agreeable to the United States." To start relations off on the right foot, his first public remarks on March 10, 1804, promised French residents that their language, education, manners, laws, and customs "shall be respected." That included their religion as well, and Stoddard advocated putting the money of the U.S. government where his mouth was. Under the Spanish regime, as Stoddard explained to his superior, Secretary of War Henry

Dearborn, the crown had supported three Catholic clergymen in Upper Louisiana. "Unless some provision be made" for their continued maintenance, the priests would depart, and some colonists might become disaffected. Better to pay each priest about three hundred dollars per year, Stoddard advised, as "this is what the people, particularly the French, are anxious for."[23]

In addition to safeguarding their spiritual needs, Stoddard sought to reassure all colonists about their material possessions. Recognizing the confusion and uncertainty surrounding Spanish land grants, the American commandant pushed first to establish an accurate record of these claims. This would have entailed the collection of original documentation from all grantees. Many, however, did not have confidence in the new regime and were reluctant to turn papers over to the U.S. government. The level of mistrust rose with the circulation of rumors that the United States was preparing to nullify all grants issued by Spanish authorities after October 1, 1800. Sensitive to popular sentiment, Stoddard dropped his call for the depositing of documents and tried to persuade his superiors not to hastily void any class of land grants. He also moved to assuage the concerns of slaveholders. Although he personally opposed slavery and judged French and Spanish masters harsher than their American counterparts, Stoddard invited those who had appealed for the restoration of the old French–Spanish black code to draw up whatever decrees were necessary to maintain "peace and security."[24]

Before the locals formulated their own regulations, the governor of the now expanded Indiana Territory, William Henry Harrison, issued a set of statutes for the District of Louisiana. Rather than French or Spanish precedent, the new slave code borrowed largely from the ordinances of Virginia and Kentucky. Contrary to Stoddard's opinion, American jurisprudence was not more protective of slave welfare than French or Spanish codes. In fact, the importation of Virginia and Kentucky statutes into the Territory of Indiana's District of Louisiana deprived slaves in the confluence region of various privileges. Under the new laws, slaves in Upper Louisiana lost the right to testify against whites in court, whereas masters were released from legal obligations to safeguard the health and well-being of their chattel.

Like Stoddard, Governor Harrison appreciated the limits of American power in the confluence region. Paying his first official visit to St. Louis in October 1804, Harrison was accompanied by a detachment of U.S. cavalry. But Harrison's tour was less a show of force than an exercise in mutual admiration and accommodation. Before his arrival, Harrison had named a number of prominent French colonists to administrative posts. Among the appointees was Pierre Chouteau, who was named Indian agent for the District of Louisiana. The Chouteaus, displaying their own hospitality and adaptability, hosted a lavish reception in Harrison's honor. Harrison came away very impressed by the ways in which the Chouteaus lived and entertained; the "state of elegance" among the elite in St. Louis he judged equal to the "first rank in Philadelphia or New York." Following their practice of cultivating ties with government officials, Auguste and Pierre Chouteau invited Harrison to become their business partner. As under the Spanish regime, the Chouteaus hoped to make American authorities more amenable by linking their fortunes together. Harrison declined this arrangement, but his brief visit abated anxieties among the Chouteaus and their clique.[25]

If the Chouteaus and some of their compatriots/competitors smoothly transferred their political loyalties, other colonists remained at odds with American governance. During the fall of 1804, the disenchanted gathered in St. Louis, Ste. Genevieve, St. Charles, Cape Girardeau, and New Madrid. These meetings resulted in a January 1805 remonstrance to Congress. A few of the planks in the memorial—that territorial officials speak French as well as English and that court records be kept in both languages—reflected the particular concerns of *habitants.* But other demands—that the United States do more to protect land and slaveholdings in Upper Louisiana, that the federal government stop encouraging eastern Indians to relocate west of the Mississippi, that the "artificial" union of the western side of the confluence region to the Indiana Territory be swiftly terminated, and that Louisiana be put on course to graduate quickly from territorial "infancy" to statehood—were grievances shared by both French and American residents.[26]

As far as separation from Indiana, the petitioners got what they wanted. In March 1805, Congress reversed the unpopular annexation, and on July 4 of that year the U.S. government officially declared the District of Louisiana independent of the Indiana Territory. Henceforth, the Louisiana Territory would have its own governor and complement of officials. But the federal government resisted calls to lift the new Louisiana Territory out of its infant status. In Congress, a Senate committee had approved a bill that would have promoted Louisiana directly to the second stage of territorial government. This would have allowed for a popularly elected general assembly within the Louisiana Territory. The final enabling legislation, however, struck this democratizing provision and created Louisiana as a first grade territory, with a governor and set of officials appointed by the president.[27]

Filling the new territory's top post was General James Wilkinson. Before assuming the governorship of the Louisiana Territory, Wilkinson had repeatedly shown himself to be a man of vaulting ambition and bottom-feeding scruples. Certainly, he had never shown himself to be a selfless conciliator. To the contrary, while serving as an officer in the Continental army during the Revolution, Wilkinson befriended Aaron Burr and Benedict Arnold. Arnold's plot against the American cause made him the most famous of traitors, but Wilkinson, too, engaged in some shady dealings. Rising to the rank of brigadier general, Wilkinson conspired to have the army's commander in chief, George Washington, replaced by Horatio Gates. When the plot was exposed, Wilkinson resigned. Remarkably, the disclosure did not permanently damage Wilkinson's reputation, and he was able to gain reinstatement to the army in the early 1790s. Once again, now Colonel Wilkinson tried to undermine his superior officer, in this case General Anthony Wayne, in hopes of securing his own advance. This time Wilkinson's perfidiousness proved profitable, for he was promoted back to the rank of brigadier general in 1792 and then succeeded Wayne as the commander of the American army in 1796. Not so profitable, though more treasonous, were Wilkinson's secret dealings with Spanish authorities in New Orleans. In exchange for sowing discontent among American colonists in the Ohio valley and thereby encouraging the secession of the "western country" from the United States, Wilkinson became a paid agent of the Spanish empire. He connived for greater fortunes by striking a deal with Spanish authorities that would give him a cut of all American commerce that made its way to New Orleans.[28]

Unfortunately for Wilkinson, the scheme to profit from trade down the Mississippi did not work out; fortunately for him, evidence of his treachery did not come out. Thus he retained his military command, and in 1805 General Wilkinson became also Governor Wilkinson, adding the title and its two thousand dollar annual salary to his portfolio. Not content with these additions, Wilkinson maintained his pattern of international intriguing. This involved continuing contacts with Spanish authorities and continuing payoffs from them. At the same time, in league with Aaron Burr and a cadre of followers in the Louisiana Territory, Wilkinson plotted a filibustering expedition into Spanish territory.[29]

In pursuit of power and profit, Governor Wilkinson aligned himself with the Chouteaus and other prominent members of the St. Louis business community. Like Harrison, Wilkinson was wined and dined by Auguste Chouteau immediately upon his arrival in St. Louis. Unlike Harrison, who had politely declined the Chouteaus' business proposition, and more like Spanish predecessors who had typically accepted payments from licensed traders, Wilkinson was happy to be a partner in any enterprise that might enrich him. For the Chouteaus and their compatriots, the advantages of having Wilkinson on their side (and in their pocket) were obvious, too. The governor could protect their trade and, just as important, he could secure their lands.[30]

In addition to the Chouteaus, Wilkinson's familiars quickly came to include most of the leading French merchants in St. Louis. Though principally engaged in trade with Indians, these men had acquired vast amounts of land, much of it from audacious speculation in Spanish grants made after 1800. The Chouteau family alone claimed several hundred thousand acres in what had been Upper Louisiana, of which close to one hundred thousand acres lay in the vicinity of the confluence of the Missouri and Mississippi rivers. A handful of the Chouteaus' business competitors—Jacques Clamorgan, Bernard Pratte, Charles Gratiot, Manuel Lisa, and Antoine Soulard—also each claimed tens of thousands of acres each. Competitors became confederates in pressing the new territorial government for confirmation of titles. In Wilkinson, they gained a weighty accomplice.[31]

Land speculators needed friends in high places, for Congress appeared intent on voiding their hoped-for engrossments. Trying to get quick control over a contentious situation, American lawmakers created a board of land commissioners in 1805 to rule on the validity of various claims. Instructions to the three commissioners seemed to negate the ambitions of would-be land magnates. Only grants issued before October 1, 1800, were eligible for confirmation, disqualifying those made by Spanish authorities between the retrocession to France and the transfer to the United States. In addition, claimants had to prove actual occupancy and improvement, which those with immense undeveloped grants could not do. Finally, engrossers came up against the provision limiting the maximum size of any confirmation to one square mile.

The legislation and the land commission bore the combined imprint of Jeffersonian idealism and rationalism. By nullifying improper Spanish grants, requiring evidence of actual settlement, and limiting maximum acreage, the law promised to open lands for small holders, for the yeoman farmers whom Jefferson venerated as God's chosen people. At the same time, Jefferson and his supporters in Congress charged the commissioners with bringing proper order to Louisiana's tangled land claims. Unable to replicate the Northwest Territory's system of surveying and selling square tracts, Jefferson expected that this enlightened design could be imposed once existing claims were sorted out. To facilitate that work, the president returned to the mechanism of a special tribunal that had been tried a quarter century earlier in Virginia by then governor Thomas Jefferson. Back in the late 1770s, Virginia had faced a similarly messy situation with regard to land claims in Kentucky, which Jefferson sought to resolve speedily by turning the matter over to a special commission. Serving as a more immediate and comparable precedent were similar tribunals convened in Detroit, Vincennes, and just across the Mississippi in Kaskaskia to rule on French land grants within what had become the Northwest Territory of the United States.[32]

In fact, the precedents were not encouraging. Rather than quieting controversies, the decisions of Virginia's commission for Kentucky lands sparked thousands of lawsuits, for many of the as yet unsurveyed claims overlapped. A quarter century later when the United States appointed commissioners to certify land grants in Louisiana, litigation that traced back to the rulings of the 1779–80 Virginia tribunal still filled the dockets of Kentucky courts.[33]

These lessons, however, were lost on the new commission when it began hearings in St. Louis in December 1805. Although so many grants did not meet the stiff conditions set out by Congress and possessed uncertain locations, two of the three commissioners consistently voted to approve the claims. Again and again, claimants came before the commission and received favorable hearings. All they needed were bits of evidence to show that they had obtained a concession from Spanish authorities (never mind at what date) and that they had made some kind of improvement to their lands (never mind if little more than a stack of logs). But once more, rather than quieting controversy, liberal determinations created lasting divisions. True, large claimants cheered the generosity of the land commission, but those with smaller claims reacted less happily as tens of thousands of acres were given away. Least happy were those without any Spanish claims to have upheld; for these newcomers, every acre confirmed was one less acre available for sale by the United States. That was also the view of William Carr, who, as land agent for the United States, argued for more stringent standards. Carr, however, could persuade only one member of the commission, John B. C. Lucas, whereas commissioners Clement Penrose and James Donaldson continued to hand out land to those with Spanish grants.[34]

The split among the commissioners reflected a much deeper rift that was emerging between pro- and anti-Wilkinson factions in the Louisiana Territory. Both Penrose and Donaldson were closely connected to Wilkinson; Penrose was the governor's nephew; Donaldson was his unsuccessful choice to be the territory's attorney general. Lining up firmly in Wilkinson's camp were the Creole merchants who had the most to gain from the commission's largesse and the governor's patronage. To Wilkinson, his adversaries were "pettifoggers," a coterie of ambitious lawyers determined to block Spanish grants because they wanted to clear the way for their own land speculations. For their part, the opposition assailed the corruption of Wilkinson's "little junto" and appealed to federal authorities to curb the excesses of the governor and the land commission. Rallying behind Carr and Lucas, the anti-Wilkinson faction presented themselves as champions of recent arrivals in the territory, whose prospects depended on thwarting Wilkinson's designs. The fact that these newcomers were almost all Americans from the Ohio valley, whereas Wilkinson's most prominent supporters were the longer established French traders of St. Louis, lent the controversies over land a potentially poisonous ethnic dimension.

Relations were particularly poisonous in the lead mining region west of Ste. Genevieve, although the contest there was not strictly a French versus American tangle. For several years, Moses Austin's denial of skimming privileges had antagonized *habitants.* Animosities escalated with the appointment of Wilkinson, the establishment of the land commission, and the belligerent actions of one John Smith T. As the recipient of an immense grant from the Spanish, Austin fit the profile of Wilkinson's chief backers. But Austin's claims predated the retrocession of Louisiana from Spain to France, and his extensive mining operation satisfied any standard for improvement. So the threat to his holdings came not from a too liberal land commission but from *habitants*, who insisted they were merely defending customary rights, and squatters, who moved onto Austin's lands and then claimed a portion as their own. The most aggressive—and ambitious—of these squatters was John Smith, late of Tennessee, or as he had restyled himself, John

Smith T, to distinguish his claims from other John Smiths. Fixed on acquiring land and power, Smith T purchased an unlocated Spanish grant and promptly located it within Austin's domain. He then made a strategic alliance with James Wilkinson, who appointed Smith T to various local offices in place of Austin. Not one to let courts work out conflicts, Smith T was ready to fight for what he considered his. Always well armed, Smith T carried "two Durks, two pairs of pistols and a Rifle," and, according to one of his many enemies, he "contributed more than any other individual . . . to make violence and disorder fashionable among the People." Indeed, interpersonal violence between colonists, rare in the Ste. Genevieve area prior to 1804, became increasingly commonplace in 1805 and 1806. The bloodshed peaked on July 4, 1806, when Smith T led an attack against Austin's headquarters at Mine à Breton. But like the Osages four years earlier, Smith T's force was turned back by the fire from Austin's cannon.[35]

By the time of this battle, Wilkinson had left the territory. Worried about the excessive generosity of the land commission and about the growing turmoil in the Louisiana Territory, Wilkinson's superiors orchestrated his removal as governor and his departure from St. Louis in May 1806. Using rising tensions between Spain and the United States over the border between Louisiana and Texas as a pretext, Secretary of War Dearborn ordered General Wilkinson to take command of troops in the Territory of Orleans. Thus Governor Wilkinson's administration came to an end. But judging by the bloodshed at Mine à Breton, the rivalries that developed during Wilkinson's tenure reached a new and more dangerous level in the summer of 1806. According to an Englishman who traveled through the confluence region that year, the population on the west bank was "composed of the dregs of Kentucky [and] France," who together made for an almost ungovernable mix. To Wilkinson's successors, then, fell the difficult task of restoring harmony and solidifying American control over a vast territory reaching from the confluence of the Missouri and the Mississippi to points still largely unknown.[36]

The Promise and Problems of Lewis and Clark

A few months after Wilkinson's exit, the return of Meriwether Lewis and William Clark brought much greater knowledge about what lay up the Missouri River, as well as the promise of better relations among the diverse inhabitants of the Louisiana Territory. It was around noon on September 23, 1806, that Lewis and Clark led the Corps of Discovery back into St. Louis. Residents ran to the shoreline to salute the members of the expedition. At a welcoming dinner and ball, at least eighteen toasts, some in English and some in French, were raised in honor of the explorers. This high note continued for several months, and the enthusiasm spread across the nation as newspapers reported the journey's completion. In the immediate aftermath, Jefferson, who had authorized the expedition and provided the explorers with their instructions, exulted that "never did a similar event excite more joy through the United States" than did the homecoming of Lewis and Clark. Yet in the confluence region, the cheers soon faded. Shortly after their return, both Lewis and Clark became territorial officials, the former as governor, the latter as superintendent of Indian affairs. In these positions, they confronted the contentious politics and increasingly combustible interethnic relations of the Louisiana Territory.[37]

At first glance, the offices that Lewis and Clark accepted appeared far less daunting than the mission they had just completed. Indeed, the journey to and from the Pacific proved far tougher than expected. Reasoning that continental geography followed a symmetrical design, Jefferson figured that the western half of North America mirrored the east. The Rockies, in his cartographic blueprint, resembled the Appalachians; the Missouri replicated the Ohio. Thus Jefferson's paramount goal for the expedition—finding the easiest route from the Mississippi to the Pacific—seemed only a matter of navigating the Missouri to its source, then locating a western "Cumberland Gap" through the Rockies and to the Columbia River. But like so many seekers of a Northwest Passage before them, Jefferson and his protégé Lewis misjudged the distances and underestimated the obstacles that awaited the explorers. Nearly a year into the journey, the

Figures 5a and 5b. Portraits of Merriwether Lewis in 1807 and William Clark in 1810 by Charles Willson Peale. Courtesy of Independence National Historical Park.

Corps of Discovery had made its way only as far as the Mandan villages (in what is now North Dakota). Leaving winter quarters at Fort Mandan in April 1805 and moving into a stretch of the Missouri River as yet unknown to traders from St. Louis and the upper Great Lakes, Lewis assumed that the Corps would quickly reach the head of the Missouri. From there, he expected a quick portage would take the party to the Columbia River and the Pacific Ocean, allowing the Corps to turn around and make its way back to the Mandans before winter. But instead of a smooth, swift passage across the Continental Divide, the Corps struggled through almost impenetrable mountains and staggered to the mouth of the Columbia in time to pass a damp and dreary winter. The return trip, which began in the spring of 1806, was considerably faster, but it involved much difficulty and danger, too. If nothing else, the journey demolished Jefferson's precepts about North American geography. The Missouri and the Rockies did not duplicate the Ohio and the Appalachians; going west from the confluence of major rivers was not the same as going east.[38]

Although the Corps failed to discover an inviting route across the continent, the expedition did follow Jefferson's instructions and did fulfill many of the president's ambitions. Putting the training he had received from his mentor and from leading scientists in Philadelphia to good use, Lewis, with Clark's assistance, collected and catalogued volumes of information about the plants, animals, and places that the Corps encountered. Lewis also received lessons in ethnography and Indian cultures, for Jefferson knew that understanding native ways was crucial to cultivating good relations. These, the president recognized, would be essential for the safe journey of the Corps of Discovery and for the American republic's establishment of control over the upper Missouri valley. Accordingly, in his detailed directive to Lewis, Jefferson urged the explorers to "make a friendly impression" on all of the Indians they encountered. At the same time, Jefferson instructed Lewis to make clear that the United States had supplanted other empires from the whole realm of the Louisiana Purchase. "You should inform" the Indians "through whose country you pass, or whom you may meet, that their late fathers the Spaniards have agreed to withdraw all their troops, from all the waters of the Mississippi and the Missouri, that they have surrendered to us all their subjects Spanish and French settled there, and all their posts and lands." But just as Spanish authorities had several decades earlier sought to win over Indians grown accustomed to the French, so Jefferson reminded Lewis to reassure natives that "they shall not have cause to lament the change" in regimes, for Americans stood ready to "become their fathers and friends" and to furnish an abundance of trade goods.[39]

Significant as this guidance from the east was, the explorers' success in dealings with Indians owed less to what Lewis learned from Jefferson's library or from his Philadelphia tutors than from instructors and experiences further west. Prior to his errand in the trans-Mississippi wilderness, Lewis had had little contact with Indians and spoke no indigenous languages. Clark, for his part, boasted more firsthand knowledge. As a soldier in the postrevolutionary conflicts with Ohio valley Indians, he had observed native life and negotiated with Indian leaders. More familiar with Indian ways than either of the captains were several *métis* recruited into the Corps. While making final preparations for the journey, Lewis and Clark also benefited from the hospitality and counsel of the Chouteaus and other St. Louis traders. Those traders provided the Corps with a variety of supplies—gunpowder, bullets, knives, awls, blankets, brass buttons, fish hooks, ivory combs, needles, textiles, tobacco, vermilion paint, and other commodities worth approximately five thousand dollars—that experience taught were in demand in Indian villages upriver. More than just trading goods, *métis* members of the Corps and French traders in St. Louis offered Lewis and Clark insights into Indian rules of exchange and diplomacy.[40]

Chief among these insights was the importance of presents to the construction of friendly relations. Like French, Spanish, and British officials, Jefferson and his subordinates did not like the expense of gifts and would have preferred to dictate rather than negotiate with Indian partners. But fearing the designs of imperial rivals, the American government supplied Lewis and Clark with "peace medals" to bestow upon Indian headmen and authorized the purchase of additional giftable items from St. Louis merchants. This supply, however, depleted long before the return of the Corps of Discovery to St. Louis, leaving the explorers even more dependent on the goods and goodwill of Indians.

That Lewis and Clark obtained the articles they needed to survive and the guidance they required to find their way to the Pacific and back to the Mississippi testified to their diplomatic talents. True, in their dealings with Indians, they tried to project strength, lecturing their counterparts about the power of the United States and the ability of the "Great Father" in Washington to provide for the welfare of his Indian "children." Following Jefferson's instructions, Lewis and Clark also repeatedly reminded Indians in the Missouri valley that the Spanish and French had departed forever and that the era of borderland competition for allies and trading partners was over. But in contrast with the way that American officials commanded Indians in the Ohio valley, Lewis and Clark had to acknowledge the weakness of American authority, especially as they moved further up the Missouri and into the country beyond. They came to understand that away from the confluence of the Missouri and

Figure 6. Among the gifts brought by Lewis and Clark were several "peace medals" for presentation to Indian leaders. This one is inscribed "You accept therewith his [the president's] hand of friendship." Courtesy of the Autry National Center.

the Mississippi, the United States could not yet impose terms of trade, nor even mediate the conflicts between Indian nations that long predated the Louisiana Purchase. Precisely because the Corps was so vulnerable, Lewis and Clark became better diplomats—more adaptable in dealings with native partners, more patient in adhering to Indian schedules for ritualized negotiations—and this made them better explorers. As Clark later summarized, "It requires time and a little smoking with the Indians, if you wish to have peace with them."[41]

In addition to the formalized negotiations carried out between

Lewis and Clark and assorted Indian men, many of the members of the Corps of Discovery engaged in more intimate diplomacy with Indian women. To be sure, the men who participated in this intercourse did not often consider themselves diplomats. Nor did Lewis (who likely abstained) or Clark (who was rumored to have fathered a child by a Nez Perce woman) appreciate the diplomatic character of sexual contacts between their men and Indian women. Raised to believe that all Indian women were "squaw drudges," the captains viewed sexual advances by Indian women as solicitations from "lechous" and "lude" prostitutes. What Lewis and Clark could not grasp was the status that Indian women held in many native societies as principal agriculturalists or the powers they acquired through sexual contact with outsiders. In part, the gains were material; as sexual partners, Indian women secured favorable access for themselves and their kin to trade goods. Just as important were the spiritual powers transmitted through copulation and, in turn, transmittable to Indian partners.[42]

With new understandings and sometimes fortuitous misunderstandings, the Lewis and Clark expedition made its triumphant entrance into St. Louis in September 1806. Along the way, the diverse membership of the exploration team had overcome internal divisions and been forged into a true corps, what Lewis and Clark called "our little community." If not American authority, Lewis and Clark had managed to establish amicable relations with most of the Indian groups they met. Together Indians and explorers traded goods and information and joined in hunting, horse racing, and sex. Such familiarity worried Lewis, who retained his conviction that "too great confidence" in the "sincerity and friendship" of Indians "has caused the distruction of many hundreds" of Americans. Yet his call for vigilance fell on deaf ears, for "so long have our men been accustomed to a friendly intercourse with the natives, that we find it difficult to impress on their minds the necessity of always being on guard with rispect to them."[43]

What Lewis and Clark accomplished and what they learned made them promising choices for the challenging assignments they received shortly after the Corps of Discovery completed its mission. On March 3, 1807, less than six months after his return from western explorations, Meriwether Lewis accepted an appointment as governor of the Louisiana Territory. A week later, William Clark was made brigadier general of the territorial militia and its superintendent of Indian affairs. As the former explorers discovered, the diverse population that resided near the confluence of the Missouri and Mississippi had not come together like their corps. Quite the opposite, relations between French and Americans had deteriorated while they had been away. Resolving conflicts between these groups and between rival camps of land claimants, then, was at the top of Governor Lewis's agenda. But even more pressing for both Lewis and Clark as they commenced their postexploration careers were the ongoing conflicts with and between assorted Indian nations.

In part, these were the same old problems that had complicated the jobs of their predecessors. In the years after the Louisiana Purchase, American territorial officials, like Spanish authorities before them, struggled to secure peace and trade with Indians while grappling with trespassing foreign traders and budget-minded superiors. Contrary to assertions of uncontested American sovereignty, the era of borderland competition did not pass immediately from the scene with the transfer of Louisiana to the United States. From posts on the Great Lakes, British traders continued to operate on both sides of the Mississippi valley, and they dominated commerce with Indian nations north of St. Louis. In 1805, Governor Wilkinson responded to these incursions by issuing yet another proclamation that purported to close the Mississippi and Missouri valleys to foreign traders. Henceforth, all traders were to traffic in American goods and to swear allegiance to the United States. Attempting to give some teeth to the edict, the federal government established a fort near the confluence of the Missouri and Mississippi rivers and considered plans to build additional posts at strategic locations further up the two major rivers. At the same time, the United States sought to cultivate better ties with Indians by opening a factory (trading post) at the junction of the Missouri and Mississippi. At this station (and other government-run factories), Indians could obtain goods at below-market prices, which it was hoped would undercut British interlopers and cement attachments to the United States. But the factory system generated strong objections from private enterprisers, who resented federal competition, and from government economizers, who blasted the expense of subsidized goods. Again and again, officials in Washington reminded their subordinates in Louisiana to keep administrative costs down and to be especially sparing in distributing presents to Indian visitors.[44]

Familiar as some issues seemed, other sources of intercultural tension were new, or at least they reached a new intensity in the years after the Louisiana Purchase. The treaty between the United States and France bound the former to execute all compacts made between Spain and Indian peoples "until by mutual consent of the United States and the said tribes or nations, other suitable articles have been agreed upon." On the heels of the transfer of Louisiana to the United States, hundreds of Indians from dozens of villages around the confluence region trekked to St. Louis. Visiting delegations expected the United States to be as generous in distributing presents as previous regimes had been. Like their English, French, and Spanish predecessors, Stoddard and his successors saw the cost of such gift giving and related entertaining as an unwelcome outlay. Initially, they accepted the necessity of these expenditures, but constant reminders from superiors to be frugal meant that Indian expectations were not always met. Moreover, as Americans moved into the confluence region in increasing numbers, the pressure on Indian landholdings grew, and violence between Indians and colonists became more prevalent. Typically, the perpetrators were young men, often inebriated and acting without the consent of territorial officials or Indian headmen.[45]

In the wake of violence, the kin and neighbors of victims, both Indians and Americans, demanded retribution, but at that point Indian and American conceptions of justice and dispute resolution parted ways. For Indian headmen, restraining retaliations meant the dead had to be "covered" in an alternative manner. Accordingly, they pressed their American counterparts to provide ritualized restitution and material compensation to the relatives of the wrongfully deceased. To avoid war in these years, American authorities generally consented, with a two hundred dollar payment becoming a standard recompense for each murdered Indian. At the same time, when American officials tried to extradite Indians whom they accused of murder, native headmen resisted. Instead of trial in American courts, Indian leaders proposed gifts, such as horses, to console victims and restore intercultural amity. American notions, however, did not think justice had been done unless individual offenders were appropriately punished. Thus incidents of intercultural violence were not easily resolved, and bad feelings from earlier episodes hung in the air when Lewis and Clark assumed office.[46]

The surge of Americans into the Ohio, Mississippi, and lower Missouri valleys also sparked more clashes between Indian groups and posed more headaches for American territorial officials. Particularly nettlesome for the governors of the Indiana Territory and then also the Louisiana Territory were altercations between Sac and Fox and Osages. Violence between these nations predated the Louisiana Purchase, but it was exacerbated by the increased flow of American settlers into the confluence region. Pushed by American colonists out of portions of their country east of the Mississippi, Sac and Fox hunting parties more frequently extended their forays south and west, across the Mississippi and to the Missouri, where they ran up against Osage hunters. Because the resulting bloodshed disturbed the peace, disrupted intercultural trade, and sometimes spilled over to injure colonists as well as Indians, American officials hastened to intercede. In negotiations with Indian leaders, Stoddard, Harrison, and Wilkinson vowed American protection for tribes who made and kept peace, while threatening to punish those who persisted in making war. With gifts worth several thousand dollars, the promise of a thousand dollar annuity, and a pledge to establish a trading factory convenient to Sac and Fox villages, Harrison persuaded a delegation of Sac and Fox chiefs to sign a treaty in 1804. By its terms, the Sac and Fox agreed to a truce with the Osages and ceded to the United States all claims east of the Mississippi. This last provision stunned Sac and Fox not included in the negotiations. Their defiant talk and ongoing raids against Osages and Americans made clear that they did not feel bound by the compact.[47]

In addition to the Sac and Fox challenge, the Osages found their regional dominance threatened by steadily rising numbers of immigrant Indians. Although Thomas Jefferson had shelved his more ambitious scheme for a wholesale transfer of Indian and Euro-American populations, the policy of encouraging eastern Indians to resettle west of the Mississippi remained in place. Prodded by the U.S. government, groups of Shawnees, Delawares, Miamis, Potawatomis, Kickapoos, Ottawas, Wyandots, Chickasaws, and Cherokees migrated to the Louisiana Territory. Emboldened by their enlarged numbers, immigrant Indians established villages in the Ozarks, and their hunting took them deeper into the Osages' heartland. Not surprisingly, conflicts ensued. By 1807, these had escalated, with a group of Shawnees appealing for assistance from other immigrants and from the United States "in order to drive [the Osages] out of their country and take possession of their lands."[48]

Try as territorial governors did to represent the "Great Father" in Washington as an all-powerful, honest broker, American authority over the confluence region remained more precarious. True, compared with French or Spanish predecessors, American officials enjoyed significant advantages. The shortage of loyal subjects, the cause of so much concern to earlier colonial administrators, was becoming less and less of an issue for American governors. Moreover, sovereignty over both sides of the Mississippi valley diminished American fears about imperial rivals. Still, in the first years after the Louisiana Purchase, the balance of population had not yet so decisively tilted in the favor of Americans as to eliminate all worries. Sporadic attacks by various Indian group against outlying settlements reminded territorial officials that the "frontiers" were hardly secure. More menacing was the possibility of a pan-Indian confederation. Rumors that Indian nations were combining and conspiring to mount a major offensive repeatedly circulated among colonists in the confluence region, causing considerable alarm and sending territorial authorities scrambling to substantiate or discredit the allegations.[49]

American officials frequently attributed possible pan-Indian confederations and other stirrings of native dissatisfaction to

Spanish and British instigations. "The excitements of the British traders," announced Governor Wilkinson in 1805, "are the main causes of [Sac and Fox] discontent." Others, too, were quick to blame the British and to warn of a general Indian attack from the north should a war between the United States and Great Britain break out. Perhaps because he spent so much time scheming with Spanish authorities, Wilkinson was particularly attentive to dangers from that quarter. His letters contained numerous accounts about "agents from St. Afee," whom he was persuaded had fanned out across the Plains in hopes of inciting Comanches, Pawnees, and Kansas Indians to "harass" American settlements in the confluence region. More disturbing were allegations that Spanish emissaries were trying to get the Osages, or some faction of the Osages, to join this anti-American confederacy, while others had reportedly crossed the Mississippi to foment unrest among the Cherokees, Choctaws, Chickasaws, Potawatomis, and Kickapoos.[50]

That American authorities worried so much about British and Spanish designs underscored the persistence of borderland conditions in the confluence region. Although the purchase of Louisiana meant that the Mississippi was no longer a border, American officials believed themselves susceptible to the machinations of imperial rivals. They were, after all, situated at a considerable distance from the seat of American power; in the first decade of the nineteenth century, it took at least two months for letters from St. Louis to reach Washington and return. By contrast, British and Spanish sites seemed very close. If some of the rumors about British and Spanish plots proved groundless, American officials were right to be concerned about the continuing interest of these empires in reacquiring all or part of the confluence region. Certainly, the British crown encouraged traders to remain active south of the Great Lakes and to work in villages on both sides of the Mississippi. British goods, ministers in London recognized, preserved ties between the British empire and Indian nations in the Ohio, Mississippi, and Missouri valleys. Meanwhile, Spanish ministers in Madrid maintained that the Louisiana Purchase was invalid because France had not fulfilled its obligations under the original retrocession treaty and had no right to sell the territory to a third party. Moreover, France and Spain had never resolved the location of the boundary between Louisiana and Texas. After the sale to the United States, Spanish officials insisted that the borders of the Louisiana Territory extended only slightly west of the Mississippi River. Thus, in the view of Spanish authorities, most of the Missouri River still belonged to the Spanish empire, and Americans who pushed upriver were trespassers.[51]

Between 1804 and 1806, Lewis and Clark avoided the Spanish parties sent to intercept their Corps of Discovery. The explorers completed their epic journey, and in the process they broadcast the claims of the United States to the Missouri valley—and to lands beyond. Their expedition, then, represented a promising start for the peaceful expansion of the American republic west of the Mississippi River. Beginning in 1807, however, Lewis and Clark, as governor of the Louisiana Territory and superintendent of its Indian affairs, inherited the intercultural and interimperial problems that had long bedeviled colonial officials in the confluence region.

The Dispossession of the Osages and the Demise of Meriwether Lewis

As governor, Meriwether Lewis waxed enthusiastic about the prospects of the Louisiana Territory. "In my opinion," he confided to an acquaintance back east, "Louisiana, and particularly the district of St. Louis, at this moment offers more advantages than any other portion of the U[nited] States to the farmer, the mechanic, [the] inland merchant or the honest adventurer who can command money or negroes." But although Lewis extolled the soil, climate, and location of the Louisiana Territory, he found its governance frustrating. Of the many challenges confronting the new governor, none loomed larger on the immediate horizon than what to do about the Osages. Upon taking office, Lewis vowed to bring that nation into line. In contrast with previous campaigns aimed at breaking the Osages, Lewis, with a significant assist from William Clark, coerced the Osages into relinquishing most of their land claims in the lower Missouri valley. Yet even as Lewis and Clark wrung concessions from the Osages, they steadfastly protected the rights of other Indians in the confluence region. Spurning demands from American squatters, the governor and the superintendent refused to countenance the illegal occupation of lands possessed by Shawnees, Delawares, and other immigrant Indians. That stand cost both Lewis and Clark politically, and it contributed to Lewis's tragic personal descent.[52]

The confrontation between the Osages and the United States traced to the Osages' aggressive defense of their country—and the government's unsympathetic response. Infuriated by the increased poachings of foreign hunters and the more permanent trespasses of immigrant Indians and American settlers, large numbers of Osages struck out against invaders. That their "depredations" sometimes expanded to include the property of colonists put the Osages on a collision course with American authorities. Particularly egregious was a raid in early 1808 in which an Osage band moved from farm to farm, pilfering "property of every description," splitting furniture "to pieces with their Tomahawks," ripping open feather beds, and rendering "useless to the owners" all goods that could not be carried away. To be sure, as Frederick Bates, secretary of the Louisiana Territory, conceded, the plunderers committed "no personal violence." But this restraint did not diminish the Americans' ardor for revenge. Nor were American officials satisfied by the Big Osage headman White Hair's contention that the perpetrators operated in defiance of his wishes. Indeed, White Hair's influence was waning, especially among young men, and on the eve of a possible battle with American soldiers, the Osages seemed on the verge of yet another fracturing in their ranks.[53]

Although Governor Lewis claimed to draw on his experiences as captain of the Corps of Discovery, he prescribed a very different course during the Osage crisis in 1807–1808. As a traveler through the upper Missouri valley and the lands beyond between 1804 and 1806, Lewis learned that the safety and success of the Corps of Discovery rested on conforming to some degree to the expectations of Indian hosts. This required that Captain Lewis offer gifts and heed native protocols. By contrast, as a territorial official pondering intercultural relations in the lower Missouri valley, Governor Lewis renounced such accommodations. He concluded that adhering to the Indians' "custom of *covering the dead*" reflected weakness and failed to purchase real peace. Likewise, paying Indian nations not to make war on one another amounted to a "tax [on] ourselves"; the policy was costly and counterproductive. Like Spanish officials a decade earlier, Lewis considered cutting off trade to be a more cost-effective strategy, and he also contemplated arming immigrant Indians as a proxy force in the fight against the Osages. "If I understand the Indian character at all," wrote Lewis, "there are but two effectual cords by which the savage arm can be bound, the one is *the love of merchandize,* and the other *the fear of punishment.*" In the interest of economy, Lewis proposed first to withhold trade before launching a military offensive.[54]

In this case, Lewis was proved right, which showed how times had changed in the confluence region. In the 1790s, Spanish threats to recall traders from the Osages had been dropped, for fear that the action would have merely opened the door to foreign commerce. At the time of the Louisiana Purchase, the power of the Osages still intimidated. Advising Lewis and Clark about the Indians whom the Corps of Discovery would meet on the journey west, Thomas Jefferson declared the Osages "the great nation South of the Missouri . . . just as the Sioux are the great [nation] north of that river." In the "quarter" of "these two powerful nations," Jefferson conceded, "we are miserably weak." But after 1804, Jefferson and other American officials downgraded their assessment of the Osages' power. In ordering a suspension of trade and declaring the Osages beyond the protection of the United States, Lewis ignored warnings about Osage retaliations or about the opportunism of alien agents. Lewis recognized that the Osages no longer occupied a territory between empires. If British traders remained preponderant in the upper Mississippi valley, and Lewis remained very concerned about an alliance between the British and tribes north of the Missouri River, Lewis understood that British goods were an insignificant presence in Osage villages. Meanwhile, Spanish wares circulated far more freely to the west of the Osages' country. Although the

Osages still outnumbered any single neighboring Indian nation, internal divisions reduced this superiority and left them more vulnerable to the combined strength of their Indian enemies. With the United States now inviting those foes to attack, the Osages faced the end of their long-held regional hegemony. Bowing to this changed balance of power, several Osage leaders signaled their readiness to parley a peace treaty so that their people might regain the trade and protection of the United States.[55]

To conduct these negotiations, Lewis turned once more to his trusted partner, William Clark. Two years after the Corps of Discovery returned to St. Louis, Clark headed back up the Missouri, although in the summer of 1808 his journey took him only as far as Fire Prairie, some eighty miles from the Osage villages. There Clark ordered his men to build a fort (to be named Fort Osage) that he and Lewis presumed would firm American control over the lower Missouri River. As a further signal of American dominance, Clark did not travel to the Osage villages. Instead, he sent his subordinate, Nathan Boone, to bring the Osages' leaders to the new fort and told his messenger to warn of "the fatal consequences" awaiting those who failed to accept this summons. Although Boone was treated rudely by the Osages, who undoubtedly resented his uninvited arrival and his threatening tone, he did persuade several score of Osages, including White Hair of the Big Osages and Walk in the Rain of the Little Osages to return with him.[56]

The talks that followed led to a treaty in which the Osages seemingly surrendered all claims east of a line from Fort Osage south to the Arkansas River. Clark justified this fifty thousand square mile cession as compensation for the property stolen by Osage "bad men." He also maintained that the treaty would bring peace and prosperity to the Osages. First, the new boundary would protect the Osages from the "continual dread of all the eastern Tribes whom they knew wished to destroy them & possess their Country." Second, it would restore the Osages' access to American trade goods, although all exchanges would take place around Fort Osage, not in Osage towns. Third, the federal government would provide the Osages with a blacksmith, a mill, and plows to improve their standard of living. As a final and immediate inducement, Clark distributed slightly over three hundred dollars of guns, powder, ball, paint, and blankets to the Osages who signed on to this agreement.[57]

News of the compact delighted Lewis, but its details enraged many Osages who claimed to have misunderstood the terms of the treaty or to have been left out of the negotiations. For Lewis, the agreement "strengthened and secured" the position of the United States in the confluence region at the least possible expense to the government. Not only did the treaty solve the most pressing problem, but the lands vacated by the Osages could also now serve as a refuge for "such Indian Nations as have long been on terms of intimate friendship with us." By this Lewis meant the Shawnees and Delawares, who, despite a record of harmonious relations with neighboring colonists in the Louisiana Territory, faced growing pressure from American squatters to abandon their lands near the Mississippi. These plans, however, ran afoul of Osage understandings. Arriving in St. Louis shortly after attending the treaty conference, an Osage delegation protested that "they had been deceived with respect to the stipulations of the treaty, and that they intended to convey" only "the privilege of hunting in that tract of country relinquished by the treaty." This involved not the fixing of a hard boundary but merely the creation of a shared hunting territory, an arrangement similar to what the Osages maintained with the Kansa and Quapaw nations. Still angrier were the complaints of Osages who had not attended the meeting at Fire Prairie and who insisted that the signers "had no right to dispose of their lands without the general consent of the nation being first obtained in council."[58]

Lewis gave little credence to the Osages' objections. Not surprisingly, he trusted Clark's assurance that the terms had been carefully explained, that the assembled Osages had assented "with cheerfulness," and that the signatories represented the will of the nation as a whole. Rather than seeing it as a reflection of any real grievances, Lewis and Clark ascribed the Osages' dissatisfaction to malicious outside influences. Specifically, they blamed Pierre Chouteau, whom they accused of manipulating the Osages in hopes that his own land claims within the ceded territory, a thirty thousand arpent Spanish grant, might be confirmed.[59]

Dismissive as Lewis was of Osage complaints, he nonetheless made an accommodating gesture by reconvening talks in the fall of 1808. The revised treaty added a few new articles intended to mollify the Osages. But the basic terms of the dispossession were not altered, and with the loss of so much land, the Osages, long the most powerful nation in the confluence region, lost that position.

Aggressive as Lewis and Clark were in ousting the Osages, they simultaneously committed to defending the lands of immigrant Indian groups in the Louisiana Territory. As Lewis asserted, these Indians had always been on friendly terms with territorial officials and white settlers, including even other newcomers from the Ohio valley with whom they shared a bloody prior history. Moreover, the advances made by many immigrant Indians merited encouragement. Particularly impressive were the strides taken by Shawnee villagers in the vicinity of Cape Girardeau. Accounts of flourishing fields and even more of large herds of livestock were seen as evidence that the Shawnees were attaining a higher state of civilization—and were fulfilling Jeffersonian hopes that Indians could soon be assimilated into the American republic. Yet by 1806 Shawnees and Delawares near Cape Girardeau and in various other settlements south of the Missouri River felt themselves besieged by the encroachments of white hunters and squatters. Painfully aware of how pioneers in other American territories had obtained preemption rights based on occupation and improvement, Indian possessors fretted that the government's continuing inaction might one day be "construed" as "consent" to the presence of intruders and then become the basis for granting titles to them. As more Americans moved into the region and trespassed on Indian claims, the pleas from Shawnee and Delaware petitioners took on greater urgency. But repeated appeals did not arouse territorial officials to take action against squatters who were numerous and armed. Finally, in April 1809, the Shawnees and Delawares gained a measure of relief when Governor Lewis ordered all intruders within five miles of the immigrant Indian towns to depart immediately. His proclamation also required "the sheriffs of the respective districts" to prosecute any squatters who defied the edict.[60]

A mixture of expediency and principle accounted for Lewis's directive. Should squatters be allowed to form "settlements so near" Shawnee and Delaware villages, Lewis warned that "discontents and disturbances will most probably arise." These, in turn, would necessitate expensive intervention that Lewis, like all budget-strained officials, wished to avoid. Eventually Lewis hoped to persuade the Shawnees and Delawares to exchange their current holdings for new tracts in the country ceded by the Osages. But like Jefferson, Lewis believed that such transfers should ideally be voluntary and contractual. Until the Shawnees and Delawares acquiesced to another relocation, their rights should be respected.[61]

The political fallout from Lewis's shielding of Indian land claims overshadowed the order's practical impact. In terms of actual enforcement, Lewis's edict was another proclamation with more bark than bite. During Lewis's tenure, squatters did evacuate settlements on the Missouri River below its junction with the Osage River. It was, however, fear of an Indian attack rather than of a crackdown by territorial law enforcement officers that induced a temporary flight. From a purely political standpoint, Lewis's words had more important consequences. In the eyes of squatters, as well as other men seeking to usurp Indian holdings, the proclamation stamped Lewis as an enemy of their cause. And the governor could not afford to make more political foes. According to the secretary of the Louisiana Territory, by July 1809 Lewis had "fallen from Public esteem & almost into the public contempt."[62]

The secretary, Frederick Bates, admittedly was not a disinterested observer—he and Lewis clashed both personally and politically—but Lewis, too, felt himself increasingly embattled. Land remained the most contentious issue. In addition to entreaties from threatened Indians and threatening squatters, the governor still faced demands from those seeking speedy confirmation of Spanish grants and from an opposing faction hoping for their nullification. Although the land commission continued to hold hearings, its decisions were too slow to satisfy those with grants and too lenient to please those without. As the number of men without Spanish grants became an ever larger majority of the territory's white population, their leaders agitated for Louisiana's elevation to second grade of territorial government. That change would create an elected territorial assembly, which presumably would be more responsive than Lewis had been to the real estate ambitions of the majority.[63]

An assembly, answerable to the majority, might also impose an American system of laws in the territory. As Bates lectured Lewis, it was past time to erase the remnants of French and Spanish jurisprudence, which he derided as "the arbitrary Rescripts of proconsular Agents." What was needed, wrote Bates, was to immediately "establish the empire of laws," under which new written statutes would trump communal customs. Echoing this sentiment, John B. C. Lucas, the land commissioner who vigorously opposed the upholding of Spanish grants, called for the replacement of "Spanish usages and regulations" by "certain and positive laws of an American stamp."[64]

For the moment, though, the substitution of "positive laws of an American stamp" for "Spanish usages" was incomplete. As Lucas conceded, he and fellow land commissioners had become "Judges of Laws of which we know nothing." Nor was this situation limited to matters of land. John Coburn, a Kentucky lawyer who emigrated to St. Louis and accepted an appointment as a judge, discovered that "to meet the wishes of the French inhabitants," he was "induced to incorporate in our Laws several leading commercial customs" that were "peculiar to the Country." Over time, Coburn expected American law to supplant local custom. But through Meriwether Lewis's tenure as governor, no such thorough overhaul occurred. Instead, as Coburn discerned, a syncretic judicial system prevailed that "assimilate[d] . . . the habits and customs of the American and French inhabitants."[65]

But if jurists managed to blend diverse habits and customs, the governor had more trouble finding and maintaining a viable middle ground. By the late summer of 1809, Lewis despaired about his political and personal fortunes. He was besieged by controversies over land and territorial governance, mistrustful of Bates and other subordinates, and out of favor with superiors in the federal government, including President James Madison, with whom Lewis lacked the close relationship he had enjoyed with Jefferson. Compounding these woes, Lewis found himself accused of financial improprieties for some unauthorized expenditures. Deciding to plead his case in person in Washington, Lewis made preparations to depart from St. Louis and ominously asked friends to handle his affairs should something happen to him.[66]

On September 4, 1809, just short of three years since his triumphant return with the Corps of Discovery, Meriwether Lewis set off from St. Louis. No cheering, singing crowds sent him on his way, and he never reached his destination. On October 10, 1809, Lewis met his end in central Tennessee. For nearly two centuries, the mysterious circumstances surrounding Lewis's death have stirred some controversy. Was he murdered? Possibly, but far more likely, the gunshots that killed Lewis were fired by his own hand. Earlier in this, his final journey, he had been drinking heavily, and he may have attempted suicide. Tellingly, when his closest friends heard about Lewis's demise, they accepted that he had taken his own life. "I fear this report has too much truth" was William Clark's initial reaction to a report that his comrade had killed himself.[67]

The death of Meriwether Lewis came near the close of a decade filled with significant transactions. In a span of ten years, the western side of the confluence region had shifted from Spanish to French to American territory, though as in earlier decades, the situation on the ground did not conform with the projections of imperial negotiators and their cartographers. Away from the confluence of the Missouri and the Mississippi, the instruments of Spanish, French, and American authority conducted their business largely at the behest of Indian hosts. Lewis and Clark learned this as they carried the U.S. flag through the Indian countries that lay up the Missouri River. Closer to the mouth of the Missouri, however, the United States increasingly gained the power to dictate terms to even the most powerful of Indian nations, as the Osages learned when Lewis and Clark compelled them to surrender much of their country.

Notwithstanding Clark's assurances to Lewis about the Osages' happiness with the terms, the agreement reached in 1808 produced much unhappiness. That was especially true among Osages not included in the negotiations or not made aware of its punitive conditions. Privately, at least, William Clark was also troubled by his part in this transfer of land from the Osages to the United States. It was, he later acknowledged, "the hardest treaty" that he ever made. Indeed, if he were "damned hereafter, it would be for making that treaty."[68]

By the time of Meriwether Lewis's death, the large-scale dispossession of the Osages seemed a certainty; still unsettled at the end of the first decade of the nineteenth century was the fate of immigrant Indian groups in the Louisiana Territory, as well as that of so many others with land claims dating back to the Spanish regime. With the demise of Lewis, Shawnees and Delawares lost a relatively sympathetic guardian. And like their enemies, the Osages, these immigrant Indians faced greater pressures and possessed fewer weapons with the apparent fading of borderland rivalries from the confluence of the Missouri, Ohio, and Mississippi rivers.

5.

Quakes

In the confluence region, the second decade of the nineteenth century began with a series of unsettling natural occurrences. In January 1811, the temperature rose to nearly eighty degrees in St. Louis. The balmy weather persisted for a couple of weeks, before plunging in a matter of days to ten below zero and leaving the Mississippi River frozen from bank to bank. With the spring thaw came a devastating flood and widespread illness. During these months of unusual happenings, a comet streaked across the night sky, which many took as a foreboding sign. Their worst fears were realized around two o'clock in the morning of December 16, 1811, when a violent earthquake with an estimated magnitude of 8.4 on the Richter scale rocked the confluence region (and shook people and structures along the entire Mississippi valley and as far east as the Atlantic coast). Near the epicenter at New Madrid, a resident described being awakened by a "very awful noise, resembling loud but distant thunder, . . . which was followed, in a few minutes, by the complete saturation of the atmosphere with sulphurious vapor, causing total darkness." Then came "the screams of the affrighted inhabitants, running to and fro, not knowing where to go, or what to do—the cries of the fowls, and beasts of every species—the cracking of falling trees, and the roaring of the Mississippi—the current of which was retrograde for a few minutes." Through that night and subsequent days and weeks, scores of sharp aftershocks kept nerves frazzled. Panic peaked anew on February 7, 1812, when another destructive tremor rumbled under the middle Mississippi valley.[1]

For the superstitious, the quakes and other phenomena of 1811–12 foretold the end of the world; for the historian, the tremors merely serve as an apt metaphor for a decade of seismic shifts in which some old worlds were shaken as never before and what had been a borderland glimpsed its future as a border state. On the heels of the great earthquakes, in which the Mississippi briefly reversed its current, a war between Great Britain and the United States broke out. For many Indians in the confluence region, the War of 1812 revived hope of a reversal of recent history and a return to the previous era of full-fledged interimperial competition. Again, however, stalemates on battlefields did not prevent the signing of what for Indians proved a catastrophic peace. Rather than resurrecting the borderland of the past, the 1810s witnessed a decisive retreat of British and Spanish influence from the confluence region and a torrent of American newcomers. To the pioneer Baptist minister John Mason Peck, who likened the rush of Americans in the immediate postwar period to "an avalanche, it seemed as though Kentucky and Tennessee were breaking up and moving" into the lower Missouri valley, with the Boon's Lick Country as the new promised land. At the risk of mixing metaphors of natural disaster, whether likened to an earthquake, an avalanche, or a flood—the newest newcomers crushed what stood before them.[2]

About one in seven of these postwar immigrants were slaves, usually swept west against their will. On the Missouri side of the confluence region, their presence excited little controversy. Not so in the nation's capital, however. There, near decade's end, debates about statehood for Missouri became entangled with sectional squabbles about slavery. These arguments sparked an unexpected firestorm, the heat of which transformed the confluence region and the nation far more lastingly than had the powerful earthquakes at decade's start.

Before the Flood

Before 1815, a rough balance of Indian and non-Indian numbers still prevailed on the western side of the confluence region. In 1810, the territorial census for Louisiana registered a little over 20,000 non-Indian inhabitants between the Missouri and Arkansas rivers; the combined Indian population was approximately the same, with the Osages accounting for about 30 percent of this total, and Shawnees, Delawares, Cherokees, and Choctaws composing most of the rest. Of course, these Indians presented no united front. Shawnees, Delawares, and Cherokees in the Louisiana Territory firmly aligned themselves with the United States and against the Osages. Among the Osages, the emergence of pro- and anti-American factions overlay earlier divisions—and further undermined Osage unity. But the non-Indian population suffered its own fractures between French minority and American majority, between fur traders and farmers, between free persons and slaves, and between advocates and opponents of the Louisiana Territory's graduation to second grade status. More than these divisions, local population densities determined local balances of power; away from the Mississippi River, American pioneers in newer, sparsely settled districts remained particularly vulnerable to Indian raids. That balance tilted further toward Indians after Great Britain and the United States declared war on one another in June 1812 and began courting Indian allies with renewed vigor. So long as the War of 1812 continued, Indians in the confluence region seemed more potent, whether as friends or as foes.[3]

On June 4, 1812, three days after President James Madison asked Congress for a declaration of war against Great Britain, he signed legislation promoting the Louisiana Territory to second grade status and renaming it the Missouri Territory (to distinguish it from the state of Louisiana, which the Territory of Orleans was renamed upon its achieving statehood, also in 1812). For proponents of this elevation, congressional approval and Madison's signature marked the successful culmination of a campaign they had been waging for several years. To its champions, graduation to the second class, which would bring inhabitants the right to elect a territorial assembly and send a delegate to the House of Representatives, was essential to the defense and development of the territory. Countering this argument, opponents charged that the new territorial classification would result only in higher administrative costs and increased taxes. Behind these oft-voiced concerns lay the generally unstated fears of the French minority and allied fur trading interests, who worried that democratization would hand governing power to an agrarian-minded and land-hungry American majority. Through the term of Meriwether Lewis, adversaries managed to check the progress of elevating legislation. But as Indian raids persisted and the threat of war with Great Britain loomed more menacingly, the campaign for second grade governance gained momentum in 1810 and 1811. By November 1811, when Congress took up the issue, opponents had largely conceded this fight. By then, most inhabitants of the soon-to-be Missouri Territory had turned their attentions to the impending conflict with England and her Indian surrogates. When word reached St. Louis in July 1812 that war had been declared (together with news of the territory's graduation and renaming), residents convened a town meeting at which they enthusiastically welcomed combat.[4]

That zeal eroded, however, in the face of real and imagined threats from British and Indian forces. On the heels of the declaration of war, rumors circulated in Missouri that ten thousand Indians had joined with the British at the Great Lakes and would soon march south. Presenting an immediate danger to outlying settlements in the confluence region, several hundred Winnebago, Iowa, Oto, and Sacs were said to be roaming north of St. Louis on both sides of the Mississippi River. Over the next two years, the level of apprehension rose as the reported size of the combined British and Indian army increased. That rumors of an imminent invasion proved false did not calm residents of the confluence region. "God only knows what our fate is to be," wrote Julia Hancock Clark, wife of William, on New Year's Day 1814.[5]

Although no large-scale invasion occurred, the Missouri Territory did experience scores of smaller incursions during the War of 1812. As in the years leading up to the war, the Boon's Lick

Country, which was then the northwestern edge of American settlements in the Missouri valley, endured the most frequent raids and sustained the greatest losses. So common were the attacks in the Boon's Lick Country that inhabitants had to take extended refuge in palisaded stations, leaving their fields untended and their herds to be plundered by raiders. In 1814 alone, it was estimated that 150 horses and 300 cattle were stolen from the region. Losses in livestock—and lives—wore down the initial enthusiasm with which Boon's Lick pioneers had greeted the declaration of war. Some retreated to safer ground closer to St. Louis; others adopted a grim determination to stick it out. In St. Louis, which was not attacked but which saw its fur trade–dependent economy badly disrupted, gloomy sentiments also took hold. "I don't see what is to prevent [the British] and Indians from overwhelming this country," opined merchant Christian Wilt in the summer of 1814.[6]

In the Boon's Lick Country, settlers blamed some of their travails on the greed of St. Louis–based fur traders. Assuming the goods that St. Louis traders sent up the Missouri River found their way into the hands of Indian raiders, Boon's Lick pioneers suggested that the merchants cared more for their profits than for their fellow citizens. Here bad feelings bore an anti-French tinge. Most of the pioneers in the Boon's Lick Country hailed from Kentucky and Tennessee, while the fur trade was still dominated by French Creoles and *métis.* Within the stations, settlers "determined to stop all trading crafts" and to commandeer the supplies for themselves.[7]

In addition to turning on one another, war-weary residents of the Missouri Territory turned on their government. Although Boon's Lick inhabitants recognized that interception of trading crafts was illegal, they justified it as self-defense: since the government of the Missouri Territory and of the United States had "refused us protection," reasoned one resident, "we determined to protect ourselves." Despite the prewar promotion to second grade status, residents throughout the Missouri Territory grumbled that local officials remained unresponsive to their needs. Lewis's successor, Benjamin Howard, preferred his old Kentucky home to his new Missouri one, and he spent long periods away from St. Louis. That absenteeism caused his subordinates to despair as they waited—and waited—for his orders. Yet Howard's presence did not help matters, at least as far as soldiers in the territorial militia were concerned. Many questioned his abilities as a commander, and one suggested that he was "universally detested," for there was "no Republicanism in the breast of old Benjamin Howard." When not carping about the inadequacies of the territorial administration, citizens and territorial officials joined in criticizing the indifference and incompetence of the national government. In mid-1812, fewer than 250 federal soldiers were stationed in the Missouri Territory, and throughout the conflict, national officials were reluctant to shift troops from what they considered the war's primary theater in the east. Needless to say, this view of the conflict disturbed inhabitants of the Missouri Territory. And because the government of the United States had not properly defended the territory, Wilt predicted that if not taken over by the British, the Spanish would return to fill the vacuum in all or part of their former Louisiana colony.[8]

That which Wilt feared, many Indian combatants cheered. The dream of "overwhelming" American pioneers and cleansing the world of malignant foreign influences animated the visions of the Shawnee Prophet Tenskwatawa. Indians from around the Great Lakes and Ohio valley flocked to Tenskwatawa's village in Indiana to hear the Prophet relate his visions of better times that were and would be again. So, too, Tenskwatawa's brother, Tecumseh, gathered partisans from the Great Lakes to the Gulf of Mexico with his appeal for a pan-Indian crusade to drive Americans back across the Appalachians. During the War of 1812, Tecumseh and his followers attached themselves to the British, recognizing that a British victory was critical to the containment of American expansion.[9]

Messianic ambitions and imperial directions only partially guided Indian military campaigns in the confluence region before and during the War of 1812. As in previous wars of a continental and transatlantic scale, Indian combatants fought primarily for their own local and more limited ends. Those Indians who aligned with the British gained access to arms, ammunition, and other goods that allowed them to stage longer and more devastating forays against exposed settlements in the Missouri Territory. By harassing American settlers and tying up at least a few American soldiers, the raids coincided with British purposes. Yet British officials could not persuade Indian allies to mount a concerted offensive against well-fortified American positions; the much rumored, and by Julia Clark and Christian Wilt much dreaded, invasion of St. Louis never materialized. Rather than waging a bloody crusade to cleanse the confluence region of Americans or bring about British control, Indian raiders aimed merely to dislodge pioneers from the Boon's Lick Country, to reclaim some hunting lands in the Missouri valley, and to secure plunder.

And why should Indians supplied by the British have done more for that empire's cause? Experience, after all, had taught Indians in the confluence region to avoid dependence on the British—or for that matter on any single empire. Substituting one power for another made no sense; instead, Indians had learned they generally fared better in a borderland. Where and when imperial claims overlapped, the resulting competition for native allies and trade had often given more power and brought more prosperity to the Indians in the advantageous, if also precarious, position between empires.

This was true as well for those Indians who sided with the Americans during the War of 1812. Rejecting the prophecy of Tenskwatawa and the strategy of Tecumseh, Shawnees in the Missouri Territory stayed on peaceful terms with American neighbors and, together with neighboring Delawares and even some Osages, played a significant role in the defense of the confluence region against British and Indian forces. Against the former, Governor Howard expressed some reservations about arming "friendly" Indians. "No man can abhor more than I do the Barbarous practice of employing Savages against civilized enemy. . . . To employ [Indians] against each other," however, he deemed, "not only Justifiable but [also] good policy." Still Howard fretted that the presence of armed Indians would be a subject of alarm to [American] inhabitants," and so he shied away from making military use of Indian allies. Howard's successor, William Clark, who was appointed governor of the Missouri Territory in 1813, shared this concern, but he concluded that the "Missouri Tribes must either be engaged for us, or they will be opposed to us without doubt." With this awareness of borderland politics, Clark dispatched Shawnees and Delawares to guard against incursions along the Missouri River. The new governor also reversed the prewar policy of restraining the Osages from attacking the Sacs. By its alliance with the British, the Sacs (or at least a portion of the Sac nation) had become the mutual enemy of the Osages and the United States. Where Clark had previously worked to weaken the Osages, he now sought to empower them (or at least that portion of the Osage nation that would fight against a common foe).[10]

While Clark catered to Indian allies, his constituents dismissed the contributions of these confederates, exaggerated the atrocities of "savages," and demanded vengeance against "every Indian from here to the Rocky Mountains." In one incident in the Boon's Lick Country, avengers surprised and killed forty-nine Indians. One Indian with a broken arm was taken prisoner. In a seeming act of kindness, Joseph Persinger recalled that the Indian was told he "could go free if he could outrun the fastest man in the company." At full speed, the Indian captive ran off, but he was soon caught and brought back to his captors. Offering another chance at freedom, the Americans instructed their Indian prisoner to run again, promising that they would hold their fire until he had gone a certain distance. Darting off, the Indian zigged and zagged. It was to no avail, however, for "the poor creature did not get far until he fell dead, with seven bullets in him."[11]

Persinger, at least retrospectively, remembered the fallen Indian as a "poor creature," but such expressions of sympathy for Indians were rare at the time. Spread by word of mouth and newspaper columns, sensationalized tales of Indian barbarism inflamed anti-native sentiments. Consider, for example, the *Missouri Gazette*'s coverage of an attack on the village of Cote Sans Dessein and its effect on readers. Initially, the newspaper headline screamed of an "AWFUL MASSACRE!" and the story described "all the houses . . . in flames, the place full of Indians, butchering all the inhabitants, whose shrieks could be distinctly heard amidst the horrid yells of the savages." Three weeks later, however, an amended version appeared in which the *Gazette* acknowledged that "the late attack . . . has not been as fatal as was [first] represented." In fact, only four of the village's two hundred inhabitants had been killed, though one of the victims had been "literally cut to pieces." Given the record of atrocities, the best policy, editorialized the *Gazette*, was that all Indians be "JACKSONIZED," meaning that both enemies and allies be subject to the kind of punitive retaliations for which Andrew Jackson was becoming famous.[12]

The "massacre" at Cote Sans Dessein occurred in the spring of 1815. Like the Battle of New Orleans, this engagement took place after the United States and Britain signed the Treaty of Ghent, ending the War of 1812. But at the Battle of New Orleans, combatants had not known about the treaty. By contrast, news of peace had reached the confluence region by the spring of 1815. That Indians attacked Cote Sans Dessein and then perpetrated a number of other depredations along the Missouri River convinced Governor Clark that Britain's native allies intended "to continue the war." Adding his voice to the chorus of revenge-minded territorial residents, Clark urged "a vigorous display of military force" to persuade these Indians to "change their disposition."[13]

But Clark rejected calls for "Jacksonizing" all Indians in the lower Missouri valley. Instead, in 1815, he convened an immense peace-making council with representatives from more than a dozen tribes, and he also stood up for the rights of the territory's Shawnees and Delawares. At the council held in the summer of 1815 at Portage des Sioux, a site just north of the confluence of the Missouri and Mississippi rivers, some two thousand Indians gathered to parley with Clark. Rather than military force, Clark fell back on gift giving to secure treaties. By the end of the session, some twenty thousand dollars in presents had been distributed. Later that year, Clark followed Meriwether Lewis's path by issuing a proclamation against the continuing encroachments of squatters on the lands of Shawnees and Delawares. Clark's December 1815 edict ordered "all white persons who have intruded and are settled upon the lands of the Indians within this territory [to] depart therefrom without delay."[14]

Clark's postwar policies were not popular among the territory's increasingly assertive citizenry. Although the treaties signed at Portage des Sioux opened new lands to American settlers, the rewards that Clark distributed to cooperating Indians rankled pioneers who wanted Indians slayed, not paid. So, too, Clark's stand on behalf of the Shawnees and Delawares defied the strongly held views of American squatters. Of course, like so many previous proclamations, the enforcement of Clark's proclamation remained problematic. Indeed, in the years immediately following the War of 1812, as borderland rivalries receded from the lower Missouri valley and a flood of Americans poured into the region, Clark's position became an increasingly difficult one to sustain.

The Flood

In the second half of the 1810s, people poured into the confluence region and across the Mississippi River in unprecedented numbers. In places, particularly around New Madrid and into the Ozark Mountains, the flow remained relatively contained. In the Ozarks, which rose to the west of the Mississippi and the south of the Missouri River, the challenges to Indian tenure and to established patterns of intercultural accommodation as yet stayed at a lower level. But at other points, along the Mississippi River from St. Louis south to Cape Girardeau and along the Missouri, especially in the coveted Boon's Lick Country, the migration of newcomers inundated Indians. Echoing John Mason Peck's description of the "avalanche" flowing from the Ohio valley, Justus Post claimed in the fall of 1816 that "it does appear as if all Kentucky are on the road for the country in the fork of the Mississippi & Missouri." This flood of Kentuckians (as well as migrants from neighboring states) contributed to a tripling of the non-Indian population of the Missouri Territory between 1810 and 1820. Pushing many Indians off of their lands, squatters swept away generations of inclusive intercultural relations. They failed, however, to secure their exclusive occupation of the land against competing claimants.[15]

One set of competing claims more or less settled was the disposition of Spanish land grants. On January 20, 1812, the Land Claims Commission issued its final report. After reviewing some 3,340 claims that predated (or supposedly predated) the Louisiana Purchase, the commissioners confirmed a total of 1,340. In addition, the commission limited the size of claims. Almost all of the confirmed grants were for less than 640 acres.[16]

These rulings opened more lands for newcomers, whose numbers overwhelmed the Indian population following the War of 1812. Absent the check provided by British intriguing, the balance between Indian and non-Indian populations quickly vanished. While the non-Indian census of the Missouri Territory surged past 60,000, the number of Indians in the region between the lower portions of the Missouri and Arkansas rivers declined. At the conclusion of the war, the Indian population in this area had fallen to around 18,000, a 10 percent decrease in five years. That tally included 4,200–6,000 Big Osages and 1,800–2,000 Little Osages, who together would still have constituted the largest single Indian nation in the area. But the Big and Little Osages were not united, and their population, scattered in various villages along the Arkansas and Osage rivers, was now easily surpassed by that of diverse immigrant Indians. Most numerous of the immigrant nations were the 5,000–6,000 Cherokees now residing on the Arkansas and White rivers. Next were the 1,200–1,500 Shawnees who inhabited three towns near Cape Girardeau, one village fifty miles west of St. Louis, and two more on the St. Francis River higher in the Ozarks. Close to the Shawnee villages near Cape Girardeau was a Delaware town, which with three other villages that were located further into the Ozarks on the White River brought that nation's population in the Missouri Territory to around 800. Approximately the same number of Sac and Fox had relocated along both sides of the Missouri River.[17]

For the most part, the migration currents that followed the war bypassed the lowlands around New Madrid and the Ozark highlands. Travelers who arrived in the Missouri Territory via the Ohio River often paused at New Madrid, but most were scared away by a landscape still scarred by the great earthquakes of 1811–12. That smaller tremors continued to occur with disturbing frequency added to the area's unwelcoming reputation. Most who thought of relocating in the Missouri Territory headed north, intent on finding good lands further up the Mississippi or along the Missouri. A small number, though, pushed inland and occupied lands within the Ozarks. Most of these pioneers hailed from Tennessee, with many tracing their roots back to Appalachian highlands.[18]

For people acquainted with the Appalachians, the Ozarks seemed a familiar and welcome environment; for outsiders, the replication of mountain ways was more disturbing. With the exception of a few plateaus, most of the Ozarks consisted of terrain that was too rough and soils that were too poor to be of interest to most farmers. But as in the Appalachians, Ozark forests offered ample forage for wandering livestock, and abundant game made the area a paradise for hunters. Deer were supposedly so plentiful that they were "hardly worth shooting." Yet mountain life involved much hardship and considerable isolation. Sparse settlement and poor roads limited contact between pioneer families and their neighbors and even more between them and the outside world. Touring the Ozarks in 1818, the geologist and ethnologist Henry Rowe Schoolcraft encountered one pioneer who knew he was living in the United States, "had some indefinite ideas about St. Louis, New Orleans, and Washington," but did not know who the president was or whether Missouri had attained statehood. Again and again during his travels, Schoolcraft commented on the primitive conditions in which inhabitants resided and the atavistic customs by which they abided. In the Ozarks, he claimed girls were "brought up with little care and inured to servile employments," while boys were raised to be excessively aggressive. "In their childhood disputes, boys frequently stab each other with knives," but "no correction is administered," for "the act is looked upon as a promising trait of character." Subsisting principally on the flesh of wild game, clothed in greasy skins, without schools or churches and thus still believers in all manner of superstitions, including witchcraft, Ozark pioneers appeared to Schoolcraft to have successfully, if unfortunately, transplanted the uncivilized culture of the Appalachian upcountry.[19]

In contrast with outsiders' commentary on Appalachian pioneers, which commonly described inhabitants as "white Indians," Schoolcraft did not liken the ways of Ozark pioneers to that of Indian cohabitants. In the Appalachians, the convergence supposedly started when white men took up hunting, but Schoolcraft recognized that hunters were not all the same. Instead, he drew a sharp distinction between how white and Indian hunters used resources. The former "destroys all before him and cannot resist the opportunity of killing game, although he neither wants the meat, nor can carry the skins." The latter "never kills more meat than he has occasion for," and in building fires "gets as much warmth as the white hunter, without half the labour, and does not burn more than a fiftieth part of the wood." In subtler ways, too, the cultures of Ozark Indians and pioneers remained apart. Take the custom of "covering the dead," by which the Osages and other Indians in the region put an end to cycles of retaliatory violence. Pioneers, however, had no equivalent, which Schoolcraft discovered when he entered one feud-ridden district. "In all probability, several lives will be lost before a pacification takes place, as both parties have their friends, and all are hot for revenge."[20]

Competition for resources and differences between cultures bred misunderstandings and conflict. Pioneers complained that the Osages often robbed white men and women and sometimes carried captives away to their villages to the west. For their part, the Osages protested against the encroachments of pioneers and rejected demands that they adopt white ways. While admitting an admiration for how whites "can do almost what you choose," the Osage headman Big Soldier nonetheless wanted nothing to do with these ways: "You are surrounded by slaves," he told an American official. "Everything about you is in chains, and you are slaves yourselves. I fear if I should exchange my pursuits for yours, I too should become a slave."[21]

Tense as relations often were in the Ozarks between Osages and American pioneers, the highlands also sustained the confluence region's tradition of peaceful cross-cultural mingling between immigrant Indians and immigrant Americans. Not only did Shawnees, Delawares, and Cherokees still unite with American pioneers against a common enemy, but they also continued to mix freely in social situations. Intermarriages between immigrants, sometimes dating prior to the movement, sometimes taking place in new Ozark homes, contributed to the blurring of cultural boundaries and the ease of intercultural associations. At least for the first years after the War of 1812, Ozark pioneers recalled days spent hunting and long nights passed gambling and dancing with immigrant Indians. In the last named activity, pioneers John Tabor and Allen Trimble remembered how neighboring Shawnees laughed at the awkwardness of white dancers. But the mocking was in good humor, and afterwards all smoked tobacco together.[22]

The fragility of these friendships was underscored by developments elsewhere in the Missouri Territory. East and north of the Ozarks, lowlands closer to the Mississippi and Missouri rivers were overrun by American newcomers. Scornful of Indian holdings, these most recent immigrants squatted where they pleased, that is, on any lands they deemed vacant. Seeking a peaceful solution, Governor Clark hoped that the Shawnees and Delawares might yet be persuaded to exchange "their possessions on the Mississippi above Cape Girardeau" for lands to the south and west in the Ozarks that had been ceded by the Osages. These mountainous lands, Clark claimed, would not attract many whites, but they contained portions that were "rich, well watered, and covered with cane," and therefore "well calculated for the convenience of the Indians." Yet like Lewis before him, Clark refused to compel the Shawnees and Delawares to move. Reiterating his defense of the claims of earlier immigrant Indians, Clark wrote to President Madison in January 1816 to affirm that Shawnees and Delawares were entitled to a vast tract by virtue of a 1793 grant from the Spanish governor of Louisiana. The boundaries of this grant ran some forty miles along the Mississippi River, from a few miles north of Cape Girardeau to the mouth of Cape Cinq Hommes Creek and extended inland in places for twenty miles. In Clark's view, the validity of the immigrant Indians' title was settled, and the preservation of intercultural amity required the immediate removal of squatters.[23]

In the same mail as Clark's letter, however, was enclosed a resolution of the Missouri Territorial Assembly that advanced an opposite view. Unlike the governor, who was appointed by the president, legislators were elected by the citizens of the territory. Alienated by Clark's Indian-protecting proclamation, nine-tenths of the territory's citizens no longer wanted Clark as their governor, or so insisted one of Clark's political adversaries. That overstated Clark's unpopularity, but the assembly's resolution of January 1816 undoubtedly reflected the views of the majority of Missouri's voters. Attributing the "great and frequent Inconveniences [that] have arisen between some of the White Inhabitants of the Counties of St[e.] Genevieve and Cape Girardeau and the Shawanese and Delaware Indians residing therein" to the "unsettled State of the Indian Claim," the assembly contended that the Spanish government never expected the "Scattered parts of Indian Tribes . . . to hold much Lands if any." As proof, the resolution cited the grants subsequently made by the Spanish to individuals within the immigrant Indians' supposed domain. Because the American land commission had confirmed most of these claims, recent immigrants assumed that the United States considered only the Shawnees' and Delawares' villages and surrounding fields to be off-limits, with the rest temporarily returned to the public domain. "Induced" by this evidence to occupy these lands and to make "considerable improvements" to them, the settlers should be spared from the execution of the governors' proclamation. The assembly also asked Congress to reduce the Indians' tract to a reasonable size and then to persuade the Shawnees and Delawares to exchange this claim for lands "in the unsettled parts of the Territory" to which many had "already removed." In a follow-up resolution in 1817, the Territorial Assembly repeated its request that the Shawnees and Delawares be relocated to "some more remote part . . . , which is better suited to Indian pursuits."[24]

Shawnees and Delawares did not embrace the proposed reduction and removal, and their leaders wondered which "pursuits" were so unsuitable to their present location. Did not their cabins resemble those of their white neighbors? Were not their fields flourishing? Was their livestock not impressive? Had they not always maintained amicable relations with European colonists in the region and demonstrated their loyalty to the United States in the late war? Did not many villagers speak English, and had they not expressed a "willingness to have their children taught to read"? The answer to all these questions was yes, and yet that hardly damned the flood of squatters. And with enforcement of Governor Clark's proclamation effectively obstructed by the assembly's opposition, the territorial government largely abdicated responsibility for guaranteeing the landholdings of immigrant Indians.[25]

Bowing to political realities, some Shawnees and Delawares once again relocated. Particularly appealing was to move villages west into the Ozarks, onto the lands surrendered by the Osages in the Treaty of 1808. There Shawnees and Delawares found a temporary refuge in a country where traditions of amicable intercultural association still prevailed.[26]

Even greater than the stream of squatters moving onto Shawnee and Delaware claims in the region north of Cape Girardeau was the deluge that engulfed the Boon's Lick Country. Named for the salt springs that were briefly operated by two of Daniel Boone's sons during the first decade of the nineteenth century, the Boon's Lick Country encompassed approximately thirty thousand square miles along both sides of the Missouri River. As of 1810, the region had attracted only a handful of white settlers. Most of these first pioneers were lured to the area by its abundant game and its luxuriant range, as opposed to its agricultural potential, which was not yet especially touted. "Elk heaven" was how one early comer described the Boon's Lick Country, which also boasted deer and buffalo in considerable numbers. Although not a site for many Indian villages, several nations claimed the region as hunting territory. Their rivalries, particularly between the Osages and the Sac and Fox, made the Boon's Lick a dangerous place, including for white poachers and settlers caught in between. During the War of 1812, continuing Indian raids curbed most migration into the region. But with the war's end and with the threat from Indians diminished, the trickle of newcomers became a torrent. Almost overnight, the

Boon's Lick Country gained a reputation as the new promised land, a "land of milk and honey." It was, wrote one observer of the postwar population rush, "the common centre of hopes, and the common point of union for the people. Ask one of them whither he was moving, and the answer was, 'to Boon's Lick, to be sure.'" The flow of people raised the population of the Boon's Lick Country to twenty thousand by 1820, an astonishing increase for a district that had been virtually unoccupied at the beginning of the decade.[27]

That so many fastened so much on the Boon's Lick Country was surprising, for the region's physical environment did not match conventional wisdom about the makeup of a promised land. Situated in a transition zone between eastern woodlands and grasslands, around 60 percent of Boon's Lick acreage consisted of prairie. For westering Americans, who traditionally rated the quality of land based on the quantity and type of trees that it supported, such meadows were often disparaged as "barrens" and usually deemed less desirable than well-wooded tracts. Accordingly, the first settlers tended to choose locations in or near forest groves. Arriving on the scene later and ascertaining that grasslands dominated the landscape (and what lands were still available), a few immigrants expressed disappointment and turned around. The majority, however, overcame their prejudices about prairie and learned how fertile these lands actually were. Reported yields of one hundred bushels of corn and fifty bushels of wheat per acre fired enthusiasm. So did the recognition that prairies did not require clearing. This advantage, remarked one settler, should not be overlooked, "for whilst" the occupant of a wooded tract "is felling timber," the prairie dweller "is plowing, sowing, and reaping, and possibly selling part of his wheat to the forrester."[28]

Delighted as occupants were with the quality of the land, they were dismayed with the difficulties in obtaining clear title to it. Most of those who arrived in the Boon's Lick Country assumed that by occupying tracts and then improving them they would gain the right to purchase under favorable terms. In 1814, however, the secretary of the treasury had ruled that the United

States had not yet extinguished Indian title in the Boon's Lick Country, and thus squatters would not be allowed to preempt lands there.

In addition to the impediments that would-be preemptors faced because of what the federal government did not do, they also suffered because of what it did enact. Specifically, squatters objected to the passage in 1815 of the New Madrid Act. Ostensibly designed to compensate individuals whose property was damaged by the earthquakes of 1811–12, the law generously authorized holders of New Madrid claims to relocate on public lands of equal quantity (up to a maximum of 640 acres) in the Missouri Territory. In effect, this provision permitted New Madrid claimants to trade up for better lands elsewhere, including tracts in the Boon's Lick Country on which growing numbers of squatters had placed their preemption hopes. Nearly one-quarter of New Madrid certificates ended up being relocated on the most coveted bottomland in the Boon's Lick Country. Very rarely, however, did these lands become the property of those for whom the New Madrid Act was meant to provide relief. Because the act did not prohibit the sale of claims, eager speculators swooped in to purchase tracts in the New Madrid district. Often these buyers, who included Governor Clark and many of his wealthy St. Louis friends, took advantage of prior knowledge about the legislation to acquire claims at bargain prices from unsuspecting holders. Ultimately, only about 4 percent of the New Madrid grants were located by the original recipients. By contrast, 385 of 516 New Madrid certificates fell into the hands of St. Louis speculators.[29]

The *inaction* of the U.S. government in failing to extend preemption privileges angered occupant-improvers; the *action* of the federal government in passing the New Madrid Act and promoting speculation infuriated them. In protest against a federal policy that favored speculators over squatters, the territorial assembly sent a memorial to Congress asking for reconsideration of an act that was "not only arbitrary and unauthorized by law, but most unjust, cruel and oppressive, towards a people who have fought and bled for the Soil they cultivate." In the Boon's Lick Country, would-be preemptors took more direct action, as the Baptist preacher John Mason Peck discovered. Traveling through the region, he "could not call at a cabin without being accosted" by suspicious residents, who demanded to know if he had "a New Madrid claim" and was "one of these land-speculators." Fortunately for Peck, he carried no New Madrid claims, and his "sympathies" were instead "wholly with the settlers." Echoing the language of the assembly's remonstrance and speaking for thousands of Boon's Lick squatters, Peck condemned the New Madrid Act as "exceedingly ungenerous, not to say dishonest," for taking "away a man's improvement, made by hard labor, and great privation, especially when these people defended this country from the Indians during the late war." If "this terrible state of things" were not corrected, Peck predicted that the animosity between squatters and speculators would end "in bloodshed."[30]

The threat of violence hardly slowed speculation. In St. Louis especially, the speculative spirit could not easily be contained. Whether staking fortunes at card games or on land games, the business community in St. Louis, both French and American, relished the chance for "high play." In this climate, New Madrid certificates presented too lucrative an opportunity to pass up. More daring—and potentially more rewarding—was the rampant gambling on town sites and urban lots in the Boon's Lick Country. Initially, attention focused on the town of Franklin, the seat of Howard County (which at its formation included the whole of the Boon's Lick Country). There, the earliest investors reaped extraordinary returns. One-acre lots at the town center that sold for twenty-five dollars in 1816 brought four hundred dollars in 1817, and eight hundred to over one thousand dollars in 1818. Looking to duplicate that score, speculators turned their gaze to other "likely" town sites, whose exceptional prospects they aggressively touted. Knowing that the surest way to guarantee a potential town's future was to have it designated as a county seat, speculators vigorously lobbied territorial legislators. By 1820, in response to rising population, the territorial assembly erected seven new counties in the Boon's Lick Country. That entailed the creation of seven new county seats and handsome profits for the backers of the selected sites. But for each site that became a seat, dozens of widely publicized locations languished in undeveloped obscurity. Spoofing the exaggerations that characterized these urban boosters, a St. Louis newspaper ran a fictitious promotion for "*Ne plus ultra*," a town whose streets were a mile wide and whose lots were full 640-acre sections.[31]

For squatters, the machinations of speculators and their confederates in government and law were no laughing matter. First, thanks to the corruption of legislators and lawyers, speculators deprived squatters of their preemption rights. Then, abetted by the same cast, they bid up the price of land beyond the means of poorer men. A poem entitled "Law Dust and Saw Dust," supposedly penned by a resident of the Boon's Lick Country, captured the frustration of occupants who watched as courts robbed them of their improvements: "To set up a village with tackle for tillage, Jack Carter he took to the saw; to pluck and to pillage that same little village, Joe Pettifog took to the law."[32]

Rhetorical salvos against rapacious speculators, crooked officials, and pettifogging lawyers were by no means unique to the Boon's Lick Country. To the contrary, for many pioneers in the lower Missouri valley, the rhetoric and their situation seemed all too familiar, a distressing replay of prior experiences in the Ohio valley. A large proportion of early settlers in the Boon's Lick Country hailed from—or at least they or their parents had spent some years trying to acquire lands in—central Tennessee and Kentucky. After the Revolution, tens of thousands of pioneers flooded into these areas, pulled across the Appalachians by the magnet of reputed new Edens in the Bluegrass of Kentucky and Tennessee. But dreams of obtaining title to a portion of these promised lands were rarely realized, the result, disappointed pioneers asserted, of the unholy alliance between speculators, lawyers, and government officials.[33]

The garb of injured innocents in which Bluegrass and later Boon's Lick pioneers cloaked themselves was an imperfect fit, however. The distinction between "us" and "them," between settlers and speculators, sometimes blurred. The occupations and improvements that squatters trumpeted often amounted to little more than a few logs thrown together (a substitute for a cabin meant to signify occupancy) and a few rows of corn barely tended (a substitute for the crop meant to signify improvement). In fact, some squatters never intended to occupy or improve; they aimed merely to acquire and then sell their preemption rights. And while squatters frequently justified their claims by invoking the blood they shed in wresting countries from Indians, they ignored the injuries done to Indians, particularly to those whose claims were swamped by the flood of pioneers into the Ohio valley after the Revolution and the lower Missouri valley after the War of 1812.[34]

The Fire Below

In addition to escalating the conflicts over land between Indian and non-Indian populations and initiating battles over the Boon's Lick Country between squatters and speculators, the postwar flow of newcomers deposited a thick residue on the territory's political and economic landscape. Overrunning some customary banks, the flood of people cut fresh channels to governing power and economic well-being. These new paths brought a different look to town streets and countrysides and threatened the political and economic dominance of old elites, particularly that of French merchants in St. Louis. But while the Missouri Territory took on an increasingly "American" guise after the War of 1812, that face was black as well as white. Locally, the presence of slaves raised a few alarms; no one in the territory, however, foresaw how the future of slavery in Missouri would start a conflagration that spread across the nation.

If not as spectacularly as the Boon's Lick Country, St. Louis also grew rapidly in the second half of the 1810s, as free people and their slaves took up residence in the town and surrounding countryside. Between 1810 and 1820, the city's population more than tripled, rising from around 1,400 to over 4,500, with 80 percent of this increase occurring after 1815. For St. Louis County as a whole, growth was somewhat slower, although its census nearly doubled during the decade, surpassing 10,000 in 1820.[35]

St. Louis attracted newcomers with varying ambitions for themselves and their city. For men seeking farms, the area around St. Louis offered some excellent, though expensive, lands. For men working as tradesmen, the scarcity of skilled laborers promoted high wages. As Christian Wilt complained, able "young men are the scarcest articles to be found in this place." As a result, artisans commanded two to three times the daily pay of their counterparts in eastern cities. For men wishing to engage in the commercial pursuits upon which St. Louis's economic vitality had always rested, the city boasted potentially greater prospects. "No commercial town in America, situated so far from the ocean," rivaled the advantages of its location, wrote Henry Schoolcraft after visiting St. Louis in 1818. Given that "the sources of its future commerce are dispersed over such an immense surface, so greatly diversified in its character and still so imperfectly explored, it is impossible to assign any probable limits to the growth of the town." Echoing and extending Schoolcraft's judgment, guidebook author William Darby declared "no position . . . more favorably situated for the accumulation of all that comprises wealth and power" than St. Louis's and predicted that "in the course of human events," the city may become "the seat of [the American] empire."[36]

That day moved closer with the appearance on August 2, 1817, of the steamboat *Zebulon M. Pike* at St. Louis docks. It was the first such craft to ascend the Mississippi above its junction with the Ohio, heralding a new era for river transportation. For the moment, the Missouri River, more difficult to navigate than the Mississippi, remained beyond the reach of the *Pike.* But boosters confidently looked forward to the not so distant time when steamboats moved regularly up and down the waterways that converged near St. Louis.[37]

Not surprisingly, those displaced by new technologies did not wholly share this enthusiasm for the new era dawning. First on the firing line were the boatmen whose job it had been to paddle and pole various crafts up and down the Mississippi, Ohio, and Missouri rivers. Because French Creoles dominated this occupation, its ebbing exemplified the Americanization of the confluence region.

Beyond the docks, St. Louis also lost some of its distinctly French character. Throughout the 1810s, the lower part of town remained chiefly inhabited by Creoles, and French was still the

Figure 7. Thomas Doney's 1847 engraving *The Jolly Flat Boat Men*, copied from the original painting by George Caleb Bingham, offers a nostalgic portrait of life on the old flatboats, before steamboats came to dominate traffic on the Mississippi, Ohio, and Missouri rivers. Courtesy of the Autry National Center.

language generally spoken on these riverine streets. A block or two from the Mississippi, however, a mixture of architecture, dress, speech, and people defined the scene. French-style upright log houses and wraparound porches sat alongside American-style dwellings, *capots*, moccasins, and headkerchiefs coexisted with American fashions, and conversations bounced between French and English.[38]

The Americanization of St. Louis and surrounding areas had significant economic and political implications. As Americans took up more and more lands and turned them into farms, the relative importance of the fur trade to the territory's economy diminished. For the French merchants in St. Louis, whose wealth and position had long depended on trade with Indians, this relative decline was compounded by a real decline in fur profits. The war had disrupted the merchants' connections with Indian nations up the Mississippi and Missouri rivers, and the immediate postwar period brought only a limited recovery. The orbit in which St. Louis–based traders operated remained more constricted than formerly, and even within this realm their commerce was not as profitable as it had once been. Much of the problem, according to the merchants, traced to competition from the federal government's factories, whose below-market prices undercut the trade and profits of private enterprises. Seeking relief, fur trading concerns discovered how much the political ground had shifted, too. Before the war, French merchants had cultivated strong ties with the governors of the Louisiana Territory, as well as with lesser officials. A continuation of their practices under the Spanish regime, these connections ensured that merchants would have powerful friends when they needed them. After the war, Governor Clark retained his close association with the Chouteaus and other French merchants. Like his predecessors, Clark entered into business partnerships with them, and he lent his influence to their interests. But that influence was also not what it once was, for in the second half of the 1810s, demographic changes in the territory brought additional democratic reforms to its governance, and these resulted in challenges to the authority of Clark and his clique.[39]

The coterie of territorial officials and French merchants found its position threatened on a variety of fronts by the increasingly assertive American majority. Needing to raise revenues and answerable to voters, the territorial assembly enacted a tax first on uncultivated lands and subsequently extended it to all lands. Because the Chouteaus and their confederates held vast amounts of land, much of it granted by Spanish authorities, yet still mostly unoccupied and unimproved, these measures were not welcomed by the little junto. Nor were they pleased when in December 1815 the territorial legislature debated the adoption of an occupying claimant statute. Modeled on a similar provision in

Kentucky's code, the bill mandated that rightful owners of land compensate squatters for any improvements. In effect, this statute would have made it cheaper to sell the land to squatters than eject them from it. Fortunately, for French merchants, they could still count on Clark to veto this and other obnoxious measures. Yet this protection also seemed to have an uncertain future, especially after 1816, when Congress elevated the Missouri Territory to third class status. Although that action did not turn the governorship into an elected office, it did give voters more control over the territory's governance. It also marked the final step on the road to statehood, which would make the governorship an elected office. Even those who feared this graduation and the further democratization it would bring reconciled themselves to it. Statehood, the little junto and their adversaries assumed, was on the immediate horizon.[40]

Certainly, neither faction anticipated that slavery would become an issue and an obstacle when Congress considered Missouri's admission into the United States. Slavery, after all, had deep roots in the confluence region. While French and Spanish officials had tried to outlaw trade in and holding of Indians as slaves, these regimes had planted and provided for African slavery in Upper Louisiana. Although the United States had banned all slave labor in the territory north of the Ohio River and east of the Mississippi, its perpetuation on the western side of the Mississippi was taken for granted. At least in St. Louis, the enduring foundations of African slavery remained audible after the War of 1812, as evidenced by a resident who observed that "the negroes of the town all spoke French."[41]

That was changing, however. As with the shifting makeup of the white population, so new migrations altered the composition—and languages—of black inhabitants. In the District of St. Louis at the time of the American takeover, there were 667 slaves, who accounted for about 15 percent of the population. By 1810, the tally of bondsmen and women had risen slightly to 740, though this represented a slight decrease as a percentage of the district's total census. Over the course of the next decade, particularly after 1814, an influx of white American settlers and their slaves raised the population of St. Louis County above 10,000, with slaves accounting for around 1,800 of this total. Into the Boon's Lick Country, where conditions were especially favorable for the cultivation of tobacco and hemp, American farmers brought nearly 2,000 bondspeople by 1820. Overall, the number of slaves in the Missouri Territory more than tripled during the 1810s (from 3,011 in 1810 to 10,222 in 1820). Most of these newcomers, like their masters, had emigrated from Kentucky and Tennessee, and their combined voices muffled, if not entirely drowned out, the sound of French speakers.[42]

American slave owners boasted that their slaves were happier than French-speaking ones. According to Timothy Flint, slaves who came from the Ohio valley arrived in Missouri with "delight in their countenances." Their happiness, masters suggested, rested on the beneficence of the new environment and the benevolence that American slaveholders displayed toward those whom they referred to as their "people" (or less humanely as their "stock"). As evidence of their concern for the well-being of slaves, many Missouri-bound masters pointed to the lengths they had gone to keep families intact. As proof of the bond between himself and his bondsmen, Frederick Bates insisted that his slaves worked without compulsion. Although government duties prevented him from closely supervising his farm, Bates employed no overseer, yet his slaves "rais[ed] a most promising crop." Overseers were, in fact, rare, for most immigrant slaveholders brought only one or two slaves with them. Upon arrival, owners and slaves lived in close quarters and shared equally in the work of establishing a new farmstead—or so masters said.[43]

Much less of what immigrant slaves said—or thought—about their relocation has come down to us. If Flint saw only happy faces, these expressions often masked discontented feelings. A few slaves voiced some objections to the move or spoke longingly of their "dear old Kaintucky memories" within earshot of their masters. But in expressing such sentiments and in acting upon them, slaves ran considerable risks. Consider, for example, what happened to York, William Clark's slave who had been a valued member of the Corps of Discovery. Upon his return from that venture, York felt he had earned his freedom. Clark, however, did not believe that York's "services" had "been so great." Instead of emancipation, Clark required that York stay in St.

Louis. Contrary to the contention of many slaveholders that they put family unity first, this decision kept York away from his wife, who resided near Louisville. So separated, York, in Clark's words, turned "insolent and sulky." Repeatedly Clark complained about York's attitude, and on more than one occasion he gave York a "trouncing." Clark also worried that York planned to run away. Should York try or should he continue "to refuse to" perform "his duty as a Slave," Clark determined to have him "Sold, or hired out to Some Severe master until he thinks better of Such Conduct." Even more ominous was Clark's threat to send York to New Orleans.[44]

York escaped this fate, and eventually he returned to Kentucky; not so fortunate was Scipio, another of Clark's slaves. Like York, Scipio incurred his master's ire for shirking work and showing a bad attitude. Like York, Scipio also felt the sting of the whip as punishment. And finally like York, Scipio faced threats of being sold, which Clark withdrew only after his slave promised to reform (and when he failed to obtain his desired price). Finally, however, fearing that he was about to be shipped down the Mississippi, Scipio shot and killed himself in 1819.[45]

The desperate lengths to which York, Scipio, and other slaves went to avoid being relocated to points south testified to the *relative* benevolence of slave regimes in Missouri, as well as in Kentucky and Tennessee. The labor required to raise hemp and tobacco was less brutal than that demanded by sugar and cotton, and the climate in the confluence region and Ohio valley was also less deadly than that further south. In addition, the same shortages that promoted high wages for free workers opened opportunities for slaves. In St. Louis in particular, slaveholders found a strong and steady demand for slaves, who could be "hired out" for half the cost of employing free laborers. Although the practice of allowing slaves to hire themselves out was officially frowned upon, many slaves were permitted to make their own deals and to keep a portion of their earnings. With a little money of their own to spend, slaves congregated on Sunday afternoons on "an open space . . . between Main and Second streets" to "dance, drink, and fight."[46]

For African Americans in St. Louis and throughout the Missouri Territory, such freedoms were tightly bounded, however.

Figure 8. Sculpture of York, who accompanied the Corps of Discovery on the 1804–1806 expedition and remained the slave of William Clark after the return to St. Louis. Sculpture by Ed Hamilton. Photo courtesy Ed Hamilton.

Few slaves saved enough to purchase their emancipation. Moreover, legal discriminations against free blacks discouraged their immigration into the territory and encouraged their emigration from it. Under American jurisprudence, blacks, whether free or slave, lost their right to testify against whites in court. The result of such discriminations was a nearly 60 percent decline in the territory's free black population between 1810 and 1820; as a proportion of the territory's population, the decrease was far sharper, from 3 percent in 1810 to .5 percent a decade later. For slaves, a series of new regulations also diminished the liberties they had possessed under Spanish and French regimes. In St. Louis, an 1808 ordinance stipulated that should more than four slaves "assemble together, unless at the house of their master or mistress," for "amusement and recreation," without first having obtained permission from town officials, they would each receive ten lashes on "his or her back." Slaves caught riding a horse without permission of their masters faced twenty stripes. An 1818 addition to the local code prohibited slaves from going out in public between 9 P.M. and daylight. At the territorial level, similar restrictions were put in place, including making it a capital offense for a "negro or other slave [to] prepar[e], exhibit, or administer any medicine."[47]

Behind this draconian statute lay fears that black doctors would poison white patients; behind the restrictions on assembly and movement were worries about slave conspiracies and insurrections. The prosecution of a couple of slaves for poisoning masters indicated that the fears were not entirely misplaced. And while no general insurrection occurred in the years before or immediately after the War of 1812, that hardly meant slaves were quiescent. But most settled for individual acts of defiance. A few suspicious fires suggested that arson was a part of the slaves' arsenal of resistance. More common were slaves who ran away, sometimes to reunite with relatives left behind in the Ohio valley and sometimes simply to find freedom. Most typical of all were slaves who disrupted the system in whatever ways they could, while hiding their defiance. "I am frequently much vexed," wrote William Clark, by slaves who "Steel a little, take a little, lie a little, Scowl a little, pout a little, deceive a little, quarrel a little, and attempt to Smile."[48]

The Firebell

Beneath the happy countenances, as Clark seemingly discerned, flared flashes of resistance, but what turned these flickers into a furious conflagration were actions taken half a continent away. In February 1819 in Washington, D.C., a New York congressman, James Tallmadge Jr., attached an antislavery amendment to a bill intended to elevate the Missouri Territory to statehood. The resulting fray exposed deep divisions between northern and southern states. To Thomas Jefferson, the sectional rancor raised by the "momentous question" of slavery and Missouri statehood was "like a firebell in the night" that "awakened and filled" him "with terror." The alarm, he feared, struck "the knell of the Union."[49]

Like a firebell in the night, the controversy was in part so terrifying to Jefferson because it was so surprising. Following the Missouri Territory's graduation to third class status in 1816, statehood advocates went into high gear, envisioning quick action from the next congress. In 1817, private petitions, asking for immediate statehood, circulated within the territory. But these memorials failed to prod the first session of the Fifteenth Congress to pass enabling legislation. To encourage matters, the territorial legislature submitted a public resolution in the fall of 1818. This memorial contended that Missouri's non-Indian inhabitants, which by an inflated estimate were said to number around one hundred thousand, were being denied their full rights. These would come only when they were residents of one of the United States. The resolution put statehood back on the legislative fast track, for in December 1818 the Speaker of the House, Henry Clay, brought it before the Congress. Two months later, the select committee approved a statehood bill. The debate of the full House, however, took an unexpected turn when Congressman Tallmadge introduced his amendment. Tallmadge's amendment was not wholly unexpected. The previous month, John Taylor, also a representative from New York, put forward an amendment to ban slavery in the Arkansas Territory (which Congress was considering creating out of the southern portion of the Missouri Territory). But where Taylor's amendment was defeated, Tallmadge's, which placed restrictions on the future emigration of slaves into Missouri and mandated that slaves born in the *state* of Missouri be freed once they reached the age of twenty-five, won a majority, with the House dividing along north-south lines. In the Senate, where slave states and free states stood equal at eleven to eleven, the antislavery provision could not secure passage, however. So there the two chambers deadlocked, derailing Missouri's bid for statehood.[50]

Back in the Missouri Territory, reaction to the news from Washington was extremely heated and, in public, entirely one-sided. At a number of well-attended gatherings in 1819, speakers condemned the Tallmadge Amendment and railed against the presumption that Congress had any right to restrict the perpetuation of slavery in Missouri. Citing the 1803 treaty with France, anti-restrictionists maintained that the United States had committed to forming the newly acquired Louisiana Territory into states, whose citizens were to enjoy all the rights and privileges of those in other states. If the question of slavery were left to the citizens of other states, then it was an issue to be decided exclusively by Missourians themselves. Reaching back even further in time, orators appealed to Missourians' republican birthright and invoked the spirit of 1776. "The Union, it is dear to us," declared Duff Green, a recent immigrant from Kentucky to the Boon's Lick Country. "But liberty is dearer." Here, Green, like many other anti-restrictionists, overlooked what proponents of the Tallmadge amendment proclaimed was obvious: that the liberty slaveholders cherished rested on their freedom to enslave others. Such candor was rare within the territory at the end of the 1810s. Neither slaves nor free blacks were allowed to offer their opinions at public meetings, and hostile audiences shouted down the few whites who openly voiced support for restrictions on slavery.[51]

At public forums and in newspaper editorials, anti-restrictionists inflamed popular sentiment by emphasizing the sectional origins and questioning the motives of their adversaries. One repeated refrain saw restriction of slavery as the work of easterners determined to impede the westward flow of population. That depiction resonated with recent immigrants from the Ohio valley, who had long complained about eastern indifference to the plight of the West. Even more specifically, anti-restrictionists identified New Englanders as their "greatest opponents," an opposition born, said one Missourian, because they "envy us." More than just jealousy, Yankees supposedly wanted to take control of the territory's valuable resources and its profitable commerce. New Englanders, in this rhetoric, had, by their allegiance to the discredited Federalist Party, betrayed the American republic during the War of 1812, and now, after the war, they plotted to deprive true western American patriots of their rewards. As Thomas Hart Benton, editor of the *St. Louis Enquirer*, put it, New Englanders were seeking "to exchange the contracted theatre, the clouds and snows, [and] the exhausted and sterile lands" of their states, for the vast region, the clear sky, the dry atmosphere, brilliant sunshine, . . . and noble rivers of the Missouri and Mississippi."[52]

Benton took the lead as well in arguing that the new state of Missouri must have expansive boundaries. In 1817, before the eruption of the slavery controversy, Benton worried that representatives from New England "wish to pare us down [un]til we are as small as themselves." In particular, he urged Congress to reject a proposal that would give the new state a northern border at the Missouri River. Instead, in his correspondence and in the columns of the *Enquirer*, Benton envisioned a state whose size "would place her in the front rank of the great states" and whose location would ensure a glorious destiny. Its extensive frontage on the Mississippi would make it the center of the American republic, while its control over the Missouri would made it the gateway to lands further west (and, awakening the old dream of a Northwest Passage to the Pacific, to the riches of Asia).[53]

Benton's grand vision and that of other statehood advocates in the Missouri Territory moved closer to reality when Congress resumed debate in February 1820. With engineers of compromise, most notably Henry Clay, working behind the scenes, the Senate approved legislation that admitted Missouri as a slave state, while preserving the previous balance by simultaneously bringing Maine into the union as a free state. In addition, the Senate version of the Missouri statehood bill included a provision prohibiting slavery in those areas of the Louisiana Territory that lay north of the 36°30' latitude—with the exception of the new state of Missouri, whose southern border was set at that line. The House of Representatives, however, defeated the Senate's limited limitation and instead passed its own bill with a prohibition on slavery in all of the remaining Louisiana Territory. Several days of political arm-twisting followed, concluding on March 3, when both House and Senate agreed to a "Missouri Compromise" in which Missouri and Maine became states and a new border between slave and free territories was drawn across the trans-Mississippi West at the 36°30' line. Three days later, President James Monroe signed the enabling legislation. To Benton's delight, the statehood act located the northern boundary of the state of Missouri well north of the mouth of the river of the same name at the 40°35' latitude, and its total area made Missouri the second largest of the United States.[54]

It was at this point, in April 1820, that Thomas Jefferson penned his "firebell" letter to John Holmes, a congressman from the Maine district of Massachusetts. The timing and destination of Jefferson's letter, after Congress had approved the compromise and to one of the northern representatives who had broken sectional ranks to allow Missouri's admission as a slave state, hints that the former president was not as frightened as he pretended. Rather, as historian Stuart Leibiger has outlined, Jefferson calculated his rhetorical alarm for political effect. Knowing that his views would be widely disseminated, "Jefferson tailored his statements about the Missouri Crisis to suit specific audiences." In this case, he intended to lend his endorsement to Holmes and other northern "dough faces" (supporters of Missouri slavery). Jefferson, in this interpretation, sought to terrify other "Yankees into fearing for the Union, causing them to abandon [further] attempts to restrict slavery."[55]

Although Jefferson wrote of his terror in the past tense, the Missouri crisis was not yet over. Under the terms of the Enabling Act, the next step toward statehood was for "people" of Missouri, which in this case included all free white males who had reached the age of twenty-one and who had resided in the territory for three months, to elect delegates to a constitutional convention. With voting scheduled for the first week in May, the campaign for the forty-one slots, apportioned among the territory's fifteen counties, was hasty, yet heated, with slavery once more generating the most fiery rhetoric. While the Missouri Compromise protected slavery within the boundaries of the new state, a few candidates did make the case for future restrictions on unfree labor. Theirs was primarily an economic, rather than moral, imperative, resting on the contention that Missouri's development would be retarded by dependence on slave labor. Anti-restrictionists rejected these claims and tarred those who raised such questions as "emancipators," which, said one candidate so accused, "was the worst name that can be given in . . . Missouri." At the polls, all restrictionists were soundly defeated.[56]

The election ensured that delegates to the convention would write a constitution that kept Missouri safe for slavery. To that end, the framers denied the state's general assembly the power "to pass laws . . . for the emancipation of slaves" without the consent of owners. The convention narrowly defeated a proviso that would have required emancipated slaves to depart the state immediately. But the proposed charter did make it a duty of the legislature to pass laws "to prevent free negroes and mulattoes from coming to, and settling in this state, under any pretext whatsoever."[57]

United in their defense of slavery, delegates did divide on a number of issues. As with previous constitutional conventions in the Ohio valley, a liberal faction championed the extension of the franchise to adult men without imposing any property qualification. These delegates, making up about one-third of the members of the convention, also pushed to put greater power in the hands of the legislative branch, which by being subject to frequent elections was most directly accountable to the "people." But while the liberal faction won the support of a majority of delegates for universal manhood suffrage, their conservative opponents, also about one-third of the members, held the upper hand on most contested issues. The result was a constitution that followed closely Kentucky's 1799 charter as opposed to the somewhat more liberal documents adopted by new states north of the Ohio River. Like Kentucky's constitution, the Missouri convention checked popular power by offering judges lifetime appointments. Conservatives further protected the independence of the judiciary by providing for high salaries that the legislature was prevented from reducing during a judge's time in office. As an additional insulation from the will of the people, the convention decided that the charter need not be submitted to the electorate for approval; instead, the constitution required only a two-thirds vote in each house of the Missouri legislature.[58]

The constitutional convention finished its work in July 1820; the following month, Missourians went to the polls to elect their first governor. The contest pit William Clark, the territorial governor, against Alexander McNair. Backed by St. Louis's little junto and by the leaders of the conservative faction that had recently dominated the constitutional convention, Clark followed the old script for electioneering. That is, he did not so much run as "stand" for office. In his sole public statement of his qualifications, he wrote a letter to the *St. Louis Enquirer* touting his "long residence" in the territory and referring "any inquiries which may concern my individual and private character" to his influential connections. In fact, Clark was back in Virginia during the month leading up to election, mourning the loss of his wife.[59]

In conducting the campaign this way, Clark demonstrated his unfamiliarity with how much the political climate had shifted since the War of 1812. He seemed not to appreciate that boasting of his friendship with the "old inhabitants and early settlers" would be a political liability with the majority of voters, who had arrived in Missouri after the war and who chafed at the control of territorial governance still exercised by the little junto. By contrast, McNair and his supporters sensed—and effectively exploited—the rising sentiment for more democratic governance. Although McNair had also been aligned with the little junto and had been elected to the constitutional convention as an anti-restrictionist, he broke with conservatives to challenge provisions for lifetime judicial appointments and blasted the high salaries offered judges. During the campaign, McNair and his surrogates called attention to these positions, while criticizing Clark for being too close to French merchants and too distant from "the people." Even more ruinous to Clark were the barrage of attacks that accused him of being "too good to the Indians." Worse still in the new political era were allegations that Clark had fathered children by Indian women. The damage became apparent when the election results were tallied. McNair received 6,576 votes, Clark just 2,656.[60]

Although Alexander McNair then became the first governor of the state of Missouri, Missouri was not yet officially a state. Its constitution still needed the consent of majorities in both houses of Congress and then the signature of the president before statehood would be finalized. The process of clearing this last hurdle began in November 1820, but discord in Washington threatened to unravel the compromise reached earlier that year. In particular, several representatives from northern states raised objections to the Missouri constitution's provision forbidding free blacks to settle in the state. Because free blacks could be citizens in their states, the northerners insisted this condition violated Section 2, Article IV of the U.S. Constitution, which held that citizens of each state should possess the privileges and immunities of citizens in the several states. The matter remained stalled until Henry Clay negotiated a second compromise. Under the new formula, which Congress ratified on March 2, 1821, Missouri legislators were to adopt a resolution indicating that the controversial clause of the state's constitution "shall never be construed to authorize the passage of any law, and that no law shall be passed in conformity thereto, by which any citizen, of either of the states in this Union, shall be excluded from the enjoyment of any of the privileges and immunities to which such citizen is entitled under the constitution of the United States." The Missouri legislature did this in June. And so at last on August 10, 1821, Missouri became the twenty-fourth state of the American republic.[61]

On February 2, 1819, just as the question of slavery and Missouri statehood was beginning to burn in Washington, George Sibley, the chief factor at Fort Osage, rang a firebell on a different subject. "I am irresistably led to the conclusion that the British Agency in Canada is again intermeddling in the Indian concerns of the Missouri," wrote Sibley to Governor Clark. The British, he maintained, were "making great exertions," attempting anew to enlist the Sacs and to extend their influence among the Osages. For the moment, Sibley felt he had persuaded the

Osages to be wary of these entreaties. "But let them once get a taste of British presents," worried Sibley, and "the blood of innocent people will stain the Shores & crimson the waters of the Missouri."[62]

Sibley's alarm and Indian hopes about a return of British gifts and a restoration of borderland possibilities were exaggerated. Although the British had not relinquished their interest in trade with Indians on the upper Mississippi and Missouri rivers, their influence no longer reached so close to the confluence of those waterways. With the withdrawal of the British (and the Spanish), the confluence region ceased to be a borderland after the War of 1812. Accordingly, the intercultural accommodations that interimperial rivalries had helped to underwrite stood on much shakier ground once the convergence of the Missouri, Ohio, and Mississippi rivers became entirely an American Confluence.

Yet even as competing international boundaries were disappearing from the region, new internal borders were being drawn. The creation of the state of Missouri mapped a fresh set of lines across the confluence region. What made these perimeters controversial was the introduction of the question of slavery. Although a compromise was found, the larger issue was not resolved. To the contrary, Missouri's course over the next half century turned on its position as a border state in the mounting conflict between slave and free states, much as its borderland location had shaped its history over the previous several decades.

6.

Closings

In November 1828, John Miller, the second governor of the state of Missouri, defended the government's policy toward Indians by declaring that "ours is a frontier State." For Miller, that situation justified the eviction of Indians living within the boundaries of Missouri, a process of ethnic cleansing that was largely carried out during the 1820s. By the definition used in this book, these expulsions closed the frontier *in* Missouri, for the elimination of independent Indian polities secured the uncontested hegemony of the United States. Indeed, by the time of Miller's declaration, much of the Indian population had been removed beyond the western borders of the state. In this sense, the frontier *in* Missouri had become the frontier *of* Missouri.[1]

Decades in the unmaking, the final stages of the frontier in Missouri transpired in the particular demographic, economic, and political climate of the 1820s. Ever since the Louisiana Purchase, Indians in Missouri, both long established nations and more recent immigrants, had faced increasing pressures on their landholdings. After the War of 1812, the retreat of British and Spanish influence deprived Indians in the confluence region of a counterforce to American expansion, and the achievement of statehood put Indians within the state's borders under additional duress. An economic downturn at the beginning of the 1820s briefly slowed the flow of American newcomers into Missouri, but what came to be known as the "Panic of 1819" offered little respite for Indians. To the contrary, the panic nurtured a more insistently democratic political culture that left Indians even more vulnerable to the land demands of the majority.

Through the first half of the 1820s, many Indians in Missouri held on to their lands, but their independence was increasingly compromised. Although the traditions of amicable intercultural association persisted in pockets, most white settlers wanted Indians banished. Against this force, Shawnees, Delawares, Osages, and other Indians in Missouri found themselves ever more dependent on American authorities, whose sympathies, though sometimes genuine, proved woefully insufficient.

And so, especially in the second half of the decade, an exodus of Indians brought the frontier in Missouri to its closure. Public officials and private citizens forwarded numerous rationales for these removals. Almost always, however, these justifications rested on flawed readings of the region's frontier past, false claims about Missouri's present situation, and fatuous understandings about the borders that would in the near future divide and redefine the confluence region.

Panic and Politics Unusual

The political crisis that accompanied Missouri's path to statehood coincided with an economic crisis that set off its own firebells in the night. While the political turmoil awakened Thomas Jefferson with a sense of dread about the future of the American union, the economic crisis sounded equally sleep-shattering alarms about the course of American society. The fallout from this twin turbulence reverberated across the nation and the new state during the 1820s, profoundly altering the rules of Missouri and American politics.

At the national level, the tumult over Missouri statehood introduced the slavery question into congressional debates and announced a stark sectional divide between northern and southern interests. As John Quincy Adams discerned, the Missouri crisis showed "the basis for a new organization of parties" that was "terrible to the whole Union, but portentously terrible to the South." In the wake of the compromise by which Missouri attained statehood, a number of politicians resolved to prevent a repetition of the Missouri crisis. To do this, they understood that slavery must be removed from national debates so that it would not again become the source of a North versus South alignment in Congress. Led by New York's Martin Van Buren, these politicians strove to rebuild the cross-sectional coalition upon which Jeffersonian dominance had rested. Essential to this revival was finding men like Van Buren, who, though a northerner, would not agitate the slavery question, or like Andrew Jackson, who, though a native of South Carolina, was identified as a westerner. Together, Jackson and Van Buren forged a new party (and a new organization of parties) that beginning in the 1820s and maturing in the 1830s temporarily succeeded in quieting the slavery question at the national level.[2]

At the state level, the slavery question also receded, not so much because the achievement of statehood settled the matter, but because in the early 1820s the attention of Missourians was diverted by economic troubles. That represented a significant turn, for in the years immediately following the War of 1812, the Missouri Territory experienced an economic boom. Fueled by rapid population growth, land prices skyrocketed. In their eagerness to acquire lands, newcomers bid up the price of acreage, particularly around St. Louis and in the much coveted Boon's Lick Country. Many took advantage of the federal government's credit system to make purchases. By the end of 1820, such purchases left Missourians over two million dollars in debt to the national government. Other newcomers bought lands that were already in private hands, extending beyond their means, but confident that rising prices would allow them to resell all or part at a substantial profit. A safe bet it would seem, for according to St. Louis editor Thomas Hart Benton, land worth thirty dollars in 1817 had appreciated to two thousand dollars by 1819. That valuation exaggerated the inflation, but it captured the spirit of the times in which investments in land reaped rich returns and handsome profits invited further speculation.[3]

A closer look at the regional and national picture might have dampened expectations. The fur trade, long a staple of the confluence region's economy, slumped noticeably. When the United States assumed control over the Louisiana Territory, the annual value of furs brought to St. Louis totaled over two hundred thousand dollars. But war disrupted the trade, and the postwar period did not bring the expected recovery. By 1819, despite the withdrawal of British competitors from the upper Mississippi, the value of furs sent to St. Louis had fallen below fifty thousand dollars. Taking note of the decline in the fur trade and of reports of hard times to the east, the *Missouri Gazette* declared in July 1819, "The signs of the times are alarming." The newspaper added that "a dark and dreadful cloud hangs over our country, which may bring the ruin of many." Still, so long as land prices continued their meteoric ascent, few of the *Gazette*'s readers paid heed to such gloomy forecasts.[4]

In 1820 and even more in 1821, land prices tumbled, and pessimistic outlooks became impossible to ignore. Especially during the latter part of 1820, it became apparent that immigration into the confluence region was down, curtailing the demand for land. Prices that spiraled up so rapidly in the previous years fell precipitously in the summer and fall of 1820 and throughout the winter of 1821. Because so many had purchased on credit, the bursting of the land bubble left debtors in a bind. Suddenly they could not find buyers to help them pay for their acquisitions. Instead, foreclosures loomed. "Such is the depreciation of the value of property," reported the *Missouri Gazette* in the spring of 1821, "that the accumulated labor of years is not now sufficient to pay a trifling debt, and property some years since which could have sold for eight to ten thousand dollars, will scarcely, at this time, pay a debt of five hundred."[5]

The problems of debtors and the woes of the economy mounted with the collapse of Missouri's two banks and the proliferation of individual bankruptcies. During the boom times, notes issued by the Bank of St. Louis and the Bank of Missouri provided a currency for buyers and sellers of land and other commodities. In theory, these bank notes substituted for specie, which was always in short supply in the confluence region, and they saved residents from the often cumbersome arrangements that bartering necessitated. The onset of hard times, however, soon reduced these enterprises to insolvency, along with scores of other banks across the trans-Appalachian West. One after another, banks closed when unable to meet the demands of creditors, who wanted notes redeemed, as promised, with gold or silver. In Missouri, the Bank of St. Louis ceased business in 1819, right at the beginning of the panic. The Bank of Missouri hung on, though its notes depreciated continually downward, losing more than three-quarters of their value between 1819 and the summer of 1821. In August, the Bank of Missouri suspended specie payments, and the directors voted to close the concern. At that point, more than half of the stores that had operated in St. Louis in 1818 had succumbed, and the pages of Missouri newspapers were filled with bankruptcy notices.[6]

Even before the Bank of Missouri went under, the deepening distress prompted Governor Alexander McNair to ask the legislature on June 4, 1821, to adopt measures "for the relief of the general depression in commerce and credit." In this message, McNair carefully deflected blame for the current situation. Discounting the speculative mania that had gripped Missourians, he contended that the panic resulted from "causes originating elsewhere." The problems, asserted one Missourian, traced to outside land speculators who, like a "flock of vampires," had descended upon the state during the boom years. Among legislators, however, the search for culprits did not focus exclusively on those at a distance. Although the decline in the fur trade, the closing of shops, and the unemployment of laborers hit St. Louis hard, rural representatives often blamed the city and its commercial culture for the troubles afflicting the rest of the state. Anti-urban and anti-commercial animus had already made itself felt during Missouri's constitutional convention, as reflected in Article VIII, which prohibited the chartering of more than one bank in the state and placed severe restrictions on its operation.[7]

In the panic-heated climate of 1821, proponents of relief demanded and received much stronger legislative remedies. Responding to the governor's call, legislators quickly approved a number of measures to calm public fears and restore economic prosperity. These included acts abolishing imprisonment for certain classes of debtors and establishing a loan office, the certificates of which would substitute for those issued by private banks and would be receivable for the payment of taxes and government salaries. In addition, the legislature enacted a stay law that either granted debtors a reprieve of two and a half years or forced creditors to accept only two-thirds of the property's appraised value. Modeled on laws passed in several other southern and western states, this stipulation assigned the appraisal to three people appointed by the local county court. That put the neighbors of debtors in a position to shield one another, at least when creditors lived outside the area.[8]

As in other states where the politics of panic inspired similar antidotes, legislative actions were bitterly contested in Missouri. Creditors complained that the stay law robbed them of their means to collect debts. Merchants grumbled that the certificates issued by the state loan office were worthless, since they would not be accepted beyond the borders of Missouri. Lawyers deemed the measures unconstitutional. But try as anti-relief leaders did to cast proponents of relief as enemies of private property, individual rights, and constitutional government, the majority of legislators (and the majority of Missouri's voters) backed the remedies. To the tune of "Yankee Doodle," advocates of relief answered their opponents: "What glorious privilege we have, to chuse the men to rule us; what dolts and blockheads we should be, to let the lawyers fool us."[9]

Relief laws had a short life in Missouri. The first test came in February 1822 when the case of *Missouri v. William Carr Lane* came before the St. Louis Circuit Court. In his decision, Judge Nathaniel Tucker overturned the loan office act, holding that the certificates were bills of credit, which the federal constitution prohibited states from issuing. Two months after this ruling, Tucker struck down Missouri's stay law in *Glasscock v. Steen.* Once again, Tucker concluded that the act impaired the obligation of contracts and thus could not pass constitutional muster.[10]

Tucker's rulings were in keeping with those of judges in other states, and so was the popular reaction in Missouri. In state after state in the early 1820s, courts invalidated relief legislation. And in state after state, these decisions generated a fiery outcry. In Missouri in the months that followed Tucker's rulings, proponents of relief condemned Tucker in particular and lawyers in general. During the campaign for the state legislature in the spring and summer of 1822, pro-relief candidates claimed that constitutional obfuscations sacrificed the common sense of the people to the "pomp and learning" of lawyers and held democratic rule hostage to the "crush of judicial oppression."[11]

Such fevered rhetoric was common across the trans-Appalachian West in the early 1820s, but in Missouri the heat dissipated more quickly than in some neighboring states. After the Kentucky Supreme Court overturned a stay law, that state's legislature responded by constituting a new highest court and naming pro-relief justices to it. For several years, Kentucky had competing supreme courts and pro- and anti-relief factions divided into "new court" and "old court" parties. Not until 1826 did anti-relief forces regain control of the legislative and executive branches of the state government and restore the "old court's" unchallenged supremacy in judicial matters. By contrast, the divisions in Missouri were not nearly so scarring or so enduring. Already in 1822, the clamor for relief had subsided. By September, the *Missouri Republican* optimistically reported that "the cry of *hard times*, which formerly almost deafened us from every quarter, has relapsed into low murmurs of complaint from only a few directions." In part, this change in public sentiment owed to the beginnings of an economic recovery that resulted from the renewed flow of immigrants into the state and the return of rising real estate prices. It also reflected a growing belief that relief measures, regardless of their constitutionality, were ineffective, at best benefiting wealthy speculators more than they did poorer debtors. For these reasons, anti-relief men won control of the legislature in 1822, putting an end to Missouri's experiment with further radical responses to the Panic of 1819.[12]

Although support for radical change ebbed, the reverberations from the panic continued to shape national and state politics throughout the 1820s, especially in the schemes advanced for distributing public lands. In 1820, Congress revamped the federal land system by lowering the minimum price to $1.25 per acre and by decreasing the minimum amount for purchase to eighty acres. In addition to these reductions, which were designed to make purchases from the public domain more affordable, Congress provided its own relief measure for those who owed money from previous sales. Under the Relinquishment Act of 1821, debtors were allowed more time to make payments and permitted to abandon a portion of their lands (as well as the moneys owed for that portion). Helpful for some past and would-be purchasers, these statutes did not go far enough for others. After all, the new minimums still required buyers to come up with $100, which was beyond the means of many. More attractive for poorer men was the "graduation-donation" proposal first floated in 1824 by Thomas Hart Benton, who had become a senator from Missouri in 1821. Benton's plan called for continuing reductions in the minimum price for public lands. Tracts that did not sell immediately would drop over the course of a few years from $1.25 per acre to 25 cents per acre. If still unsold, these lands would be donated in small parcels to actual settlers. And if no private owners accepted the donation, then the remaining parts of the national domain would be turned over to the states in which they were located.[13]

Benton's attachments before joining the Senate made him an unlikely advocate for such a populist program. As an ambitious lawyer and editor of the *St. Louis Enquirer*, Benton had aligned himself with the interests of that town's elite French merchants. In the *Enquirer*, Benton had emphasized the importance of the fur trade to Missouri's economic well-being and had pushed for liberal confirmation of Spanish land grants. In the Senate, Benton maintained these positions, urging the federal government to be generous in validating still unconfirmed old land claims and winning passage of legislation to abolish the factory system. That measure, particularly dear to the trading community in St. Louis, eliminated the federal government as a competitor in commerce with Indians. Yet Benton was careful not to reveal the extent of his association with the Chouteaus and other St. Louis merchants, and he also stressed the broader public interests that were served by these positions.

Moreover, Benton's views on various matters shifted during and after the Panic of 1819. Personally stung by the failure of Missouri's banks, Benton abandoned his previous support for such institutions. After the banks went under, Benton became a staunch supporter of an economy based exclusively on "hard money," an advocacy that earned him the moniker "Old Bullion." Early in the 1820s, Benton also recognized that Missouri's voters were demanding more accountability and control over government at local levels. Riding that sentiment, he introduced an amendment to the first session of the Eighteenth Congress (1823–24) to scrap the electoral college system in favor of direct popular election of the president of the United States. The disputed result of the 1824 presidential election, in which Congress awarded the election to John Quincy Adams despite Andrew Jackson having won more votes, boosted support for Benton's amendment. It also led Benton into an unexpected alliance with Jackson (unexpected because a decade earlier when Benton was still residing in Tennessee, he and Jackson had been involved in a bitter personal dispute, culminating in a brawl in which Benton shot Jackson and several of Jackson's friends then stabbed Benton). But time healed these wounds, and in the second half of the 1820s, Benton emerged as the leader of Missouri's nascent Jacksonian party.[14]

In this role, Benton championed the entwined causes of Jackson, popular democracy, and land graduation-donation. Playing to the discontent of westerners, Benton blasted the existing system for distributing federal lands for creating inequalities between old and new states. Where "the old States have a right to make primary disposition of the soil within their limits; the new ones have not. . . . The Federal Government has no jurisdiction over the soil, timber, grass, and water of the old States; they assert and exercise jurisdiction over all those in the new States." This "condition of inequality" Benton held "to be inconsistent with the terms and spirit of the Constitution." By contrast, graduation-donation favored neither old nor new states, "comprehend[ing] within its liberal scope the essential interest of every State in the Union." Making a pragmatic case, Benton claimed that graduation-donation made good fiscal sense. Though prices would drop, land sales would still produce more revenue, enough "to eliminate the public debt and the necessity of raising additional federal revenues through tariffs." Benton's version of supply-side economics would then reduce the tax burdens for all Americans. Yet more important than these fiscal benefits, Benton spoke of "the wider horizon" opened by graduation-donation: by "pass[ing] public lands cheaply and easily into the hands of the people," the "adoption of this great measure" guaranteed "the durability and prosperity of this Republic—the number of tenants diminished[,] the class of freeholders increased," the nation ever populated by "virtuous and independent farmers."[15]

Benton's glorious vision, however, remained only that, blocked by political foes in the Congress, with some of the strongest opposition to graduation-donation coming from his fellow senator from Missouri, David Barton. Like Benton, Barton began his political career as a protector of property, sharing with his wealthy supporters a suspicion of the tyranny of the majority (as evidenced in the relief controversies). Also like Benton, Barton was committed to an expanded role for the national government, particularly to an extensive program of internal improvements. But while Benton's ideas swung to embrace broader popular democracy and reject augmented federal power, Barton stayed the ideological course. And while Benton aligned with Jackson, Barton lined up with John Quincy Adams and Henry Clay. On almost every major issue, then, Benton and Barton found themselves on opposing sides, nowhere more so than on the politics of land distribution. Rather than increasing the predominance of freeholders, Benton's scheme, in Barton's view, would enable wealthy speculators to acquire lands at bargain prices. The result of graduation-donation would be the establishment of "the most alarming and oppressive land aristocracies." What is more, the policy injured those who had purchased public lands at earlier higher prices, for the value of these properties would also be reduced.[16]

In the Senate during the 1820s, Barton won his battle against Benton's land distribution policy, but in Missouri politics, Benton (and Jackson) won the war. As Benton later recognized, his vigorous promotion of graduation-donation "had more effect upon the public mind than upon federal legislation." Although Benton could not as yet enlist sufficient congressional support to get his plan enacted, he did gain the backing of the Missouri General Assembly. In 1829, the legislature approved a resolution praising the graduation bill and instructing Senator Barton to vote for it. More significant in the new political era in which popular support mattered as never before, Benton's proposal gained the backing of "the people." "Benton's proposition," suggested one congressional opponent, "had stimulated all the people of the Western country to madness." Or, as Barton summarized, the popularity of "graduation hung like a guillotine" over his political head. The clearest evidence of the triumph of Benton and his politics within Missouri came in the 1828 presidential election. That year, Andrew Jackson carried the state in a landslide, polling over 70 percent of the popular vote in Missouri.[17]

To their partisans, the victory of Jackson and the support for Benton's land policy signaled the burgeoning of popular democracy. To be sure, a few men turned away from the political contests of this world. As one Methodist preacher put it, "There are many kinds of ticks but none of them so injurious . . . as Polly Ticks." But during the 1820s many more Missourians became engaged in politics, rejecting older ideals about deferring to their betters and demanding that their voices be heard and heeded. That clamor burst forth in 1820 when upstart Alexander McNair overwhelmed incumbent William Clark in the state's first gubernatorial election. It built the following year in the uproar for relief, and it reached a new peak with the election of Jackson to the presidency in 1828. The rise of "Jacksonian Democracy" had important repercussions for Missouri, especially in debates about the distribution of the national domain. And because public lands were often still in Indian hands, the Panic of 1819 and

Figure 9. John Sartain's 1854 engraving *The County Election*, copied from the original painting by George Caleb Bingham, captures the spirited character of popular democracy in the age of Jackson. Courtesy of the Autry National Center.

its political fallout also had a profound impact on intercultural relations within the state of Missouri.[18]

The Twilight of the Frontier *in* Missouri

At the end of the 1820s, wrote Hattie Anderson, a historian of the "peopling" of frontier Missouri, the new state had become "a true melting pot." By this, Anderson meant that newcomers to the state had enriched its demographic diversity. Yet, at the same time that Missouri was adding people from points near and far, the state was shedding most of its remaining Indian population and losing the traditions of intercultural association and accommodation that had formerly made the confluence region a truer melting pot.[19]

After slowing briefly during the economic troubles at the beginning of the decade, Missouri's population soon regained its upward trajectory. Thanks to the renewed influx of newcomers, the 1830 census registered 140,455 residents, more than double the 1820 count. Among the newest Missourians, former residents of Kentucky and Tennessee predominated, their numbers augmented by smaller migrations from neighboring states in the Ohio valley, as well as from Virginia and North Carolina. These migrations included both free persons and slaves, with the latter's numbers rising at a slightly faster clip than the former. Thus, in 1830, Missouri's census included more than 25,000 slaves, who accounted for nearly 18 percent of the state's census; by contrast, in 1820, Missouri's 10,000 slaves made up approximately 15 percent of the population.[20]

As in the second half of the previous decade, the chief destination for Missouri-bound slaves and slaveholders in the 1820s was the Boon's Lick Country. For transplants from Kentucky and Tennessee, the Boon's Lick Country replicated the fine climate and soil for growing tobacco and hemp found in those states. The location of the Boon's Lick Country, though, offered easier and cheaper shipment to the Deep South (where hemp was in high demand as rope for bundling cotton). Such attractions also encouraged the settlement of lands further away from the banks of the Missouri and further upriver. As in Kentucky and Tennessee, most settlers in Missouri's expanding core of tobacco and hemp cultivation owned only a few slaves. A small number, however, arrived with, or built up, substantial holdings. During the 1820s, planters ploughed tobacco and hemp profits into larger land and slaveholdings and replaced log cabins with two-story brick houses. These new showplaces lent an air of aristocratic distinction to their owners and to the surrounding countryside. With the establishment of plantations, the Boon's Lick Country, whose name resonated with frontier times, evolved into Missouri's "Little Dixie," a sobriquet that suggested the particularly southern flavor of that part of the state.[21]

In contrast to the growing southernness of the Boon's Lick Country and its developing plantation agriculture, St. Louis was slower to recover from the effects of the panic, and it continued to attract a more diverse set of newcomers. Not until 1828 did the value of assessed real estate in St. Louis again reach its pre-panic level, and as of that year the city's population had increased by less than 10 percent since 1820. Still, signs of renewed vitality appeared. In 1829, a visitor described the place as being "in a very improving condition," with new buildings of "the most permanent and beautiful kind . . . springing up in every direction" and small, unimproved lots on Main Street selling for four to five thousand dollars apiece. New buildings were needed for new businesses and new residents, who were a heterogeneous assortment. Touring St. Louis in 1827, the Englishman Charles Sealsfield found "Kentucky manners" prominent amidst a complex blend of accents and origins. As Timothy Flint explained, "Very few towns in the United States, or the world, have a more mixed population." Americans, from "all parts of the states," now "predominate over the French . . . with a sprinkling of people from all quarters of the world."[22]

A number of factors contributed to St. Louis's economic revival and demographic stew. Of particular import was the surge in steamboat traffic, which brought goods and people in and out of St. Louis. By decade's end, the number of steamboats docking in St. Louis averaged almost one per day. Once again, St. Louis's geographic advantages served it well. Above St. Louis, shallower waters demanded different steamboats than those that navigated the lower Mississippi. Thus goods traveling up and down the Mississippi had to be transshipped at St. Louis, rousing the town's commerce.[23]

Additional stimulus came with the rebound in the fur trade. This renewal was spurred in part by steamboat transportation, which not only sped journeys up and down the Mississippi but also opened the upper reaches of the Missouri to navigation by steam-powered vessels. The enlivening of the fur trade resulted as well from an injection of capital and competition from outside the confluence region. In St. Louis, what had been a relatively closed community of still primarily French traders grudgingly opened after the German-born, New York–based entrepreneur John Jacob Astor located a branch of his American Fur Company there in 1819. During the 1820s Astor, who was on his way to becoming the wealthiest man in the United States, conducted business on a

Figure 10. An 1840s watercolor by an unknown artist, depicting St. Louis. Courtesy of the Autry National Center.

transcontinental and transoceanic scale, but he made St. Louis the base for his operations along the Missouri River, on the Great Plains, and in the Rocky Mountains. St. Louis's established French traders most certainly did not welcome the competition from Astor's well-financed enterprise, although their hostility diminished after Astor brought in one of their own, Bernard Pratte, as a partner in 1826. By then, other Boston and New York family firms had also joined the fray, often sending younger brothers and sons to oversee operations out of St. Louis. Lumped together as "Yankees" by southern-born residents of Missouri, these migrants from the Northeast altered both the traditional ways of acquiring and merchandising furs as well as the cultural mix of St. Louis.[24]

Of the various restructurings that the fur trade underwent, the most daring originated with a help-wanted posting in the *Missouri Republican* on March 22, 1822. Placed by William Henry Ashley, who had come to Missouri from Virginia two decades earlier and had been elected the state's first lieutenant governor in 1820, the advertisement sought "enterprizing young men" for a fur-gathering expedition to the upper Missouri. Described by a St. Louis acquaintance as "a most interesting man," at once "modest and reserved," yet with "a singular passion . . . for perilous adventures," Ashley proposed an audacious gambit with profound implications for intercultural relations. Not only did Ashley take on Astor and the French traders of St. Louis, but he also took on the system of trade that relied on Indian men to hunt and trap animals and Indian women to prepare pelts for exchange. Instead, Ashley's scheme cut Indian hunters and trappers out by employing or sometimes merely outfitting his own men to gather skins in the Rocky Mountains.[25]

As Ashley's "mountain men," Astor's agents, and French traders worked north and west from St. Louis, traveling up the Missouri and into the Rockies, a new commercial avenue opened to the south and west. In 1821, William Becknell, a merchant in the Boon's Lick town of Franklin, ushered the start of what soon grew into a considerable trade between Missouri and Santa Fe. From the initial European colonization of the confluence region, dreams of a southwest passage between the Mississippi and the Spanish capital of New Mexico had intrigued traders. But Spanish authorities' commitment to protectionist policies prohibited French and British traders, and even after Spain acquired Louisiana, the difficulties of journeying overland across the plains kept the volume of trade minimal. Following the Louisiana Purchase, Spanish officials again attempted to defend New Mexico and adjacent provinces against any encroachments by foreign traders. That meant trying to intercept American expeditions sent across the southern and central plains. Captured parties faced confiscation of goods, stiff fines, and imprisonment, with release only coming after promises were extracted not to return. Aware of the hostile reception awaiting American interlopers, Becknell's advertisement made no mention of trespassing into Spanish territory. Rather, the men who accompanied him would go across the plains and to the Rockies "for the purpose of trading for horses and mules and catching wild animals of every description." Becknell's timing was fortuitous, however, coinciding with the achievement of Mexican independence and with the new nation's relaxation of trade barriers. Consequently, when Becknell's company and its caravan of pack horses reached Santa Fe, they received an unexpectedly warm official greeting and found inhabitants eager to trade for American goods.[26]

From this beginning, trade between Missouri and New Mexico took off quickly. Each spring wagons drawn by teams of oxen and laden with cotton and woolen cloth, tools, cutlery, and miscellaneous goods set off from Missouri. From trailheads at the point where the Missouri River turned north (at the western border of the state), caravans embarked on the two- to three-month journey to Santa Fe. There freighters exchanged their wares for furs, horses, mules, and silver. The last item was especially valued back in Missouri, where specie was always in short supply. By the second half of the 1820s, the Santa Fe commerce averaged between one and two hundred thousand dollars annually. Unlike the commerce up the Missouri, the Santa Fe trade was not monopolized by a few firms. Instead, about half of its revenues flowed to a variety of St. Louis firms, with the rest divided among merchants in smaller towns along the lower Missouri River.[27]

To this amalgam of peoples and economic activities, Missouri mixed in what developed into a substantial population of German immigrants. By 1850, almost one-third of St. Louis's inhabitants hailed from Germany. At the beginnings of this wave of immigration in the late 1820s and early 1830s, however, most of the German newcomers intended to resettle themselves on Missouri farmlands.[28]

Principal promoter of this first wave of German immigration was Gottfried Duden. A native of Remscheid in the Duchy of Berg, Duden settled in the lower Missouri valley in 1825. His letters, which were published in Germany in 1829, depicted the state of Missouri as a most inviting place, encouraging a flow of immigrants that built during the 1830s and crested in the 1840s and early 1850s. In most respects, Duden's glowing account of Missouri mirrored the promotional literature aimed at potential emigrants to America. Like so many other boosters, Duden extolled Missouri as a region where men of humble means could get ahead more easily and more readily. These advantages began with extraordinarily fertile soils that yielded immense harvests of grain, ideal pasturage that kept stock well fed, and a climate whose benevolence Duden, in the tradition of real estate propagandists, overstated. Scoffing at what his American neighbors called the "rough season," Duden insisted that Missouri had barely "any winter," with little snowfall and frost "so slight that the fire was needed only in mornings and evenings." Subsistence, too, required little effort. Not only was farmland and forage unusually productive, but in Missouri there was also "so much game . . . that a good shot can easily supply a large family with meat." At the same time, in the Missouri, which was "exceedingly rich in fish," were found buffalo fish, eel, pike, trout, salmon, and catfish weighing "more than one hundred pounds"! Here again Duden displayed a penchant for exaggeration that was common in similar texts, although Duden's work was clearly meant for would-be immigrants from German-speaking lands. For these readers, deprived by European game laws of the right to hunt, Duden's promise that "hunting and fishing is absolutely free" on "land that is not fenced in" carried special appeal. Duden's guarantee that beer "could easily be brewed," thanks to "great quantities of hops" that "are found in the woods," made Missouri seem the best poor German's country.[29]

During the 1820s, newcomers to Missouri also included a continuing stream of westering Indians, but, in contrast with the hospitality shown southerners, Yankees, and Germans, these eastern transplants, along with longer settled Indians, felt increasingly unwelcome within the borders of the state. Although Thomas Jefferson's scheme of a population transfer in which eastern Indians swapped places with trans-Mississippi European colonists had never been implemented, the federal government continued to encourage half of that exchange: prodding Indians to resettle on lands west of the Mississippi. From the Spanish era, the Missouri side of the confluence region had been a favored destination for westering Indians, and it remained so during the first years of American rule. Thus in 1820, after decades of migrations across the Mississippi, the Reverend Jedidiah Morse counted nearly 1,400 Shawnees living in villages on Apple

Creek, to the south of Cape Girardeau, and along the Meramec River. Morse also found 1,800 Delawares in towns on the Current and White rivers. To these numbers of transplanted eastern Indians now residing within the boundaries of Missouri, Morse added almost 100 Peorias (on the Current River) and more than 200 Piankashaws (on the St. Francis River). Four years later, the War Department enumerated similar totals for the Shawnees and Delawares. Its census also registered over 8,000 other Indians, including more than 2,000 Kickapoos, who had recently moved from the other side of the Mississippi into Missouri. By the mid-1820s, however, hostility from various quarters discouraged any more Indians from entering Missouri, except to pass through it on their way to new homes beyond the state's western border. And even Shawnees and Delawares, who had gotten along so well for so long with American neighbors, faced increasing pressure to trade their Missouri claims for tracts to the west.[30]

For decades the most aggressive opposition to the tide of immigrant Indians came from the Osages, but their ability to dominate neighboring Indians had diminished considerably by the early 1820s. An 1818 treaty further reduced the Osages' domain by nearly two million acres, though some of the lands in this cession were claimed by Iowas who vigorously protested the transfer. Their country reduced, the Osages still numbered over five thousand, but with divisions unreconciled and villages scattered across southwestern Missouri and the Arkansas Territory, they could no longer stand up to the combined power of immigrant tribes. In both Missouri and Arkansas, reported Indian agent Richard Graham, "emigrating Indians," having gained "an idea of the great riches of the Osage Country, . . . openly avow their intentions of taking possession of it."[31]

As in the territorial era, the Osages' ongoing efforts to prevent such encroachments sparked rounds of retaliations that American officials feared would escalate into a more general intertribal war. Charged with keeping peace, Graham and William Clark, who returned to his post as superintendent of Indian affairs after losing the gubernatorial election, spent much time and energy arranging truces between the Osages and neighboring Indians. But violence proved hard to contain. In the fall of 1824, for example, just a few months after Clark confidently assured the secretary of war that there was "no prospect" of conflict between Indians in Missouri, a group of Osages stole horses from a Delaware hunting party. The Osages also killed Kikthawenund, the son of a Delaware chief, while he was attempting to recapture the horses. Immediately, kinsmen of the slain Delaware sought revenge, launching a series of attacks against Osage hunters. More disturbing from the perspective of American officials, aggrieved Delawares invited Shawnees and Kickapoos to join in a concerted campaign aimed at permanently dislodging the Osages.[32]

Even as American officials sought to mediate disputes between Indians in Missouri, the policies of the U.S. government exacerbated intertribal conflicts by pushing more Indians across the Mississippi and by providing inadequately for the newcomers. In contrast with earlier migrations that eastern Indians had chosen for themselves, the years following the War of 1812 witnessed the development of state-sponsored evictions and forced relocations. A series of treaties with Indians north of the Ohio River mandated their relocation west of the Mississippi River. For Shawnees and Delawares in Ohio and Indiana, these agreements sometimes meant rejoining tribal brethren who had previously settled in Missouri. More typically, the latest newcomers occupied their own towns, which as Secretary of War John C. Calhoun advised Richard Graham should be "as far west and as near the Osage boundary as possible." Often treaties called for Indians evicted from the Ohio valley and Great Lakes regions to move west of the Osages' country and outside the state of Missouri. Always treaties guaranteed the removed good lands, generous annuities, and ample supplies. Again and again, however, corruption, incompetence, and tight budgets deprived Indians of what they were promised, leaving them "destitute of means of support" on the exhausting journey west and in "great need" after they arrived at their new homes.[33]

Significant as conflicts between Indians were, what most jeopardized the well-being of Missouri's Indians were increasingly contentious relations with non-Indians. In general, disputes involved property damages or thefts, though occasionally altercations also resulted in persons injured. In the early 1820s, the most serious outbreak of raids and retaliations occurred in the newly established counties of Chariton, Randolph, Ray, and Clay, which lay north of the Missouri River and represented a westward extension of the Boon's Lick settlements. In the fall of 1820, according to a white resident, bands of Sac, Fox, and Iowas, "under the pretense of hunting," were "annoying the inhabitants by firing the woods, . . . stealing cattle," and "terrifying women and children." As with inter-Indian conflicts, such incidents between whites and Indians had the potential to escalate quickly into more serious—and violent—intercultural conflicts.[34]

Adjudicating squabbles between Indians and whites and preventing them from erupting into murderous raids and retaliations kept American authorities amply occupied. To their credit, William Clark and his subagents succeeded in containing violence. Despite growing friction between Indians and whites, Clark did not allow the frontier in Missouri to devolve into a bloody ground during the 1820s. In part, that success owed to the sympathy that Clark displayed toward Indians and to his equitable handling of complaints. As Clark wrote Jefferson in 1825, "In my present situation of Superintendent of Indian Affairs, it would afford me pleasure to be enabled to meliorate the condition of those unfortunate people placed under my charge, knowing as I do their [w]retchedness and their rapid decline."[35]

Yet Clark's compassion also attested to the dwindling power of Indians in the confluence region. In the not so distant past, Indians had insisted that intercultural disputes be resolved according to their own understandings of justice, such as provisions for "covering the dead." By the 1820s, however, Indians in Missouri had no choice but to rely on American authorities and American courts to mete out fair punishments to offenders and provide appropriate compensation for victims. That marked a crucial loss of political autonomy.

Searching for the causes of Indian–white conflicts, American officials frequently identified alcohol as the source of frontier problems. Both state and federal law banned trading liquor to Indians, but the flow of alcohol into Indian villages in the lower

Missouri valley was on the rise in the 1820s. Faced with shrinking margins, fur traders relied more and more on strong drink to lock up better deals with Indian partners. Moreover, traders who could not or would not supply liquor risked losing business to rivals who could and did. Indian leaders complained repeatedly to American authorities that the furnishing of alcohol threatened their people with economic ruin and fueled intercultural violence. As one government agent put it, if the supplies of whiskey and brandy were not shut off and the suppliers expelled, the Delawares would be "a lost people" within "two years." But the laws against alcohol, like so many previous proclamations and edicts, had little impact in the lower Missouri valley in the 1820s.[36]

Although alcohol had a destructive impact on Missouri's Indians and undoubtedly contributed to discordant intercultural relations, the key to conflict was not liquor but land. Reduced to its essence, the problem was simple and familiar: more white people wanted more land, which required Indians to be displaced. The country ceded by the Osages in western and southwestern Missouri satisfied some of the rising demand, but more attractive were the holdings of Shawnees and Delawares in the eastern and southeastern parts of the state. Not waiting for government sanction, squatters occupied ever larger portions of the Shawnees' and Delawares' domain. The result, declared Senator Thomas Hart Benton in 1824, left the Shawnees and Delawares, along with the other Indians who remained in Missouri, as mere "remnants," all "surrounded, or pressed upon, by the white population."[37]

Amid the rising clamor for the removal of these "remnants" and the opening of their lands, Indians found a few sympathizers among missionaries, traders, and government officials. Emblematic of the first group was the Reverend Nathaniel Dodge from the United Foreign Missionary Society of New York. In 1821 Dodge had established the Harmony Mission in western Missouri. This mission was about fifteen miles from a small Big Osage village and a larger Little Osage town. Living close by the Osages, Dodge made little headway in converting "these poor heathen" to Christianity, but he and members of his family voiced compassion for the Indians' plight in this world. At the very least, the Osages were "preffable" to the "set of white people" who had invaded their country.[38]

Missouri's Indians could also count on some traders for support. In the past, economic interests and familial ties had bound French merchants in St. Louis with Indian trading partners in the lower Missouri valley. But recent changes in the fur trade had loosened those links. The entrance of Boston and New York firms and the influx of Yankee traders created new enterprises that lacked historical and blood connections to the Osages and neighboring Indians. More important, by the 1820s, population growth and overhunting had significantly depleted the once abundant wildlife in the Ozarks and the lower Missouri valley, forcing St. Louis–based traders to shift their focus to Indians and lands further up the Missouri River. Still, a number of traders remained who catered to Missouri's Indians and who spoke up for them and for the symbiotic relations that had once prevailed between whites and Indians. Along the St. Francis River, the presence of Shawnees and Delawares was still welcome, maintained trader Samuel Goode Hopkins. Responding to a rumor that the Shawnees and Delawares in the area were to be evicted, Hopkins asked Richard Graham to stop any removal. First, the "portion of the country" in which the Shawnee and Delaware villages were located had little appeal to whites, for earthquakes were "so common." At the same time, "there is just enough fish, fowl, and game to minister to" the "subsistence" of Indians, "without encroaching upon the rights" of those whites who had moved into the area. In fact, these "industrious" Indians had shown themselves to be very "useful" to their white neighbors. Relocating the Shawnees and Delawares would end the "little trade" that Hopkins deemed "a great convenience" to the white community. And echoing the sentiments of the Dodge family, he added that the presence of these Indians saved the area from "worse [white] neighbors."[39]

Such pleas received a sympathetic hearing from Graham and William Clark. True to the convictions that had contributed to his electoral defeat, Clark remained a foe of squatters who illegally occupied Indian lands. In the spring of 1824 in response to the latest incursions, he determined that whites "settled on lands designed for the Delawares and Shawnees will be required to remove." Those words sounded very much like the proclamation he had issued in 1815, suggesting that Clark's views had not changed.[40]

But the frontier in Missouri certainly had. The demographic and political situation that had rendered Clark's proclamation of the previous decade ineffective obtained to a far greater extent in the mid-1820s. By then, the numerical imbalance between whites and Indians had grown considerably. In addition, the rise of popular democracy made the will of the majority much harder for the Indians' sympathizers to buck. Already in the first half of the 1820s, Indians within the boundaries of the new state had lost a significant degree of their political independence, a development that pointed to the closing of the frontier in Missouri. In the second half of the decade, the frontier in Missouri moved toward a definitive end; this involved the expulsion of Indians from inside the state's borders, a final solution that enlisted even William Clark in its service.

Removal and Racial Borders

Thomas Hart Benton had an explanation for why the ouster of Missouri's Indians was imperative: "To remove the Indians" would "make room for the spread of slaves." Stripping away layers of often contradictory justifications, Benton plotted Missouri's post-frontier social topography. Gone were the blurred boundaries that had made the region a confluence of cultures, replaced in Missouri and surrounding states by a stricter color line and a starker divide between slave and free.[41]

Calls for ridding Missouri of its Indian population were not new, but the demands gained greater force in the 1820s. From the acquisition of the Louisiana Territory, some of the newly arriving Americans objected to any Indian presence in their environs. During and after the War of 1812, the clamor for "slaying every Indian from here to the Rocky Mountains" grew louder. In postwar years, popular opinion turned strongly against Governor William Clark's protection of Indian landholdings and the federal government's policy of encouraging eastern tribes to relocate in the lower Missouri valley. Statehood further raised the pressure on Missouri's Indians. First, in 1820, voters, now able to elect their governor, ousted Clark. The following year, the Missouri General Assembly appealed anew to the federal government for a halt to Indian resettlements in Missouri and for the removal of Indians from Missouri. As far as legislators were concerned, the federal government's actions (in promoting Indian immigration to Missouri) and inactions (in failing to promote Indian emigration from Missouri) were of a piece with the intrusion by outsiders on the question of slavery during the statehood debate. In both cases, the national government offended the rights of Missourians and undermined Missouri's equality with other states. As Thomas Hart Benton put it, the existence of independent Indian communities within Missouri was "a palpable evil, an anomaly in government, and a direct inconsistency with the policy and jurisdiction of a sovereign state."[42]

Removal of Indians was deemed the best political remedy for this wrong. Touted as practical, economical, and humane, it required only that Indians in Missouri exchange their lands within the state for "equal" holdings from the public domain to the west. This swap, proponents argued, made good sense for all parties. Missouri would finally gain equality with older states, and fertile lands would become available to its citizens (and their slaves). At the same time, the federal government could easily recoup the expenses of moving and resettling Indians by selling the lands they left behind. Indians, too, would embrace the trade, for in Benton's opinion, they understood that theirs was a "temporary" situation. "Fully sensible to the disadvantages of their present position" in which "the power of the state is against them" and from which "sooner or later they must go," Missouri's Indians would welcome the opportunity to occupy "a fixed and permanent home beyond its boundaries." On this point, political rivals closed ranks. Indians, David Barton declared, were "desirous of selling" their lands in Missouri. Besides, what choice did they have? If they held out, warned Duff Green, one of Benton's political allies, "the arms of our frontier inhabitants" would make removal an offer the Indians could not refuse.[43]

Just as violence by Americans against Indians was often excused as appropriate vengeance, so, too, removal was sometimes rationalized as a response to Indian raids. In his annual message in 1822, Governor McNair warned that Missouri's citizens "suffer much" from Indian attacks. McNair's successor, John Miller, included similarly dire updates in his yearly messages. Missourians, he claimed, were "surrounded by the most powerful and warlike tribes" and were "at all times liable to Indian depredations." Such rhetoric was not new, but its persistence was curious, since Indian raiding was far less of a problem in the 1820s than it had been in the previous decade. Moreover, in the years after statehood, it was Missouri's Indians who felt increasingly encircled. Still, the rhetoric turned violence against Indians into mere retribution and made removal seem reasonable.[44]

That hatred was endemic and violence unavoidable became a frequent, if historically amnesiac, refrain. When in the mid-1820s Timothy Flint described the "countenances of the frontier people, as they relate numberless tragic occurrences . . . between them and the savages," he merely repeated many old tales of "horrible barbarities and murders" perpetrated by Indians. What was different in Flint's telling was how thoroughly he erased the history of congenial minglings and peaceful accommodations from his account of intercultural relations in the confluence region. To be sure, Flint allowed for the "facility with which the French and Indians intermix." But he contrasted the "affinity" between French and Indians with the "repulsion between the Anglo-Americans and them." He judged this "antipathy" to be "fixed and unalterable." Although "monstrous exceptions" might occur in which American men formed fleeting connections with Indian women, lasting peace and truly "affectionate intercourse" were unimaginable "between the two races."[45]

Flint's view—that intercultural mixings were heinous, racial divisions insurmountable, and Indian–American enmities inevitable—was historically inaccurate, but it was less disputed in the 1820s. Like Flint, more and more Missourians had no personal experience with a frontier in which rituals of conciliation were performed, cross-cultural attachments (sexual and otherwise) consummated, and peaceful accommodations realized. For the vast majority who had arrived in Missouri from points east after the War of 1812, Flint's version of the frontier as a zone of collisions accorded with their own sense of history.

Yet even those who remembered the not so distant past—when collusions also distinguished the frontier in the confluence region—went along with removal. Thus John Scott, who came to the confluence region shortly after the Louisiana Purchase and held a variety of territorial offices before being elected to Congress, knew that Shawnees and Delawares on the western side of the Mississippi had usually gotten along with their French and American neighbors. Scott recognized that the conflicts which did occur were not the result of the stark cultural divide between "savagery" and "civilization" imagined by Flint. Instead, it was the advances made by Shawnees and Delawares that caused "disturbances," such as ensued from the "intermingling of the stock." Because the "safety" of Indians, whites, and livestock was frequently "jeopardized" by this confluence of herding cultures, Scott concluded that Shawnees and Delawares must go—for their own protection. In truth, safeguarding Indians and their stock were at best secondary concerns. At the top, Scott acknowledged, was the bottom line: the tracts held by the Shawnees and Delawares were "very valuable," too valuable to remain the property of Indians. Moreover, as Scott conceded, "the land proposed to be received in exchange" was "not of an equal quality by a great difference."[46]

Among American officials, William Clark had the most direct personal experiences and strongest memories of an accommodationist frontier, yet he, too, came around on removal. In fact, he became its chief local architect during the 1820s, work that seemed to undo much of what he had learned about Indian diplomacy on his western exploration and much of what he had stood for as a territorial official. On a number of previous occasions, he had demonstrated his commitment to Indian property rights. His 1815 proclamation in defense of Shawnee and Delaware claims, though politically costly and practically unenforceable, attested to Clark's principles. In 1824, against overwhelming public opinion, he courageously reaffirmed this stand on behalf of the Shawnees and Delawares. But Clark's support for Indian landholdings had hardly been absolute. Back in 1808, he had negotiated the Osages' first vast cession; ten years later, he helped impose another treaty—and another land forfeiture—on the Osages. Under Clark's direction, an 1823 treaty with the Iowas and an 1824 agreement with the Sacs and Foxes cleared Indian claims from that portion of Missouri lying north of the Missouri River. Three more accords followed in 1825. The first extinguished the Kansa Indians' claims in the western part of Missouri. The second expunged the Osages' last holdings within Missouri. Finally, in November 1825, Clark came to terms with Shawnees in the much coveted Apple Creek region of Missouri. Barely eighteen months after his latest proclamation in defense of Shawnee claims, he affixed his signature to a treaty by which those same Shawnees relinquished their lands near Cape Girardeau. In exchange for giving up their Spanish grant, the Shawnees received $14,000 and a tract near the junction of the Kansas and Missouri rivers, just beyond the western border of Missouri.[47]

Clark maintained that pragmatism partially explained these actions. Accepting the inevitability of removal, he determined in 1823 that since "the Government will sooner or later have to do this, . . . the sooner it was done the better." Waiting would only increase "the difficulties of purchasing" Indian lands and deepen the dissatisfactions among those forced to abandon their improvements. The challenge facing Clark during the 1820s was to make removal as orderly as possible. Accordingly, in June 1829, Clark once more decried "the encroachment of the whites" onto "that part of Shawnee lands yet remaining on White River." By this time, however, Clark's "regret" was not the trespassings themselves. What upset Clark was that the incursions interfered with the efficient execution of "the removal of those Indians," which "would most probably have been effected in the course of the next year."[48]

More than pragmatism or efficiency, Clark justified removal as the most compassionate policy left to him and for Indians. In the mid-1820s, he explained that the changing circumstances of Indians now necessitated their departure "from within the limits of the States" (including of Missouri). With the Indians' power "broken, their warlike spirit subdued, and themselves sunk into objects of pity and commiseration, . . . justice and humanity require us to cherish and befriend them." That entailed transplanting them to a country "where they could rest in peace," by which he did not mean, as some other Americans wished, they would go to die. Rather, Clark retained Thomas Jefferson's idealistic hope that, given time and proper instruction, Indians might yet be fully incorporated into the American republic. To that end, Clark understood that removal imposed an obligation on the government of the United States "to teach them to live in houses, to raise grain and stock, to plant orchards, to set up landmarks, to divide their possessions, to establish laws for their government, [and] to get the rudiments of common learning, such as reading, writing, and ciphering."[49]

In the end, the differing explanations for removal made little difference. Although Benton, Flint, Scott, and Clark voiced a range of opinions about the history of Indian–white relations, the extent of racial divisions, and the causes of intercultural conflicts, their views converged on the solution to all problems. That was removal, and throughout the 1820s, the government of the United States pursued this ethnic cleansing of Missouri.

In the end, the views of Indians mattered little, too. Although Benton, Flint, Scott, and Clark sometimes claimed to speak on behalf of Indians, only Clark had spent much time speaking with Indians. And even Clark's intercultural conversations were hardly what they had once been. Twenty years earlier, Clark had learned that successful negotiations with Indian peoples in the Missouri valley followed an elaborate choreography and involved both symbolic and substantive give and take. By the 1820s, however, the geopolitical conditions that sustained frontiers of accommodation had withered away. Numbers and power were now overwhelmingly on the American side. Borderland competition that had effectively constrained American expansion was a thing of the past. On occasion in the 1820s, American officials in the upper Mississippi and Missouri valleys alleged that British agents still meddled in Indian affairs. As late as 1829, Clark blamed "British influence" on certain chiefs for holding up one planned removal. But most accusations of foreign interference were quickly discredited, and borderland memories barely registered when Clark laid down terms of removal.[50]

Indians had few options but to give up their lands and take the inferior tracts and inadequate payments they were offered in return. In previous decades in the Ohio valley, American encroachments had spurred prophetically inspired opposition, but in the 1820s, no significant visionaries emerged to catalyze Indian resistance within Missouri. Nor did young men, who once defied their own leaders to carry out raids against American settlements, mount any meaningful attacks. Even the most defiant seemed to accept the futility of a militant last stand. But contrary to Benton's prediction that Indians would welcome removal, there was no enthusiasm in Indian villages for the enforced swap of lands, only resignation and resentment.[51]

The slowness with which Indians moved toward removal attested to that reticence. Although the Shawnees on Apple Creek signed a removal treaty in November 1825, their departure did not occur until the spring of 1830. In part, these and other delays owed to the government's inability to organize the exodus. In the case of the Apple Creek Shawnees, the government's failure to provide promised supplies also increased the hardships of the journey and made the first seasons in new homes along the Kansas River even tougher. But while some Indians reluctantly relocated, others lingered in Missouri. Disavowing the treaty of 1825, scores of Osages held on in Missouri, and many of the removed returned to the state to hunt. Among the Shawnees as well, numbers "continue to loiter in and occupy the country," complained Governor Miller in November 1830. Indeed, months after the supposed removal of the last Shawnees, Miller claimed the greater portion of the tribe still remained within the boundaries of his jurisdiction.[52]

Some who lagged asserted that their mixed heritage exempted them from expulsion. In the 1825 treaty with the Osages, the United States seemingly affirmed this differentiation by awarding 640-acre grants to forty-two *métis* who had worked as traders and interpreters while living among their Indian kin. That the government did not mandate removal and instead set aside nearly 27,000 acres for individuals with European fathers and Indian mothers suggested that *métis* were placed in a separate category from Indians.[53]

The government's distinction, however, did not alter the changing social climate, which drew racial lines in such a way that *métis* were made as unwelcome in Missouri as their "full-blooded" kin. Rather than battle the prejudices of American neighbors, most children of French, as well as of English and American, traders opted to move west with their Indian kin. Especially for the offspring of American traders, staying within Missouri often brought rejection from fathers for whom Indian-born sons and daughters were now viewed as an embarrassment. Persisting *métis* suffered worse opprobrium from other Americans, who, like Flint, denigrated them as "monstrous" mongrels. By contrast, within relocated Indian societies, persons of mixed ancestry continued to enjoy the advantages of being between peoples. Beyond the borders of Missouri, *métis* still benefited from the dual lineages that had long made them valuable intermediaries in cross-cultural trade.[54]

Within Missouri, the fixing of racialized borders adversely affected persons of African as well as Indian ancestry. Particularly consequential were statutory revisions undertaken by the state legislature during its 1824–25 session. Taken together, these laws closed a variety of opportunities once available to "negroes and mulattoes" (the latter now defined as having one-fourth "negro blood") in Missouri. Slaves lost the right to do business without the permission of their owners and saw their mobility curtailed by similar requirements for ferry transportation. Free blacks also faced additional discriminations, including acts prohibiting their carrying firearms without a special license or settling in Missouri unless they were citizens of the United States. But for constitutional restrictions, the legislature might well have passed a complete ban on the migration of free blacks or ordered the expulsion of those already residing in the state. Clearing "free people of color" from the state did become a founding principle of the Missouri Colonization Society. Formed in 1825 in St. Louis, the Colonization Society promoted its own plan for removal, with the proposed destination—Africa—lying far beyond the borders of the state. This removal did not occur during the

1820s, but the general unwelcome mat made Missouri a far less appealing place for free people of color. While the number of free blacks in Missouri rose from 347 in 1820 to 569 in 1830, this increase of about 60 percent was only half that of the state's population growth as a whole.[55]

Despite efforts to tighten the social and legal boundaries between white and black Missourians, racial lines remained permeable at a few points. Try as lawmakers did to erect firm racial barriers, these ran up against the legacy of decades of mixing. Thus enforcing laws aimed at restricting free persons of color proved difficult, especially in the cases of mixed heritage individuals who found it possible to "pass" for white. The law, too, left some important openings. Into the 1830s, mulattoes could legally marry whites. Although free blacks were enjoined from testifying in court against whites, they retained their right of *habeas corpus.* In 1825, slaves gained the right to sue in state courts for their freedom. This legislation reaffirmed an earlier territorial statute that had first been used by the descendants of Marie Jean Scypion. In that case, the plaintiffs contended that since Scypion was of mixed Indian and African heritage, they should be emancipated, since colonial laws forbade Indian slavery. They won, and in following decades scores of Missouri slaves obtained their emancipation after satisfying courts that they had been wrongfully held in bondage.[56]

In a number of cases that underscored Missouri's location on the border between slave and free states, Missouri slaves sued on the basis of having lived in neighboring polities where slavery was prohibited. Because of the Northwest Ordinance of 1787 and the Missouri Compromise of 1821, Missouri was surrounded on three sides by such jurisdictions, including the state of Illinois through which thousands of Missouri-bound slaves had traveled. During the 1820s and 1830s, Missouri's Supreme Court rejected claims to freedom from slaves who had merely passed through Illinois. But those same justices generally upheld suits where slaves could prove to having dwelled—sometimes as briefly as one month—on free soil. Too much, though, should not be made of the aperture opened by the 1825 statute. Generous as Missouri's Supreme Court justices initially were in emancipating slaves for temporary residency in free states, these rulings touched only a tiny fraction of the state's enslaved population. In that sense, it left a door barely ajar, only enough for most of Missouri's slaves to glimpse the freedom that in coming decades tempted them to move across the state's Mississippi River border.[57]

Traveling in Missouri in the 1820s, Timothy Flint passed through several villages that had been home to hundreds of Indians until their recent removal. According to Flint, the scene in which "every house was deserted" presented a "desolate contrast" to the "bustle and life" he had seen "a few months before." But while Flint confessed to some "melancholy emotions," he, like most Americans in Missouri, did not renounce removal. Rather, as Governor Miller rejoiced, the clearing of Indians from Missouri constituted actions "of the most desirable and praiseworthy character." In fact, Miller's only regret was that the relocation still left Indians so "near our borders." Nonetheless, "the alternative of having them on our frontier was more acceptable than their remaining within . . . the limits of our own State." Better, in short, for Missouri to *have* a frontier than to *be* a frontier.[58]

That the closing of the frontier in Missouri followed so quickly on the heels of statehood was no coincidence. The tumultuous advent of statehood together with the panic-driven changes in political culture empowered Missouri's citizenry. Those citizens, most of whom had come to Missouri relatively recently, had no acquaintance with the confluence region's traditions of intercultural association and wanted no part of that kind of frontier. State officials felt popular pressure most directly, and they advocated most aggressively for Indian removal. But more insulated federal authorities bent, too, and even the most even-handed, like William Clark, came to see removal as an idea whose time had come.

The closing of the frontier transformed the character of Missouri's borders. With the exiling of Missouri's Indians during the 1820s, the state lost the internal boundaries that had made it a frontier. Henceforth, the frontier in the lower Missouri valley shifted primarily to the western border of the state of Missouri. At the same time, the eastern border of Missouri emerged as a meeting point between slave and free states. Over the next several decades, developments along both of these borders profoundly shaped the future of Missouri and of the United States.

Epilogue

On September 1, 1838, William Clark died in St. Louis. Hundreds of mourners soon gathered at the home of his son Meriwether Lewis Clark. Thousands poured onto the streets of St. Louis for the funeral procession. "The name of GOVERNOR CLARK must ever occupy a prominent place on the pages of the history of this country," a Missouri newspaper eulogized.[1]

In fact, the names of William Clark and his partner, Meriwether Lewis, became ever less prominent on the pages of nineteenth-century histories. By midcentury, school primers devoted little space to Lewis and Clark. Other explorers enjoyed far more renown, most notably John C. Frémont, the son-in-law of Missouri's longtime senator Thomas Hart Benton. Whereas the route that Lewis and Clark took up the Missouri and across the Rockies turned out not to be a viable way to move large numbers of people to the Pacific, Frémont's "discovery" of South Pass opened up the "far West" to American colonization in the 1840s and 1850s. St. Louis became a chief staging area for this mass migration, with a number of towns along the western border of the state of Missouri serving as "jumping off" points for the overland trek through Indian territories and to Oregon farms and California gold fields.

In the years after William Clark's death, Missouri became the major gateway to frontiers that lay to the state's west. Except for a few straggling bands, the state itself had largely been cleansed of its Indian population. To the extent that Indians continued to be a "problem" for state officials, it was primarily a matter of policing borders. Within the boundaries of the state, other ethnic, cultural, and religious conflicts—some old, some new—took precedence.

The problem that came to dominate Missouri's place in national affairs was slavery. During the 1840s and 1850s, questions about the expansion of slavery into territories to the west of Missouri ignited a new firestorm. In the aftermath of the Mexican-American War, the politics of slavery's extension focused particularly on the future disposition of the frontiers *of* Missouri. Yet this matter could not be contained outside the boundaries of the state. Instead, in the 1850s, Missouri emerged as America's elemental border state.

The Legacy of Lewis and Clark

The publication of this history of the Missouri frontier coincides with the two hundredth anniversary of the journey of Lewis and Clark. Not since the bicentennial of the Declaration of Independence has the American history industry been so alive with commemorations. The fascination with Lewis and Clark has stretched from coast to coast, but fittingly the Missouri Historical Society in St. Louis has mounted the official national exhibition. After all, St. Louis was where their great journey ended and where their post-exploration careers were centered.

The current heat about the Lewis and Clark expedition has been building for some time, but the American public has not always displayed so much enthusiasm for the captains, the Corps of Discovery, and their explorations. Although the Corps received a heroes' welcome upon their return to St. Louis, the acclaim soon faded. Once it became clear that the expedition had not fulfilled Thomas Jefferson's hopes of finding a water route across the continent, political opponents stepped up their attacks against what they derided as a wasted expenditure. Such

Figure 11. Lewis and Clark plush toy: Epitomizing the new "feel good" version of the Lewis and Clark saga, this toy features Lewis's dog, Seaman, at the bow of a canoe with Clark, Sacagawea, York, and Lewis all happily together. Photo by the author.

charges did not unseat Jeffersonians from power, but they created some embarrassment, and the alleged failings contributed to diminishing interest in the explorations of Lewis and Clark. The resurrection of Lewis and Clark and the transformation of their journey into *the* great national epic occurred during the twentieth century. The centennial of the expedition brought major expositions in St. Louis and Portland that saluted the Lewis and Clark expedition. Only in the last few years, though, with the approach of the bicentennial, has the Lewis and Clark journey reached the level of popular phenomenon.[2]

What the public has embraced today is quite different from previous incarnations of the Lewis and Clark myth. Whereas the centennial expositions tied the exploration to a story of American progress and empire, current interpretations tend to celebrate the Corp of Discovery's multicultural character and the expedition's peaceful encounters with native peoples. In recent tellings, the journey's central cast often features four leads, with York and Sacagawea joining Lewis and Clark in the spotlight. In what might be called the "feel good" version of the Lewis and Clark tale, the foursome's journey affords a glimpse into a kinder, gentler frontier history and offers a beacon to a better future. With York's elevation to a position of equality within the Corps, we escape the brutality of bondage, entering what appears to be a far more humane interracial landscape. Likewise, stories of the captive Indian woman Sacagawea captivate us because they turn a history of violent conquests and dubious dispossessions into one of peaceful accommodations and mutual acculturations. In that sense, the feel good myth of the Lewis and Clark epic tells us less about who we were or even who we are than it does about who we would like to be.[3]

As this book has emphasized, the history of the confluence region *before* Lewis and Clark provides ample evidence of such accommodations and acculturations. On frontiers, which opened long before any newcomers from across the Atlantic arrived at the meeting point of the Missouri, Ohio, and Mississippi rivers, peoples from the north, the south, the east, and the west mingled. Cohabitations invited competition for vital resources, sometimes leading to violence. Yet the precolonial record also pointed up numerous examples of peaceful exchanges between cultures and adjustments among peoples. So, too, the entrance of European colonizers brought forward new maps and new mixings. If the confluences were occasionally rough, the eighteenth-century history of the region more typically featured accommodationist and inclusive frontiers. This was certainly true of the relations established between French traders and Indian occupants in what the former designated the Illinois Country or Upper Louisiana. For the French, the construction of middle grounds with Indians had precedent in territories to the north and east, although the society created by colonists in the confluence region was distinct from precursors in the St.

Figure 12. Life-size bronze sculpture by Richard Greeves portrays the Shoshone woman known as Sacagawea, who in recent years has become as prominent as Captains Lewis and Clark in accounts of the expedition. Courtesy of the Autry National Center.

Lawrence valley and the Great Lakes. More surprising than the adjustments and accommodations in evidence between French and Indians were those fashioned by European rivals, who followed the French into the heart of North America. In the case of the Spanish, British, and Americans, there was little prior history with accommodations of the type that developed in the confluence region during the second half of the eighteenth century. But confronted by borderland rivals, Spanish and British officials, as well as the earliest American pioneers, adjusted the style and substance of their intercultural relations.

In many respects, borderland assumptions shaped the expedition of Lewis and Clark and shaped the way they subsequently governed. Behind the search for the most "practicable" water route to the Pacific and the bid for Indian allegiances lay concerns that if the United States did not soon secure commercial and political control over its vast Louisiana Purchase, its imperial competitors would. On the trail, these fears, together with the Corps' vulnerability in the face of powerful Indian nations, caused Lewis and Clark to modify their diplomatic stance. As it turned out, various misunderstandings—about the meaning of gifts, the role of fathers, and the functions of sexual intercourse—worked to the advantage of American explorers. But the success of Lewis and Clark depended also on what they came to know about dealing with Indians, beginning with their willingness to adapt to native rituals and protocols. Back in St. Louis, Governor Lewis and General, later Governor, Clark continued to be occupied by British and Spanish intrigues. To the end of the War of 1812, years which encompassed Lewis's brief tenure and the beginning of Clark's governorship, the explorers turned territorial officials sought to curb the excesses of American expansion, lest pioneer trespassings alienate still threatening Indian groups and drive them into the arms of imperial rivals.

The defense of Shawnee and Delaware landholdings by Governors Lewis and Clark should not, however, be attributed exclusively to borderland exigencies. Defying squatter demands carried great political cost, which contributed to Lewis's personal troubles and underwrote Clark's electoral downfall. Contemporaries vigorously condemned what territorial secretary and Lewis nemesis Frederick Bates deemed the "harsh and mistaken" measures on behalf of the Shawnees and Delawares. That Lewis stood fast has been seen by historians as evidence of how the very traits that made him an ideal exploration commander undermined his ability to govern. Yet what Bates saw as Lewis's inflexibility "in error" may now be credited as testament to his undaunted political courage, a trait that William Clark similarly displayed in the years after Lewis's death.[4]

But how to reconcile Lewis and Clark, the protector of Shawnees and Delawares, with Lewis and Clark, by the latter's confession, "damned hereafter" for dispossessing the Osages—and ultimately also displacing the Shawnees and Delawares? The 1808 treaty that Clark considered his "hardest" and that prompted his fears for the afterlife was by no means the last land cession he compelled Indians to make. In fact, during more than thirty years as governor and superintendent, Clark negotiated another thirty-six treaties that received congressional approval. That total represented one-tenth of the pacts made between Indian nations and the United States. Add in agreements concluded by agents under his supervision and Clark's tally rises to more than one-fifth of all Indian treaties ratified by the United States. And at the end of his days, the bottom line was clear: together the agreements made by Clark ejected Shawnees, Delawares, Osages, and other "natives" from inside Missouri, moving them and tens of thousands of other Indians to lands to the west of the state.[5]

Almost all of these treaties happened after the War of 1812, after the eclipse of borderlands lifted one of the major constraints on American expansion in the Mississippi and Missouri valleys. Shortly after the war, Clark convened a council at Portage des Sioux, near the junction of the Mississippi and Missouri rivers. There he reached agreement on thirteen separate pacts. These treaties merely affirmed "peace and friendship" between specific Indian nations and the United States, leaving Indian landholdings intact for the moment. But only for the moment: in the years and treaties that followed, land cessions became an essential component of Clark's treaties. Increasingly, too, Clark and his subordinates dictated, rather than negotiated, terms with Indian nations who lacked the numbers, the weaponry, and the European backer to resist American demands.

Nowhere were the results of bygone borderlands and unchecked American expansionism more dramatic than in the country of the Osages. For decades, the Osages had reigned as the most powerful nation in the lower Missouri valley, their regional hegemony spreading east to the Mississippi River and west onto the Great Plains. Recognizing the Osages' dominion, French and Spanish traders and imperial officers generally respected Osage rights and rites. But the balance of power swung quickly in the wake of the Lewis and Clark exploration, as demonstrated by the 1808 land cession arranged by Governor Lewis and Superintendent Clark. This was followed by treaties

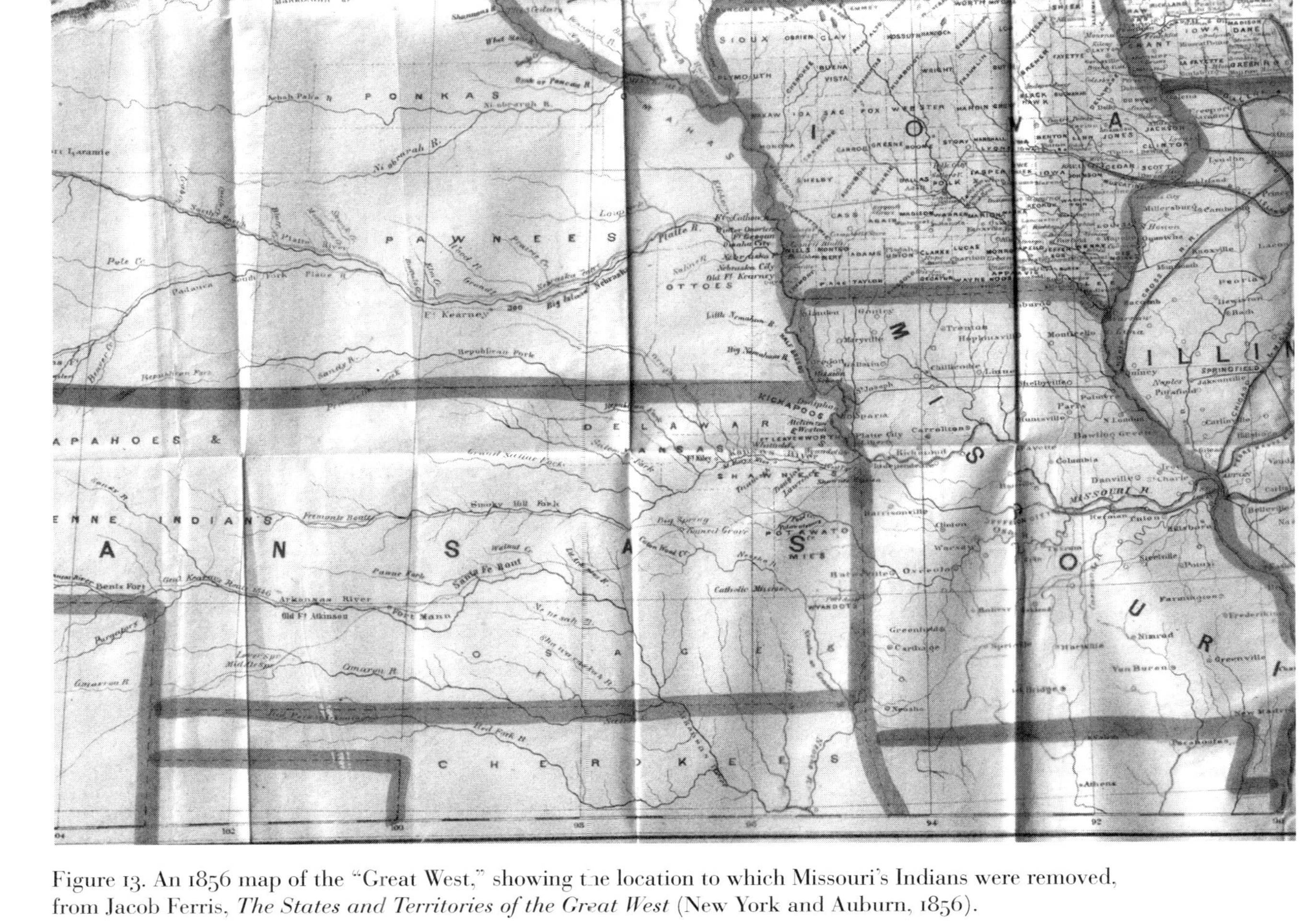

Figure 13. An 1856 map of the "Great West," showing the location to which Missouri's Indians were removed, from Jacob Ferris, *The States and Territories of the Great West* (New York and Auburn, 1856).

in 1818 and 1825 that further reduced the Osages' holdings and left only small numbers still resident in Missouri. The presence of even a few Osages, though, still occasionally triggered alarms among American settlers. In 1832, for example, the Boon's Lick Country became "almost wild with excitement" on rumors that thousands of Osages were massing south of the Missouri River, preparing to attack. In fact, there were no such plans, and the Osages, diminished by warfare and disease, could no longer assemble a war party anywhere near that size. Five years later, several raids by Osage bands in the western part of the state led Governor Lilburn Boggs to call out the militia. A corps of five hundred men marched off to punish the raiders, but the force managed to apprehend only a handful of Osage women. Federal troops arrived on the scene and freed these captives before additional harm was done to them. Rather than disband as ordered, however, the Missouri militiamen seized some Osage families, beat them, and drove them out of the state.[6]

In comparison with contemporaries, who removed Indians without regard for their well-being, Clark retained a devotion to protecting well-behaved Indians. If Clark used military force—or the threat of military force—to discipline Indian groups deemed hostile to the United States, he insisted that peaceful peoples be treated humanely. To that end, he sought to perpetuate the factory system by which Indians were supposed to be supplied with quality goods at below-market prices. After Congress closed government-operated posts in the early 1820s, Clark advocated strict regulation of traders to prevent their taking advantage of Indians. In carrying out removals, Clark also tried to safeguard Indians on their way to and at their new homes. Indeed, Clark justified removal as necessary to save Indians from complete destruction. Away from the corrupting elements of frontier contact, Clark hoped that Indians might be converted to Christianity and American-style agrarianism and perhaps within a generation assimilated into American society. These hopes were a rhetorical commonplace among Jacksonian champions of removal. The difference was that Clark genuinely believed that if Indians were "kept close to [agricultural] work and dissuaded from hunting as much as possible," they could become like white Americans. And Indians of the Mississippi and Missouri valleys appreciated the difference, continuing to put greater faith in Clark than in other American officials.[7]

At the expedition's bicentennial, it is more difficult to preserve any feel good sentiments about Lewis and Clark on matters of slavery and the fate of black Americans. York, we must acknowledge, was never treated as an equal member of the Corps. Also no longer in dispute is York's continuing enslavement after the Corps of Discovery returned to St. Louis. Although Clark later suggested that he freed York upon the completion of the journey, recently discovered—and now published—letters from William Clark to his brother Jonathan decisively refute this uplifting ending. As with Native Americans, Clark claimed his relationship with York and his other African American slaves was governed by a benevolent paternalism. But for Clark, as for so many like-minded Jeffersonians, African American slaves and free blacks were not a generation away from assimilation and equality. As territorial governor, Clark clashed with squatters and legislators over Indian rights. On questions of slavery, however, Governor Clark marched in perfect step with the majority of citizens, categorically rejecting any outside restrictions on Missouri's admission to the union or on its future development as a slave state.[8]

The Last Frontier in Missouri

William Clark made his last trip up the Missouri River in the fall of 1836. The scenery was familiar from previous ventures, including, of course, his first trip three decades earlier. So was the goal of the journey—to clear the claims of Indians occupants—although this purpose was quite different from the instructions Jefferson had given Lewis and Clark in 1803. Over the next few months, Clark completed a new set of treaties that formally opened what is now northwestern Missouri and led to the shifting of the state's western boundary to the Missouri River. The last frontier in Missouri then closed.

When Missouri became a state, its western boundary ran straight north and south from the confluence of the Kansas and

Missouri rivers at 94°37' West longitude. This line left a triangle-shaped territory containing slightly more than three thousand square miles between the original western boundary of the state and the Missouri River (extending to the northern border of Missouri at 40°35' North longitude). During the 1820s, federal officials envisioned this area, which came to be known as the "Platte Country," as a district to which eastern Indians would be relocated. Accordingly, treaties in 1830 and 1833 with the Potawatomis designated the Platte Country as the place for their resettlement. Here, though, national plans once more conflicted with the objectives of American settlers. As with so many previous government-drawn lines, enforcement proved a problem. Lured again by exuberant descriptions of the region's fertility, increasing numbers of squatters entered the supposedly off-limits area, then complained about Indian depredations and pressed the government to oust the Indians and confirm their holdings.[9]

Following as well a recurring script, politically minded government officials aligned themselves with the rights of white squatters. To reserve the territory for Indians, wrote one, "would be attended with the most ruinous effects, . . . alike injurious to the Indians and whites." The presence of Indians populated the region with "a poor, drunken miserable set of beings" and ensured "constant broils with their white neighbors." Moreover, by excluding enterprising Americans, it kept first-rate lands from being properly improved and kept the population of northern Missouri from transporting goods via the Missouri River. In the nation's capital, Missouri senators Lewis F. Linn and Thomas Hart Benton lobbied fellow legislators to delete the Platte Country from the Potawatomi treaties. In Missouri's capital, Governor John Miller called for pushing the western boundary of the state to the Missouri River, an annexation, he asserted, that would greatly enhance the economic development of the state. And, in a common rhetorical twist in which victims were turned into victimizers, Miller added that the transfer of sovereignty "would greatly protect that frontier from the invasion of hostile Indians."[10]

Through the first half of the 1830s, the federal government and the superintendency of William Clark tried to uphold the rule of law, if not the rights of Indians. A September 1835 proclamation ordered all trespassers out of the Platte Country, giving them time to harvest their crops before vacating their homes. In February 1836, a company of dragoons burned the cabins of two families still living in the area. But no sooner had the troops exited than the squatters returned to their claims, certain that their perseverance would shortly be rewarded by government certification of their preemption rights.[11]

Recent history gave squatters good reason to hope, and, sure enough, the federal government quickly came around. In May 1836, the efforts of Linn and Benton resulted in a bill that attached the Platte Country to the state of Missouri once remaining Indian claims were extinguished. A few months later, William Clark negotiated the necessary agreements. These received Senate approval in early 1837, and on March 28 of that year, President Martin Van Buren made Missouri's new border official.[12]

Unlike the lengthy and deadly trail over which many eastern Indians were then being escorted, the ejections from the Platte Country involved much shorter, though still tearful, removals. Some were pushed north of Missouri's border; more were resettled across the Missouri River. To ease initial hardships and encourage the transition to "civilization," Clark's subordinates oversaw the construction of log houses, provided livestock and farming utensils, and broke and fenced lands. But these actions were insufficient. Short of food, the removed consumed the cattle and hogs. Short of fuel, they burned the logs in houses and fences. Impoverished and demoralized, many "kept constantly drunk," a condition that compounded their impoverishment and demoralization.[13]

In the wake of Indians rushed American settlers. Already before the official opening, several hundred families had established residences, mostly in the southern part of the Platte Country. By 1840, the federal census recorded over 15,000 inhabitants, and four years later, a state survey showed a population

Map 6. Missouri Boundaries, Showing the Platte Purchase.

of 37,000. Most came to farm, but a substantial number commenced mercantile enterprises. Trading posts along the eastern bank of the Missouri served as entrepots for commerce in and out of the Platte Country, but even more these businesses profited by supplying army garrisons and Indian settlements across the river. Where once the "Indian trade" had been synonymous with the "fur" or "skin" trade, merchants in northwestern Missouri in the late 1830s and early 1840s more typically exchanged goods for government payments. Although illegal, much of the trade with Indians involved alcohol, which was amply available thanks to the presence of five distilleries located near the state line. Tempted by returns of 200 to 400 percent, three-quarters of the traders in the Platte County, by one government agent's estimate, smuggled whiskey across the state's western border.[14]

During the 1840s, commercial outposts and the towns that grew up around them on the Missouri River expanded the scope of their operations. In addition to attending to populations in western Missouri and across the state's border, businesses boomed by outfitting overland travelers headed for Oregon and California. The most rapid growth occurred in Independence and surrounding towns that were located at the point where the Missouri River turned north. In the 1820s and 1830s, these villages had served as the western outposts for trade with Santa Fe. In the 1840s, their orientation turned to take advantage of new migrations to the Pacific slope. As with the commerce with Indians in alcohol, equipping overland parties offered the possibility of windfall profits, stimulating competition in the form of new enterprises and new towns further up the Missouri River.[15]

The closing of the last frontier in Missouri marked an end and a beginning. After the demise of the Platte Country as a refuge for the removed, some Indians hung on within the state's borders. But no Indian political entities were left to contest the state's borders, which by the 1840s took their "modern" shape. The 1840s also saw economic and political horizons shift away from the frontiers *in* Missouri to the frontiers *of* Missouri, to the opportunities that came with being the principal gateway to America's newest West.

To Border State

"Henceforth," declared a westering traveler in 1848, "Missouri is not to be regarded as a frontier state; but, possessing within her own limits all the elements of mighty empire, she is destined to become the heart of the republic." This grand vision excited many of Missouri's promoters in the decade after the state ceased to be a frontier. Especially after the Mexican War, Missouri seemed ready to claim its centrality. From this hub went multiplying numbers of overland travelers. As important, the exponential growth of steamboat traffic positioned Missouri as the thriving junction for peoples and products moving in and out from all directions. In terms of people, the influx more than matched the outflow. The state's population of 66,557 in 1820 more than doubled to 140,455 in 1830, jumped to 383,702 in 1840, reached 682,044 in 1850, and added another half million by 1860. Yet in the midst of economic and demographic booms,

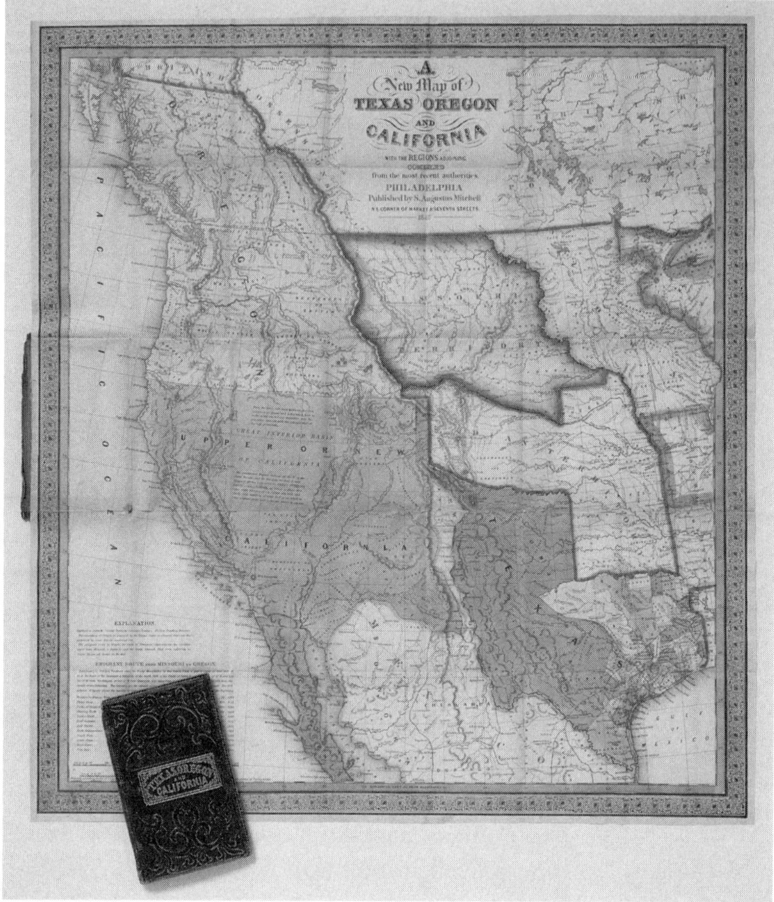

Figure 14. *A New Map of Texas, Oregon, and California: With the Regions Adjoining*, 1846, made by Samuel Augustus Mitchell, reflects Missouri's position as a gateway to points further west. Courtesy of the Autry National Center.

deep divisions within the state and around its borders dashed the dreams of boosters. During the 1850s, intensifying altercations over slavery on the frontiers of Missouri and in Missouri itself darkened once bright horizons.[16]

Slavery caused the loudest arguments, though slaves were becoming a smaller proportion of Missouri's population. In 1830, slaves accounted for approximately 18 percent of Missouri's census. That percentage dropped to 15 in 1840, and to around 13 in 1850. By 1860, fewer than one in ten Missourians were enslaved, yet that decade witnessed the most explosive quarrels over the issue of slavery.[17]

So noisy did the contentions over slavery become that they drowned out other ongoing sources of strife within post-frontier Missouri. Nearly silent yet of great historical significance were the divisions between men and women crossing the frontier of Missouri. At midcentury, as in earlier times among pioneer families moving to Missouri, decisions to go west were almost always made by men. Sometimes husbands and fathers requested and received the consent of wives and children. But as scores of diaries kept by women on the overland trail from Missouri confided, the determinations of patriarchal heads of households often conflicted with the wishes of their female dependents. For the most part, reluctant female emigrants confined their regrets to private journals, where they did not become a subject of noisy controversy.[18]

In the post-frontier era, conflicts between French and American ways occasionally still intruded into public debates, but not with the same volume as they once had. The quieting of these contentions traced largely to the diminishing prominence of persons of French ancestry. Because the state's surging population included very few French-speaking newcomers and because the economy moved away from its fur-trading origins, the old French mercantile elite saw its influence ebb. This decline was apparent as early as Missouri's first gubernatorial election in which William Clark, despite strong support from St. Louis's French merchants, suffered a landslide defeat. In the decades after statehood, demographic trends and democratic politics further eroded the place of French merchants and encouraged *métis* descendants to seek refuge among their Indian kin.[19]

The waning of French ways was paralleled by the waxing of German ones. By 1860, nearly one in seven Missourians had been born abroad, and slightly more than half of these immigrants (approximately 7.5 percent of the state's total population) hailed from German-speaking lands. St. Louis, in particular, became a city of immigrants. By 1850, foreign-born residents outnumbered native-born ones. Owing considerably to the German influx, the city's population nearly quintupled in the 1840s alone, with perhaps half of that increase coming in the last two to three years of the decade and consisting primarily of central European refugees.[20]

If the majority of white Missourians increasingly viewed St. Louis as an alien place, it was not simply because of the city's fading veneer of Frenchness or its fresh German facade. What made St. Louis "foreign" to many Missourians was also its "Yankee" character. About half of the newcomers to St. Louis during the 1840s arrived from the northeastern states. To be sure, as historian Jeffrey Adler has discerned, Yankees were "more conspicuous than they were numerous," comprising only about 10 percent of the city's population in 1850. But together with its immigrant influx, St. Louis's concentration of Yankees made it stand apart from the state as a whole, where more than two-thirds of the population traced their origins back to the states of the Upper South (principally Virginia, North Carolina, Kentucky, and Tennessee). To keep more northerners from moving to St. Louis, one Virginia-born circuit court judge playfully decreed that "no Yankee should" be allowed to "cross the Mississippi River." When asked how this regulation might be enforced, the judge suggested that "every ferryman" would be instructed to ask each traveler to "pronounce the word *cow*," and if the person "said 'in keow' he would not be permitted to cross."[21]

Jokes aside, the estrangement between northerners and southerners within Missouri was no laughing matter. Although the firebell that awakened Thomas Jefferson seemed to quiet after Missouri attained statehood, the ringing—within Missouri and across the United States—was only temporarily muffled. In fact, in the 1830s, violence between northerners and southerners in Missouri provided a terrifying taste of what Jefferson feared.

This first eruption of sectional strife did not, however, follow a fight over slavery. Instead, religious differences reignited the north versus south firestorm during the 1830s. Specifically, the migration to western Missouri of thousands of Mormons, most of whom traced their roots back to New York and New England, sparked a series of conflicts with non-Mormon neighbors, most of whom were from the Upper South. Inspired by prophet Joseph Smith's vision of the New Jerusalem located in Missouri "on the borders by the Lamanites" (Indians), these Yankee pioneers settled initially in Independence in 1831. But as growing numbers of "Saints" gathered in and around Independence, "gentiles" in Jackson County turned combative. In the summer and fall of 1833, mobs attacked Mormons, damaging homes and whipping men. The nastiest assault occurred on November 4, 1833. It left several dead and wounded and led more than one thousand Saints to flee Jackson County, establishing new homes north of the Missouri River in Clay County. But the relocation provided only a temporary haven, and renewed conflicts in the mid-1830s forced Mormons to move once more. Again, the respite from persecution was brief. Threatened by the arrival of thousands of new Saints in 1838, western Missouri's non-Mormons returned to the attack. Extremists among the Mormons answered by forming mobs and vigilante groups of their own. Quickly acts of intimidation and retaliation escalated, culminating in what came to be called the "Mormon War," which riled the western Missouri countryside between August and November of 1838.[22]

Responding to these hostilities, Governor Boggs adopted the state's favored policy toward Indians. He ordered the Missouri militia to expel the Mormon populace from the state and, if they resisted, to bring about their "extermination." As with Indian removals, due process was denied to the evicted and compensation fell well short of the value of lost property.[23]

If the resemblance to Indian removals recalled the recent closing of the Missouri frontier, other aspects of the Mormon War anticipated—and overlapped with—conflicts to come. Certainly, the antislavery views held by many of the Saints contributed to the animosities of the 1830s. Still, at the time, slavery was only one of several issues that divided Mormons from non-Mormons. Most obvious, the theology of Mormons, including their claims to various spiritual gifts and powers, marked them as different. In addition, the Saints' interest in converting the "Lamanites" and their too friendly dealings with Indians on the borders of Missouri aroused suspicions. The communalism of the Saints also stood in contrast with the ways of their neighbors. Perhaps, above all, the increasing numbers of Mormons portended a political takeover. As one non-Mormon in the Clay County battleground summarized, the Mormons "intend to Emigrate here till they outnumber us," and "then they would rule the Country at [their] pleasure." Non-Mormons were determined to avoid that situation, and they resorted to extralegal violence to ensure their continuing numerical and political dominance. To defend themselves, western Missouri's Mormons had little choice but to take the same steps. Here, then, was a rehearsal for the fears about demography and democracy that emerged when the question of slavery on Missouri's borders moved front and center. As in the Mormon War, the recourse to mob terror became a defining feature of Missouri's border state politics in the mid-nineteenth century.[24]

For the most part, tussles over slavery stayed within legal avenues during the 1830s and the first half of the 1840s. And for a time, slaves gained some victories in Missouri courts. Through the 1830s, the Missouri Supreme Court continued to adopt a liberal interpretation of the statutes that allowed slaves to win freedom on the basis of evidence of wrongful enslavement. Proof of prior emancipation or of birth by a free mother remained the slaves' surest route to freedom. More controversial—and consequential—were cases in which slaves sued on the basis of having spent time in a state or territory where slavery was prohibited. That was a potential godsend for Missouri slaves, since under the Missouri Compromise the state was surrounded on three sides by such places and the most common route into the state brought migrants through Illinois. Adhering to an 1828 precedent, the Missouri Supreme Court refused to accept a slave's merely having traveled through a free state or territory as a standard for emancipation. Instead, the court required a period of residency before setting a slave free, but that tenure might be as little as one month. In addition, during the 1830s, the justices generally deferred to the laws of neighboring Illinois and to the antislavery provisions of the Northwest Ordinance and Missouri

Compromise, opening for Missouri slaves what historian Robert Moore Jr. has termed "a ray of hope."[25]

If judicial decisions posed a modest challenge to slavery in Missouri, legislative actions sought to extinguish the hopes of African Americans and silence the voices of opponents of slavery. In 1836 and 1837, Missouri lawmakers attempted to quash antislavery efforts by making it a crime to "by word or writing, incite the negroes to obtain their freedom or tr[y] to remove them from their present situation." Convicted offenders faced being "sentenced to slavery from three months to one year." In the early 1840s, the legislature upped these penalties, stipulating that anyone convicted of helping a slave escape be imprisoned for five years. New laws in the late 1830s and early 1840s also tightened restrictions on the movements of free black into and around Missouri and placed a variety of other legal oppressions on them, all of which violated the Missouri Compromise.[26]

Like Mormons, free blacks learned they could not count on the power of the state to protect them against extralegal oppressions either. Serving notice of this was the fate of Francis McIntosh, a free black steamboat steward, who, in 1836, was arrested for interfering with sheriff's deputies while they were apprehending a felon. McIntosh evidently panicked and stabbed two of the officers, one of whom died. McIntosh was in custody for only a few hours before a mob took him from the St. Louis jail, tied him to a tree, and burned him to death. The lynching, reported the *Missouri Argus* approvingly, should serve as a lesson to "impudent free negroes to be cautious."[27]

By the 1840s, the Missouri judiciary had joined in the unequivocal defense of slavery and white supremacy. Already in the late 1830s, the number of freedom suits filed by slaves had gone into decline, in part as a result of the threats directed at plaintiffs and their attorneys. In court, too, plaintiffs confronted a more hostile climate as ardently proslavery justices replaced more liberal predecessors. Emblematic of the new temper was the opinion of Justice William B. Napton in the 1841 case of *Renick v. Chloe*. "Color raises the presumption of slavery," ruled Napton, "and until the contrary is shown, a man or woman of color is deemed to be a slave." Under Napton's jurisprudence, it became much harder for any slave to show the contrary, even for those who could demonstrate that they had resided in one of the free states or territories across Missouri's borders.[28]

The reversal of freedom suit precedents put Missouri courts in opposition to those of its neighbors and made Missouri slaveholders more sensitive to their precarious geographic position. While little could be done about the aversion to slavery in the polities to the east and north, proslavery Missourians mobilized in the late 1840s and early 1850s to take control of the territory across the state's western border. Those lands, which were occupied by a diverse mix of previously removed Indian peoples, were, according to the Missouri Compromise, supposed to be off-limits to slavery. But Missourians had already proven that Indians could be removed more than once and that provisions of the Missouri Compromise could be ignored by the state's lawmakers and judges.

Initially, in the mid- to late 1840s, some of Missouri's political leaders tried to keep the question of expansion into the Indian countries to the west separate from that of slavery's extension there. In his biennial message of 1844, Governor Meredith Marmaduke claimed that the overwhelming majority of people in Missouri favored the annexation of Texas, because it would break the power of "the immense hordes of Indians" that the "general government has located on our borders." Two years later, the *St. Louis Daily Union* avowed that "the question of slavery has no connection whatever with the war against Mexico." That certainly was the wish of Senator Thomas Hart Benton, who embraced territorial expansion as an antidote to sectional division.[29]

Benton's logic, in which westward expansion promoted the unification of North and South with Missouri at the center of the enlarged republic, failed to account for the fervor that the question of slavery brought to American politics in the aftermath of the Mexican War. For Missouri governor Austin King, the wrangling over whether newly organized western territories would be slave or free replayed the debate surrounding Missouri's admission to statehood. Once again, declared King in his 1848 inaugural address, the "proper maintenance of our rights" meant "deny[ing] to the General Government any power to debar us from an equal participation in that territory, or to impose terms on us in reference to our property, which would not bear alike upon every member of the Union." For Benton, the statehood controversy had shown the ascending power of "the people" over electoral politics. During the 1820s, he curtailed his association with the old elite, the little junto, and recast himself as the champion of Jacksonian Democracy. After the Mexican War, however, Benton's longstanding leadership of Missouri's Jacksonians came under attack by those who accused him of being insufficiently democratic, meaning insufficiently committed to the unfettered extension of slavery. When Benton voted for a bill excluding slavery from the Oregon Territory, firebrands led by Claiborne Jackson pushed a series of resolutions through the Missouri General Assembly directing the state's representatives in Washington to insist that Congress had no right to decide whether territories would be slave or free. That determination, the resolutions held, belonged exclusively to the people of a territory. Ratcheting up the rhetoric, the "Jackson Resolutions" further promised Missouri's cooperation with other slave states for "mutual protection against the encroachments of northern fanaticism."[30]

To Benton, such talk was treasonous. Congress, retorted Benton, did indeed have the authority to legislate for the territories and to prohibit slavery in them. "A high wall and a deep ditch" divided his views from those of proslavery agitators. But the forces on the other side of wall and ditch were growing bolder, and in January 1851 they joined with Whig legislators to deprive Benton of reelection.

With Benton unseated, firebrands in Missouri turned their attention to the impending organization of the territory on the state's western border. This territory, wrote Claiborne Jackson, must be established without "any infernal restrictions." Missourians must be allowed to settle there "with all our property of every kind." If slavery were prohibited across another of the state's borders, then Missourians might as well emancipate their slaves, "for we can hardly keep our Negroes here now." Better, in that case, to "let the Indians have it *forever*," for "they are better neighbors than the abolitionists, *by a damn sight*."[31]

Of course, firebrands like Jackson, or his close confederate Senator David Rice Atchison, were not sitting idly awaiting congressional action. In the early 1850s, they pressed their cause, employing political pressure and extralegal tactics. Atchison especially took the lead as both a political spokesman and an officer in the paralegal militia. With proslavery and abolitionist factions facing off across Missouri's western border, Atchison informed his friend Jefferson Davis that "we intend to 'Mormanise' the Abolitionists."[32]

Atchison's willingness to do unto opponents of slavery what had been done to the Mormons suggested the parallels between the conflicts, but his position also pointed to the greater polarization that took hold in western Missouri and across its borders. In the earlier conflict between Missourians and Mormons, Atchison had, for the most part, played a moderating role. In 1838, as a general in the Missouri militia, Atchison had been ordered by Governor Boggs to restore peace in western Missouri. Having previously worked as an attorney for western Missouri's Mormons, Atchison had some sympathy for the Saints' plight. "I do not feel disposed to disgrace myself, or permit the troops under my command to disgrace the State and themselves by acting the part of a mob," he wrote Boggs. In the 1850s, by contrast, Atchison saw no room for compromise, no means other than mob terror to exterminate the opponents of slavery and ensure that Kansas was safe for Missouri slaveholders.[33]

In 1856, the fight over slavery across Missouri's western border bloodied Kansas and deepened sectional divisions across the nation; the following year, the Supreme Court's decision in the case of *Dred Scott v. Sandford* showed how great a divide the confluence of rivers had become. The Dred Scott case began its judicial life ten years earlier as an 1847 suit in Missouri courts. As with so many similar cases, the plaintiff's argument rested on his residence in free territory. Specifically, during the 1830s Scott had been taken by his owner, military surgeon John Emerson, to live in Illinois and then in the Wisconsin Territory. Although Scott's contention had ample precedent in Missouri courts, a legal technicality led the St. Louis Circuit Court to reject Scott's suit. At a second trial in 1850, however, Scott gained a favorable ruling. His owner then appealed the case to the Missouri Supreme Court, whose recent decisions boded ill for Scott. Indeed, the judicial climate had become even more hostile to emancipation suits after 1851, when a new law made membership on the high court's bench an elective office. Sure enough, in March 1852 the Missouri Supreme Court reversed the lower court's ruling and returned Scott and his family to slavery. In a two to one decision, the majority asserted that changing times nullified earlier precedents, that Missouri courts were bound neither by the laws of other states nor by congressional legislation, and that slavery was, in fact, God's will. At that point, Scott shifted his appeal to the federal courts, where it eventually reached the Supreme Court.[34]

Far from settling the matter, the ruling of the nation's highest court against Scott further split the nation. In the wake of the bloodshed on its frontier and the Supreme Court's decision in the Dred Scott case, Missouri solidified its reputation as a border state between the realms of slave and free labor. And the confluence of the Missouri, Ohio, and Mississippi rivers, so long the place where north and south, as well as east and west, came together, became the site at which the United States came apart.

Notes

Introduction

1. For a fuller discussion of the outlines of what I have called a "greater western history," see Stephen Aron, "Lessons in Conquest: Towards a Greater Western History," *Pacific Historical Review* 63 (May 1994): 125–47.

2. Robert Tignor, Jeremy Adelman, Stephen Aron, Steve Kotkin, Suzanne Marchand, Gyan Prakash, and Michael Tsin, *Worlds Together, Worlds Apart: A History of the Modern World from the Mongol Empire to the Present* (New York: W. W. Norton, 2002). For an attempt to frame the comparative and common histories of North American states and societies, see Jeremy Adelman and Stephen Aron, "From Borderlands to Borders: Empires, Nation-States, and the Peoples in between in North American History," *American Historical Review* 104 (June 1999): 814–41. See also the criticisms of this framework and our rejoinder in "Forum Essay: Responses: Borders and Borderlands," *American Historical Review* 104 (October 1999): 1221–39.

3. Among historians of the American West, the foremost critic of the term *frontier* has been Patricia Nelson Limerick. See Limerick, *The Legacy of Conquest: The Unbroken Past of the American West* (New York: W. W. Norton, 1987), 17–32; Limerick, "What on Earth Is the New Western History?" in Patricia Limerick, Clyde Milner, and Charles Rankin, eds., *Trails: Toward a New Western History* (Lawrence: University Press of Kansas, 1991), 81–88; and Limerick, "The Adventures of the Frontier in the Twentieth Century," in James R. Grossman, ed., *The Frontier in American Culture* (Berkeley: University of California Press, 1994), 66–102. The most notable "new western history" in which the frontier goes unmentioned is Richard White, *"It's Your Misfortune and None of My Own": A New History of the American West* (Norman: University of Oklahoma Press, 1991). On the changing meanings of frontier, see John Mack Faragher, "The Frontier Trail: Rethinking Turner and Reimagining the American West," *American Historical Re-*

view 98 (February 1993): 106–17; John T. Juricek, "American Usage of the Word *Frontier* from Colonial Times to Frederick Jackson Turner," *Proceedings of the American Philosophical Society* 110 (February 1966): 10–34; Lucien Febvre, "*Frontière:* The Word and the Concept," in Peter Burke, ed., *A New Kind of History: From the Writings of Febvre* (London: Routledge and Kegan Paul, 1973), 208–18; Fulmer Mood, "Notes on the History of the Word *Frontier,*" *Agricultural History* 22 (April 1948): 78–83; Laddis K.D. Kristof, "The Nature of Frontiers and Boundaries," *Annals of the Association of American Geographers* 49 (September 1959): 269–82; Kerwin Lee Klein, *Frontiers of Historical Imagination: Narrating the European Conquest of Native America, 1890–1990* (Berkeley: University of California Press, 1997).

4. Jack D. Forbes, "Frontiers in American History and the Role of the Frontier Historian," *Ethnohistory* 15 (Spring 1968): 207; Peggy Pascoe, "Western Women at the Cultural Crossroads," in Limerick, Milner, and Rankin, eds., *Trails*, 46; Howard Lamar and Leonard Thompson, "Comparative Frontier History," in Limerick, Milner, and Rankin, eds., *The Frontier in History: North America and Southern Africa Compared* (New Haven: Yale University Press, 1981), 7–8. See also William Cronon, George Miles, and Jay Gitlin, eds., "Becoming West: Toward a New Meaning for Western History," in their book *Under an Open Sky: Rethinking America's Western Past* (New York: W.W. Norton, 1992), 3–27, an introduction that makes "border-setting" crucial to the understanding of frontier processes.

5. Adelman and Aron, "From Borderlands to Borders," 815–17.

6. Colin G. Calloway, *New Worlds for All: Indians, Europeans, and the Remaking of Early America* (Baltimore: Johns Hopkins University Press, 1997); Robert V. Hine and John Mack Faragher, *The American West: A New Interpretive History* (New Haven: Yale University Press, 2000), 71. For historical observations of the confluence of the Missouri and Mississippi and geological explanations for the turbulence of their meeting, see Kate L. Gregg, ed., "The Missouri Reader: Explorers in the Valley," pts. 1 and 2, *Missouri Historical Review* 39 (April 1945): 354–88; 39 (July 1945): 505–44; Gerald T. Dunne, *The Missouri Supreme Court: From Dred Scott to Nancy Cruzan* (Columbia: University of Missouri Press, 1993), 1; Walter Schroeder, "Environmental Setting of the St. Louis Region," in Andrew Hurley, ed., *Common Fields: An Environmental History of St. Louis* (St. Louis: Missouri Historical Society Press, 1997), 27–29; Larry McMurtry, "Life on the Missouri," *New York Review of Books* 48 (November 15, 2001): 53–55.

7. Francis Parkman, "The Jesuits in North America in the Seventeenth Century," in David Levin, ed., *France and England in North America*, 2 vols. (New York: Viking Press, 1983), 1:432.

8. Stuart Banner, *Legal Systems in Conflict: Property and Sovereignty in Missouri, 1750–1860* (Norman: University of Oklahoma Press, 2000), 8.

1. Openings

1. James Davis, *Frontier Illinois* (Bloomington: Indiana University Press, 1998), 24–29; J. Joseph Bauxar, "History of the Illinois Area," in Bruce G. Trigger, ed., *Handbook of North American Indians*, vol. 15: *Northeast* (Washington, D.C.: Smithsonian Institution, 1978), 594–601; Raymond E. Hauser, "The Illinois Indian Tribe: From Autonomy and Self-Sufficiency to Dependency and Depopulation," *Journals of the Illinois State Historical Society* 69 (May 1976): 127–38; Robert T. Bray, "The Missouri Indian Tribe in Archaeology and History," *Missouri Historical Review* 55 (April 1961): 213–25; Carl H. Chapman and Eleanor F. Chapman, *Indians and Archaeology of Missouri* (Columbia: University of Missouri Press, 1983), 99–117.

2. William R. Iseminger, "Relationships between Climate Change and Cultural Change in Prehistory," *Illinois Antiquity* 25 (Spring 1990): 2–4; Walter Schroeder, "Environmental Setting of the St. Louis Region," in Andrew Hurley, ed., *Common Fields: An Environmental History of St. Louis* (St. Louis: Missouri Historical Society Press, 1997), 13–37; Sally A. Kitt Chappell, *Cahokia: Mirror of the Cosmos* (Chicago: University of Chicago Press, 2002), 7–49; Chapman and Chapman, *Indians and Archaeology of Missouri*, 27–97; Leonard Hall, "Wildlife in Missouri," *Missouri Historical Review* 60 (January 1966): 207–15.

3. Bruce D. Smith, with C. Wesley Cowan and Michael P. Hoffman, *Rivers of Change: Essays on Early Agriculture in Eastern North America* (Washington, D.C.: Smithsonian Institution Press, 1992), 201–203; Alan Gallay, *The Indian Slave Trade: The Rise of the English Empire in the American South, 1670–1717* (New Haven: Yale University Press, 2002), 23–39; Chappell, *Cahokia*, 46–49; Alfred E. Johnson, "A Steed-Kisker Effigy Pipe," *Plains Anthropologist* 39 (May 1994): 185–93.

4. Chapman and Chapman, *Indians and Archaeology of Missouri*, 71–87; Chappell, *Cahokia*, 65–68.

5. William R. Iseminger, "Culture and Environment in the American Bottom: The Rise and Fall of the Cahokia Mounds," in Hurley, ed., *Common Fields*, 44–51.

6. Ibid., 51–57; Peter Peregrine, "A Graph-Theoretic Approach to the Evolution of Cahokia," *American Antiquity* 56 (January 1991): 66–75.

7. Robert L. Hall, "Cahokia Identity and Interaction Models of Cahokia Mississippian," in Thomas E. Emerson and R. Barry Lewis, eds., *Cahokia and the Hinterlands: Middle Mississippian Cultures of the Midwest* (Urbana: University of Illinois Press, 1991), 23–33; William I. Woods and George R. Holey, "Upland Mississippian Settlement in the American Bottom Region," in ibid., 59–60; Thomas E. Emerson, "Some Perspectives on Cahokia and the Northern Mississippian Expansion," in ibid., 221–36; Patricia J. O'Brien, "Steed-Kisker: The Western Periphery of the Mississippian Tradition," *Midcontinental Journal of Archaeology* 18 (Spring 1993): 61–96; Iseminger, "Culture and Environment in the American Bottom," 50–51.

8. Chappell, *Cahokia*, 71–75.

9. Chapman and Chapman, *Indians and Archaeology of Missouri*, 99–117; Bray, "The Missouri Indian Tribe in Archaeology and History," 213–25; Gilbert C. Din and Abraham P. Nasatir, *The Imperial Osages: Spanish-Indian Diplomacy in the Mississippi Valley* (Norman: University of Oklahoma Press, 1983), 3–6; Alfred E. Johnson, "Kansa Origins: An Alternative," *Plains Anthropologist* 36 (1991): 57–65; John Joseph Mathews, *The Osages: Children of the Middle Waters* (Norman: University of Oklahoma Press, 1961), 1–94.

10. Information in this and the following three paragraphs is drawn primarily from James R. Christianson, "The Early Osage: 'The Ishmaelites of the Savages,'" *Kansas History* 11 (Spring 1988): 2; J. Frederick Fausz, "'Becoming a Nation of Quakers': The Removal of the Osage Indians from Missouri," *Gateway Heritage* 21 (Summer 2000): 29–30; Willard H. Rollings, *The Osage: An Ethnohistorical Study of Hegemony on the Prairie-Plains* (Columbia: University of Missouri Press, 1992), 5, 14–99; William E. Foley, *The Genesis of Missouri: From Wilderness Outpost to Statehood* (Columbia: University of Missouri Press, 1989), 10–12; Tanis C. Thorne, *The Many Hands of My Relations: French and Indians on the Lower Missouri* (Columbia: University of Missouri Press, 1996), 14–17; Din and Nasatir, *The Imperial Osages*, 8–24; Mathews, *Children of the Middle Waters*, 80–86; Kirstie C. Wolferman, *The Osage in Missouri* (Columbia: University of Missouri Press, 1997); David A. Horr, ed., *Osage Indians*, 5 vols. (New York: Garland, 1974). For a full bibliography of works on the Osages, see Terry Wilson, *Bibliography of the Osage* (Metuchen, N.J.: Scarecrow Press, 1985).

11. Patricia Galloway, ed., *The Hernando de Soto Expedition: History, Historiography, and "Discovery" in the Southeast* (Lincoln: University of Nebraska Press, 1997); Dan F. Morse and Phyllis A. Morse, "The Spanish Exploration of Arkansas," in David Hurst Thomas, ed., *Columbian Consequences*, vol. 2: *Archaeological and Historical Perspectives on the Spanish Borderlands East* (Washington, D.C.: Smithsonian Institution Press, 1989), 197–208; Lawrence A. Clayton, Vernon James Knight Jr., and Edward C. Moore, eds., *The De Soto Chronicles: The Expedition of Hernando de Soto to North America in 1539–1543*, 2 vols. (Tuscaloosa: University of Alabama Press, 1993); Richard Flint and Shirley Cushing Flint, eds., *The Coronado Expedition to Tierra Nueva: The 1540–1542 Route across the Southwest* (Niwot: University Press of Colorado, 1997); Janet Lecompte, "Coronado and Conquest," *New Mexico Historical Review* 64 (July 1989): 279–304.

12. Waldo R. Wedel, "After Coronado in Quivira," *Kansas Historical Quarterly* 34 (Winter 1968): 369–85; Peter H. Wood, "The Changing Population of the Colonial South: An Overview by Race and Region," in Peter H. Wood, Gregory A. Waselkov, and M. Thomas Hatley, eds., *Powhatan's Mantle: Indians in the Colonial Southeast* (Lincoln: University of Nebraska Press, 1989), 35–103; Richard White, *The Roots of Dependency: Subsistence, Environment, and Social Change among the Choctaws, Pawnees, and Navajos* (Lincoln: University of Nebraska Press, 1983), 5–15; David H. Dye, "Warfare in the Sixteenth-Century Southeast: The de Soto Expedition in the Interior," in Thomas, ed., *Columbian Consequences*, 211–21.

13. Colin G. Calloway, *One Vast Winter Count: The Native American West before Lewis and Clark* (Lincoln: University of Nebraska Press, 2003), 267–312; David J. Weber, *The Spanish Frontier in North America* (New Haven: Yale University Press, 1992), 187–89; Carl Waldman, *Atlas of the North American Indian* (New York: Facts on File, 1985), 56; Elliott West, *The Contested Plains: Indians, Goldseekers, and the Rush to Colorado* (Lawrence: University Press of Kansas, 1998), 39–40, 44–57; James F. Brooks, *Captives and Cousins: Slavery, Kinship, and Community in the Southwest Borderlands* (Chapel Hill: University of North Carolina Press, 2002), 174–80; Pekka Hamalainen, "The Western Comanche Trade Center: Rethinking the Plains Indian Trade System," *Western Historical Quarterly* 29 (Winter 1998): 485–513.

14. Rollings, *The Osage*, 82–89.

15. For colonial designs of France and Spain, compare Weber, *The Spanish Frontier in North America*, 17–25, and W. J. Eccles, *The Canadian Frontier, 1534–1760*, rev. ed. (Albuquerque: University of New

Mexico Press, 1983), 1–59. For overviews and reviews of the literature on comparative colonization projects, see Jay Gitlin, "Empires of Trade, Hinterlands of Settlement," in Clyde A. Milner II, Carol A. O'Connor, and Martha Sandweiss, eds., *The Oxford History of the American West* (New York: Oxford University Press, 1994), 79–113.

16. My thinking about how and why colonial regimes came to differ from one another has been strongly influenced by Eric Hinderaker and Rebecca Horn. In their paper "Inventing Indians: Kings and Caciques in Colonial American Histories" (presented at the "Greater American Histories?" conference, Huntington Library, San Marino, 2001), Hinderaker and Horn persuasively argue that the differences between colonial regimes owed less to the original designs of colonizers than to the nature of the indigenous societies they encountered.

17. R. Cole Harris, ed., *Historical Atlas of Canada*, vol. 1: *From the Beginning to 1800* (Toronto: University of Toronto Press, 1987), 113–16, plates 46, 51, 52, 53, 55, 56; Eccles, *The Canadian Frontier*, 83–102.

18. For an incisive analysis of French missionary practices, see James Axtell, *The Invasion Within: The Contest of Cultures in Colonial North America* (New York: Oxford University Press, 1985).

19. Eric Hinderaker, *Elusive Empires: Constructing Colonialism in the Ohio Valley, 1673–1800* (New York: Cambridge University Press, 1997), 53–54; Eccles, *The Canadian Frontier*, 103–31; Susan Sleeper-Smith, *Indian Women and French Men: Rethinking Cultural Encounter in the Western Great Lakes* (Amherst: University of Massachusetts Press, 2001).

20. The literature on the fur trade is now as vast as the terrain across which *voyageurs* and *coureurs de bois* traversed. As starting points for understanding the relations between French traders and Indians in Canada and the Great Lakes region, see Cornelius J. Jaenen, *Friend and Foe: Aspects of French-Amerindian Cultural Contact in the Sixteenth and Seventeenth Centuries* (New York: Columbia University Press, 1976), and Bruce G. Trigger, *Natives and Newcomers: Canada's "Heroic Age" Reconsidered* (Kingston, Ont.: McGill-Queen's University Press, 1985).

21. My summary of French–Indian relations in the western Great Lakes borrows heavily from, and simplifies considerably, the account in Richard White, *The Middle Ground: Indians, Empires, and Republics in the Great Lakes Region, 1650–1815* (New York: Cambridge University Press, 1991). For Iroquois invasions and their impact on the Indians of the Ohio Valley and Great Lakes, see Daniel Richter, *The Ordeal of the Longhouse: The Peoples of the Iroquois League in the*

Era of European Colonization (Chapel Hill: University of North Carolina Press, 1992), esp. 50–74, 144–49, 162–89; Hinderaker, *Elusive Empires*, 14–16.

22. Kate L. Gregg, ed., "The Missouri Reader: Explorers in the Valley," pt. 1, *Missouri Historical Review* 39 (April 1945): 355.

23. Dale Miquelon, "Jean-Baptiste Colbert's 'Compact Colony Policy' Revisited: The Tenacity of an Idea," *Proceedings of the Annual Meeting of the French Colonial Historical Society* 17 (May 1991): 12–23.

24. Marquette quoted in F. Terry Norris, "Where Did the Villages Go? Steamboats, Deforestation, and Archaeological Loss in the Mississippi Valley," in Hurley, ed., *Common Fields*, 75; Gregg, ed., "The Missouri Reader: Explorers," 355–65; Timothy Severin, *Explorers of the Mississippi* (London: Routledge and Kegan Paul, 1967), 66–91.

25. "Voyage of P. Jacques Marquette [toward New Mexico]," in Reuben Gold Thwaites, ed., *The Jesuit Relations and Allied Documents*, 73 vols. (Cleveland: Burrows Bros., 1896–1901), 59:133, 135; Gallay, *The Indian Slave Trade*, 102, 105–10.

26. Gregg, ed., "The Missouri Reader: Explorers," 365–66; Severin, *Explorers of the Mississippi*, 92–143.

27. Marquette quoted in Gregg, ed., "The Missouri Reader: Explorers," 364; La Salle quoted in ibid., 367; Virgil J. Vogel, "The Origin and Meaning of 'Missouri,'" *Bulletin of the Missouri Historical Society* 16 (April 1960): 213–22.

28. Gregg, ed., "The Missouri Reader: Explorers," 382, 387, 385.

29. Ibid., 383.

30. Rollings, *The Osage*, 103–23.

31. Carl H. Chapman, "The Indomitable Osage in Spanish Illinois (Upper Louisiana), 1763–1804," in John Francis McDermott, ed., *The Spanish in the Mississippi Valley, 1762–1804* (Urbana: University of Illinois Press, 1974), 293–95; Christianson, "The Early Osage," 5–6. On the trading of Indian slaves in regions bordering the domain of the Osages, see Gallay, *The Indian Slave Trade*, 101–27; Brooks, *Captives and Cousins*, 59–68.

32. DuTisné to M. de Bienville, November 22, 1719, Indian Collections, Missouri Historical Society, St. Louis.

33. R. David Edmund and Joseph L. Peyser, *The Fox Wars: The Mesquakie Challenge to New France* (Norman: University of Oklahoma Press, 1993), 55–118.

34. Glenn R. Conrad, "Administration of the Illinois Country: The French Debate," *Louisiana History* 36 (Winter 1995): 31–53.

35. Dorothy Penn, ed., "The Missouri Reader: The French in the

Valley," pt. 1, *Missouri Historical Review* 40 (October 1945): 95–103; Miquelon, "Jean-Baptiste Colbert's 'Compact Colony Policy' Revisited," 12–23; Conrad, "Administration of the Illinois Country," 31–53.

36. Penn, ed., "The Missouri Reader: The French," pt. 1, 103–106; Carl J. Ekberg, *French Roots in the Illinois Country: The Mississippi Frontier in Colonial Times* (Urbana: University of Illinois Press, 1998), 31–88.

37. Ekberg, *French Roots,* 5–30.

38. Walter A. Schroeder, *Opening the Ozarks: A Historical Geography of Missouri's Ste. Genevieve District, 1760–1830* (Columbia: University of Missouri Press, 2002), 37–39, 28.

39. Ibid., 207; Stuart Banner, *Legal Systems in Conflict: Property and Sovereignty in Missouri, 1750–1860* (Norman: University of Oklahoma Press, 2000), 67–71.

40. Winstanley Briggs, "Le Pays des Illinois," *William and Mary Quarterly,* 3rd. ser., 47 (January 1990): 30–31.

41. Heloise H. Cruzat, trans., "Records of the Superior Council, XVI," *Louisiana Historical Quarterly* 5 (July 1922): 408.

42. Briggs, "Le Pays des Illinois," 30–56; Carl J. Ekberg, *Francois Vallé and His World: Upper Louisiana before Lewis and Clark* (Columbia: University of Missouri Press, 2002), 7–10, 22.

43. Penn, ed., "The Missouri Reader: The French in the Valley," pts. 3 and 4, *Missouri Historical Review* 40 (April 1946): 407–30; 40 (July 1946): 562–78; Briggs, "Le Pays des Illinois," 52–53; Winstanley Briggs, "Slavery in French Colonial Illinois," *Chicago History* 18 (Winter 1989–90): 66–81; Davis, *Frontier Illinois,* 19.

44. Ekberg, *French Roots,* 172–75, 191–96.

45. Davis, *Frontier Illinois,* 49–50.

46. Marie George Windell, ed., "The Missouri Reader: The French in the Valley," pt. 5, *Missouri Historical Review* 41 (October 1946): 81–83.

47. John L. Kessell, *Spain in the Southwest: A Narrative History of Colonial New Mexico, Arizona, Texas, and California* (Norman: University of Oklahoma Press, 2002), 223–51; John Francis Bannon, S.J., *The Spanish Borderlands Frontier, 1513–1821* (New York: Holt, Rinehart and Winston, 1970), 92–142; Weber, *The Spanish Frontier in North America,* 147–91.

48. John Francis Bannon, S.J., "Black-Robe Frontiersman: Gabriel Marest, S.J.," *Bulletin of the Missouri Historical Society* 10 (April 1954): 357–64.

49. Penn, ed., "The Missouri Reader: The French," pt. 1, 106;

William E. Foley, *A History of Missouri*, vol. 1: *1673–1820* (Columbia: University of Missouri Press, 1971), 12–14.

50. David D. Denman, "History of 'La Saline': Salt Manufacturing Site, 1675–1825," *Missouri Historical Review* 73 (April 1979): 307–308.

51. Carl J. Ekberg, ed., "Antoine Valentin de Gruy: Early Missouri Explorer," *Missouri Historical Review* 76 (January 1982): 146–48.

52. Christianson, "The Early Osage," 3–4.

53. Rollings, *The Osage*, 84–87.

54. Ibid., 65–66.

2. Traditions

1. For a review of the controversies over the date of Ste. Genevieve's founding, see Carl J. Ekberg, *Colonial Ste. Genevieve: An Adventure on the Mississippi Frontier* (Gerald, Mo.: Patrice Press, 1985), 13. In addition to this book, Ekberg has authored two other studies that superbly detail the history of Ste. Genevieve and upon which the following paragraphs are largely drawn. See also Ekberg, *French Roots in the Illinois Country: The Mississippi Frontier in Colonial Times* (Urbana: University of Illinois Press, 1998), esp. 88–96; Ekberg, *Francois Vallé and His World: Upper Louisiana before Lewis and Clark* (Columbia: University of Missouri Press, 2002).

2. Ekberg, *Francois Vallé*, 42–43, points out that during its first decade, villagers also sometimes called their town "St. Joachim, after the parish of that name in Canada." By the 1760s, however, Ste. Genevieve was the accepted name.

3. Walter A. Schroeder, *Opening the Ozarks: A Historical Geography of Missouri's Ste. Genevieve District, 1760–1830* (Columbia: University of Missouri Press, 2002), 207; Ekberg, *French Roots*, 111–37; Stuart Banner, *Legal Systems in Conflict: Property and Sovereignty in Missouri, 1750–1860* (Norman: University of Oklahoma Press, 2000), 14, 67–73.

4. Ekberg, *Colonial Ste. Genevieve*, 458, 415.

5. Ibid., 240–83.

6. Amos Stoddard, *Sketches, Historical and Descriptive, of Louisiana* (Philadelphia: Mathew Carey, 1812), 323; "First Spanish Detailed Statistical Report of Ste Genevieve and St. Louis, Dated 1772," and "Census of Piernas for 1773," in Louis Houck, ed., *The Spanish Regime in Missouri: A Collection of Papers and Documents Relating to Upper Louisiana Principally within the Present Limits of Missouri during the Dominion of Spain, from the Archives of the Indies at Seville*, 2 vols.

(Chicago: R. R. Donnelley and Sons, 1909), 2:53–54, 61; Susan C. Boyle, "Did She Generally Decide? Women in Ste. Genevieve, 1750–1805," *William and Mary Quarterly*, 3rd. Ser., 44 (October 1987): 775–89; Winstanley Briggs, "The Enhanced Economic Position of Women in French Colonial Illinois," in Clarence Glasrud, ed., *L'Héritage Tranquille: The Quiet Heritage* (Moorhead, Minn.: Concordia College, 1987), 62–69.

7. Ekberg, *Francois Vallé*, 120, 128–29, 228; Teresa Blattner, *Divorces, Separations, and Annulments in Missouri, 1769–1850* (Bowie, Md.: Heritage Books, 1993).

8. Ekberg, *Francois Vallé*, 52, 173–74; Kristen Kalen Morrow, "Ste. Genevieve's First Family . . . A Chronicle of the Vallés," *Gateway Heritage* 8 (Fall 1987): 25–28.

9. Winstanley Briggs, "Slavery in French Colonial Illinois," *Chicago History* 18 (Winter 1989–90): 75–81; Ekberg, *French Roots*, 152, provides a table based on the 1752 census of the slave and free populations for each of the Illinois Country villages in 1752.

10. Ekberg, *French Roots*, 147; Christine Williams, "Prosperity in the Face of Prejudice: The Life of Free Black Woman in Frontier St. Louis," *Gateway Heritage* 19 (Fall 1998): 5–6; Gilbert C. Din, *Spaniards, Planters, and Slaves: The Spanish Regulation of Slavery in Louisiana, 1763–1803* (College Station: Texas A&M University Press, 1999), 3–34.

11. Briggs, "Slavery in French Colonial Illinois," 78–81.

12. Ibid., 79–81; Russell M. Magnaghi, "The Role of Indian Slavery in Colonial St. Louis," *Bulletin of the Missouri Historical Society* 31 (July 1975): 264–72.

13. Willard H. Rollings, *The Osage: An Ethnohistorical Study of Hegemony on the Prairie-Plains* (Columbia: University of Missouri Press, 1992), 124–29.

14. William E. Foley, *A History of Missouri*, vol. 1: *1673–1820* (Columbia: University of Missouri Press, 1971), 15; Ekberg, *Colonial Ste. Genevieve*, 41–43; Ekberg, *French Roots*, 91, 259–63.

15. Marie George Windell, ed., "The Missouri Reader: The French in the Valley," pt. 6, *Missouri Historical Review* 41 (January 1947): 206; Patricia Cleary, "Contested Terrain: Environmental Agendas and Settlement Choices in Colonial St. Louis," in Andrew Hurley, ed., *Common Fields: An Environmental History of St. Louis* (St. Louis: Missouri Historical Society Press, 1997), 62.

16. James E. Davis, *Frontier Illinois* (Bloomington: Indiana University Press, 1998), 50–53. For the best comprehensive survey of the global conflict, see Fred Anderson, *Crucible of War: The Seven Years'*

War and the Fate of Empire in British North America, 1754–1766 (New York: Vintage Books, 2000).

17. For a brief survey of the negotiations regarding the fate of Upper Louisiana, see John Francis Bannon, S.J., "The Spaniards and the Illinois Country, 1762–1800," *Journal of the Illinois State Historical Society* 69 (1976): 110–18.

18. Laclède quoted in William E. Foley and C. David Rice, *The First Chouteaus: River Barons of Early St. Louis* (Urbana: University of Illinois Press, 1983), 5.

19. Chouteau quoted in Don Rickey Jr., "The Old St. Louis Riverfront, 1763–1960," *Missouri Historical Review* 58 (January 1964): 176.

20. St. Ange to Dabbadie, August 12, 1764, in Clarence W. Alvord and Clarence E. Carter, eds., *The Critical Period, 1763–1765*, Collections of the Illinois State Historical Library, vol. 10 (Springfield: Trustees of the Illinois State Historical Library, 1915), 292; Cleary, "Contested Terrain," 64; Penn, ed., "The Missouri Reader: The French," pt. 1, 115; William E. Foley, *The Genesis of Missouri: From Wilderness Outpost to Statehood* (Columbia: University of Missouri Press, 1989), 28; Tanis C. Thorne, *The Many Hands of My Relations: French and Indians on the Lower Missouri* (Columbia: University of Missouri Press, 1996), 70.

21. Selwyn K. Troen and Glen E. Holt, eds., *St. Louis* (New York: New Viewpoints, 1977), xviii; John Francis Bannon, S.J., "The Spaniards and the Illinois Country, 1762–1800," *Journal of the Illinois State Historical Society* 69 (May 1976): 115; Cleary, "Contested Terrain," 70.

22. Foley and Rice, *The First Chouteaus*, 8–17.

23. Sterling to Gage, December 15, 1765, in Clarence W. Alvord and Clarence E. Carter, eds., *The New Regime, 1765–1767*, Collections of the Illinois State Historical Library, vol. 11 (Springfield: Trustees of the Illinois State Historical Library, 1916), 125; Eric Hinderaker, *Elusive Empires: Constructing Colonialism in the Ohio Valley, 1673–1800* (New York: Cambridge University Press, 1997), 177.

24. Beverly W. Bond Jr., ed., "Notes on Proposed Settlements in the West, 1755–1757," Historical and Philosophical Society of Ohio, *Publications* (Cincinnati: R. Clarke & Co. for the Historical and Philosophical Society of Ohio, 1925), 42.

25. George Croghan to Sir William Johnson, August 17, 1765, in Milton Wheaton Hamilton et al., eds., *The Papers of Sir William Johnson*, 13 vols. (Albany: University of the State of New York, 1921–62), 11:900. Information in this and the following five paragraphs is drawn largely from Gregory Evans Dowd, *A Spirited Resistance: The North American*

Indian Struggle for Unity, 1745–1815 (Baltimore: Johns Hopkins University Press, 1992), 25–40; Dowd, *War under Heaven: Pontiac, the Indian Nations, and the British Empire* (Baltimore: Johns Hopkins University Press, 2002); Anderson, *Crucible of War*, 457–75, 535–46, 617–37; Davis, *Frontier Illinois*, 56–64.

26. Dowd, *War under Heaven*, 221.

27. My understanding of the Acadian precedent and of the broader history of state-sponsored "ethnic cleansing" in North America that it initiated owes to John Mack Faragher, *A Great and Noble Scheme: The Tragic Story of the Expulsion of the French Acadians from Their American Homeland* (New York: W. W. Norton, 2005).

28. Ysabel Sandoval, trans., "The Beginning of Spanish Missouri: Instructions, D'Ulloa to Ríu, 1767," *Missouri Historical Society Collections* 3 (April 1908): 145, 159; Gilbert C. Din, "Captain Francisco Ríu y Morales and the Beginnings of Spanish Rule in Missouri," *Missouri Historical Review* 94 (January 2000): 121–45.

29. Sandoval, "Beginning of Spanish Missouri," 152, 160; John C. Ewers, "Symbols of Chiefly Authority in Spanish Louisiana," in John Francis McDermott, ed., *The Spanish in the Mississippi Valley, 1762–1804* (Urbana: University of Illinois Press, 1974), 272–73.

30. Sandoval, "Beginning of Spanish Missouri," 160; "Secret Instructions of Ulloa to Captain Ríu, Dated January 7, 1767," in Houck, ed., *The Spanish Regime in Missouri*, 1:26; Abraham P. Nasatir, *Borderland in Retreat: From Spanish Louisiana to the Far Southwest* (Albuquerque: University of New Mexico Press, 1976), 9.

31. Foley, *The Genesis of Missouri*, 39; Carl H. Chapman, "The Indomitable Osage in Spanish Illinois (Upper Louisiana), 1763–1804," in McDermott, ed., *The Spanish in the Mississippi Valley*, 287–308.

32. "Report of Indian Traders, Given Passports by Don Francisco Cruzat, Dated November 28, 1777," in Houck, ed., *The Spanish Regime in Missouri*, 1:139; Rollings, *The Osage*, 137.

33. Janet Lecompte, "Don Benito Vasquez in Early Saint Louis," *Bulletin of the Missouri Historical Society* 26 (1970): 289.

34. "Secret Instructions of Ulloa to Captain Ríu," 1:27; Jerningham to Ulloa, November 28, 1767, in Lawrence Kinnaird, ed., *Spain in the Mississippi Valley, 1765–1794*, pt. 1: *The Revolutionary Period, 1765–1781*, Annual Report of the American Historical Association for the Year 1945, vol. 2 (Washington, D.C.: Government Printing Office, 1949), 36–37.

35. Ulloa to Grimaldi, October 26, 1768, in Kinnaird, ed., *Spain in the Mississippi Valley*, 77–81; R.E. Chandler, "Ulloa's Account of the 1768 Revolt," *Louisiana History* 27 (Fall 1986): 407–37.

36. Nasatir, *Borderland in Retreat*, 12–14.

37. "Instructions for Holding Council with the Indians" and "General Instructions of O'Reilly to the Lieutenant Governor of the Villages of Ste. Genevieve, St. Louis, etc., Dated February 17, 1770," in Houck, ed., *The Spanish Regime in Missouri*, 1:46–47, 76–83.

38. Banner, *Legal Systems in Conflict*, 17; Robert R. Archibald, "From 'La Louisiane' to 'Luisiana': The Imposition of Spanish Administration in the Upper Mississippi Valley," *Gateway Heritage* 11 (Summer 1990): 26–33.

39. Proclamation by O'Reilly, December 7, 1769, in Kinnaird, ed., *Spain in the Mississippi Valley*, 126.

40. Din, *Spaniards, Planters, and Slaves*, 35–47; Ekberg, *Colonial Ste. Genevieve*, 208–25.

41. Banner, *Legal Systems in Conflict*, 26.

42. For descriptions of various British North American regions as good poor man's countries, see R. C. Ballard Thruston, ed., "Letter by Edward Harris, 1797," *Filson Club History Quarterly* 2 (July 1928): 166; Carl Bridenbaugh, ed., "Patrick M'Robert's Tour through Part of the North Provinces of America," *Pennsylvania Magazine of History and Biography* 59 (April 1935): 136; Robert Beverly, *The History and Present State of Virginia* (1705; repr., Chapel Hill: University of North Carolina Press, 1947), 275; Bernard Bailyn, *Voyagers to the West: A Passage in the Peopling of America on the Eve of the Revolution* (New York: Knopf, 1986), 504.

3. Newcomers

1. On the American occupation of the Ohio Valley and the conflicts with Indians that ensued, see Stephen Aron, *How the West Was Lost: The Transformation of Kentucky from Daniel Boone to Henry Clay* (Baltimore: Johns Hopkins University Press, 1996); John Mack Faragher, *Daniel Boone: The Life and Legend of an American Pioneer* (New York: Holt, 1992); Elizabeth A. Perkins, *Border Life: Experience and Memory in the Revolutionary Ohio Valley* (Chapel Hill: University of North Carolina Press, 1998); Daniel P. Barr, "Contested Ground: Competition and Conflict on the Upper Ohio Frontier, 1744–1784" (Ph.D. dissertation, Kent State University, 2001).

2. Michael N. McConnell, *A Country Between: The Upper Ohio Valley and Its Peoples, 1724–1774* (Lincoln: University of Nebraska Press, 1992); Thomas Hatley, *The Dividing Paths: Cherokees and South Carolinians through the Era of the American Revolution* (New York: Ox-

ford University Press, 1993); and Colin G. Calloway, *The American Revolution in Indian Country: Crisis and Diversity in Native American Communities* (New York: Cambridge University Press, 1995), provide particularly valuable insights into Indian and intercultural politics in the Ohio Valley before, during, and after the American Revolution.

3. James Alton James, ed., *George Rogers Clark Papers, 1771–1781,* Collections of the Illinois State Historical Library, vol. 8 (Springfield: Trustees of the Illinois State Historical Library, 1912), 40–63; Paul L. Stevens, " 'To Invade the Frontiers of Kentucky'? The Indian Diplomacy of Philippe De Rocheblave, Britain's Acting Commandant at Kaskaskia, 1776–1778," *Filson Club History Quarterly* 64 (April 1990): 205–46; Robert M. Sutton, "George Rogers Clark and the Campaign in the West: The Five Major Documents," *Indiana Magazine of History* 76 (December 1980): 334–45; John D. Barnhart, ed., *Henry Hamilton and George Rogers Clark in the American Revolution with the Unpublished Journal of Lieut. Gov. Henry Hamilton* (Crawfordsville, Ind.: R.E. Banta, 1951); Lowell H. Harrison, *George Rogers Clark and the War in the West* (Lexington: University Press of Kentucky, 1976).

4. Lawrence Kinnaird, ed., "Clark–Leyba Papers," *American Historical Review* 41 (October 1935): 92–112.

5. Janet Lecompte, "Don Benito Vasquez in Early Saint Louis," *Bulletin of the Missouri Historical Society* 26 (1970): 294; William E. Foley, *A History of Missouri,* vol. 1: *1673–1820* (Columbia: University of Missouri Press, 1971), 28–29.

6. Letter of Governor Miró to Don Joseph Galvez, 1782, in Louis Houck, ed., *The Spanish Regime in Missouri,* 2 vols. (Chicago: R.R. Donnelley and Sons, 1909), 1:209; Document no. 88, Petition by the inhabitants of Ste. Genevieve, July 3, 1779, in A. Lloyd Collins, comp., "Ste. Genevieve Archives: Translated from the Original French Language into English," typescripts at Western Historical Manuscripts Collection, State Historical Society of Missouri, Columbia; Abraham P. Nasatir, *Borderland in Retreat: From Spanish Louisiana to the Far Southwest* (Albuquerque: University of New Mexico Press, 1976), 35–66.

7. H.W. Beckwith, ed., "*George Rogers Clark's Conquest of the Illinois,*" in Collections of the Illinois State Historical Library, vol. 1 (Springfield: Trustees of the Illinois State Historical Library, 1903), 208.

8. See esp. Gregory E. Dowd, *A Spirited Resistance: The North American Indian Struggle for Unity, 1745–1815* (Baltimore: Johns Hopkins University Press, 1992).

9. Colin G. Calloway, *Crown and Calumet: British–Indian Rela-*

tions, 1783–1815 (Norman: University of Oklahoma Press, 1987); Robert S. Allen, *His Majesty's Indian Allies: British Indian Policy in the Defence of Canada, 1774–1815* (Toronto: Dundurn Press, 1992); Larry L. Nelson, *A Man of Distinction among Them: Alexander McKee and British-Indian Affairs along the Ohio Country Frontier, 1734–1799* (Kent, Ohio: Kent State University Press, 1999); Wiley Sword, *President Washington's Indian War: The Struggle for the Old Northwest, 1790–1795* (Norman: University of Oklahoma Press, 1985).

10. See esp. the speech of Indian negotiators in Colin G. Calloway, ed., *The World Turned Upside Down: Indian Voices from Early America* (Boston: St. Martin's Press, 1994), 181–82, For an interpretation that stresses the Indians' search for a return of the French, see Richard White, *The Middle Ground: Indians, Empires, and Republics in the Great Lakes Region* (New York: Cambridge University Press, 1991), 315–412.

11. Extracts from a Report of Carondelet as to the Situation and Military Condition of Louisiana, 1793, in Houck, ed., *The Spanish Regime in Missouri,* 2:12; Robert R. Archibald, "From 'La Louisiane' to 'Luisiana': The Imposition of Spanish Administration in the Upper Mississippi Valley," *Gateway Heritage* 11 (Summer 1990): 24–37.

12. Nasatir, *Borderland in Retreat,* 36; William E. Foley, *The Genesis of Missouri: From Wilderness Outpost to Statehood* (Columbia: University of Missouri Press, 1989), 57; Lowell Harrison, "James Wilkinson: A Leader for Kentucky?" *Filson Club History Quarterly* 66 (July 1992): 334–68; John Thornton Posey, "Rascality Revisited: In Defense of General James Wilkinson," *Filson Club History Quarterly* 74 (Fall 2000): 309–51.

13. "Immigration to Be Encouraged, 1778," in Houck, ed., *The Spanish Regime in Missouri,* 1:152, 154, 156.

14. Carl J. Ekberg, *Colonial Ste. Genevieve: An Adventure on the Mississippi Frontier* (Gerald, Mo.: Patrice Press, 1985), 430; James E. Davis, *Frontier Illinois* (Bloomington: Indiana University Press, 1998), 99; Selwyn K. Troen and Glen E. Holt, eds., *St. Louis* (New York: New Viewpoints, 1977), 8.

15. Cruzat's orders are printed in Troen and Holt, eds., *St. Louis,* 19, 20; for changing slave population, see Carl J. Ekberg, *French Roots in the Illinois Country: The Mississippi Frontier in Colonial Times* (Urbana: University of Illinois Press, 1998), 155–56.

16. Perez's order, dated November 24, 1787, is quoted in Troen and Holt, eds., *St. Louis,* 21.

17. Cruzat to Miró, August 23, 1784, in Lawrence Kinnaird, ed.,

Spain in the Mississippi Valley, 1765–1794, pt. 2: *Post War Decade, 1782–1791*, Annual Report of the American Historical Association for the Year 1945, vol. 3 (Washington, D.C.: Government Printing Office, 1946), 117.

18. The largest settlement of immigrant Indians was located near Apple Creek above Cape Girardeau, with other new villages established along Saline Creek below Ste. Genevieve and along the Meramec River about twenty miles below St. Louis. See Carl J. Ekberg and William E. Foley, eds., *An Account of Upper Louisiana by Nicholas de Finiels* (Columbia: University of Missouri Press, 1989), 34–35, 41, 49; Walter A. Schroeder, *Opening the Ozarks: A Historical Geography of Missouri's Ste. Genevieve District, 1760–1830* (Columbia: University of Missouri Press, 2002), 70, 373; Daniel H. Usner Jr., "An American Indian Gateway: Some Thoughts on the Migration and Settlement of Eastern Indians around Early St. Louis," *Gateway Heritage* 11 (Winter 1990–91): 42–51; Lynn Morrow, "Trader William Gilliss and Delaware Migration in Southern Missouri," *Missouri Historical Review* 75 (January 1981): 148–50; Nathaniel Sheidley, "Unruly Men: Indians, Settlers, and the Ethos of Frontier Patriarchy in the Upper Tennessee Watershed, 1763–1815" (Ph.D. dissertation, Princeton University, 1999), 229–30; Gilbert C. Din, "The Immigration Policy of Governor Estéban Miró in Spanish Louisiana," *Southwestern Historical Quarterly* 73 (October 1969): 155–75.

19. Official Letters of Louis Lorimier, 1787–93, in Houck, ed., *The Spanish Regime in Missouri*, 2:50–51; "Letter of Instructions: Carondelet to Howard," *Missouri Historical Society Collections* 3 (January 1908): 86; Tanis C. Thorne, *The Many Hands of My Relations: French and Indians on the Lower Missouri* (Columbia: University of Missouri Press, 1996), 90–96.

20. Official Letters of Louis Lorimier, 1787–93, 2:51.

21. Ruby Matson Robins, ed., "The Missouri Reader: Americans in the Valley," pt. 1, *Missouri Historical Review* 45 (April 1951): 280–82; Letter of Colonel George Morgan to Don Diego de Gardoqui, in Houck, ed., *The Spanish Regime in Missouri*, 1:286–309.

22. Jefferson quoted in Gilbert C. Din, "Spain's Immigration Policy in Louisiana and the American Penetration, 1792–1803," *Southwestern Historical Quarterly* 76 (January 1973): 255.

23. Protest of Governor Miró against Grant to Col. George Morgan, Dated 1789, in Houck, ed., *The Spanish Regime in Missouri*, 1:276–77; Din, "The Immigration Policy of Governor Esteban Miró," 155–75; C. Richard Arena, "Land Settlement Policies and Practices in Spanish

Louisiana," in McDermott, ed., *The Spanish in the Mississippi Valley*, 51–60.

24. Howard C. Rice, ed., *Barthélemi Tardiveau: A French Trader in the West* (Baltimore: Johns Hopkins University Press, 1938), 43; Letter of Barthélemi Tardiveau to Count Aranda, Proposing to Establish a Great French Colony in Upper Louisiana, in Houck, ed., *The Spanish Regime in Missouri,* 1:361, 363.

25. Letter of Carondelet in Regard to the Formation of American Settlements on the Mississippi below New Madrid, 1793, in Houck, ed., *The Spanish Regime in Missouri,* 1:413; Carondelet Reports on Danger of an American Settlement at the Ecores a Margo, 1793, in ibid., 2:15–20.

26. Lynn Morrow, "New Madrid and Its Hinterland, 1783–1826," *Bulletin of the Missouri Historical Society* 36 (July 1980): 241–50.

27. J. B. Martigny to *Monsieur* [Galvez], October 30, 1779, quoted in Abraham P. Nasatir, ed., *Before Lewis and Clark: Documents Illustrating the History of Missouri, 1785–1804,* 2 vols. (1952; repr., Lincoln: University of Nebraska Press, 1990), 1:71; Jack D. L. Holmes, ed., "A 1795 Inspection of Spanish Missouri," *Missouri Historical Review* 55 (October 1960): 10; Marie George Windell, ed., "The Missouri Reader: The French in the Valley," pt. 5, *Missouri Historical Review* 41 (October 1946): 105.

28. In part, climate contributed to the decision by St. Louis traders to save their finer furs for northern posts. In cooler climes, beaver and otter pelts kept better, reducing losses from spoilage. Against these advantages, however, the Chouteaus and others had to weigh the greater costs and difficulties in moving goods to the Great Lakes—and then to Montreal as well as all the way down the St. Lawrence—as compared with the relatively simple navigation between Upper Louisiana and New Orleans. But price considerations tipped the balance to the north. For excellent studies of the Chouteaus and problems faced by other St. Louis traders in these years, see William E. Foley and C. David Rice, *The First Chouteaus: River Barons of Early St. Louis* (Urbana: University of Illinois Press, 1983), 37–38; William E. Foley, "The Lewis and Clark Expedition's Silent Partners: The Chouteau Brothers of St. Louis," *Missouri Historical Review* 77 (January 1983): 131–33; LeCompte, "Don Benito Vasquez in Early Saint Louis," 285–305; Thorne, *The Many Hands of My Relations,* 90.

29. For official prohibitions on the distribution of alcohol, see Troen and Holt, eds., *St. Louis,* 16–17; "Notice to the Police at the post of Ste. Genevieve to arrest anyone selling spirituous liquors to Indians," Janu-

ary 18, 1794, in Collins, comp., "Ste. Genevieve Archives." For lists of tribes receiving presents in St. Louis and inventories of gifts distributed, see Recapitulation of Indian Tribes of Missouri River, November 15, 1777, Papers from Spain, Missouri Historical Society; Abraham P. Nasatir, ed., "An Account of Spanish Louisiana, 1785," *Missouri Historical Review* 24 (July 1930): 525.

30. Report of Gov. Miró to the Marquis Sonora of Outrages Perpetrated by the Osage Indians, in Houck, ed., *The Spanish Regime in Missouri*, 1:255; Nasatir, ed., "An Account of Spanish Louisiana, 1785," 532; Manuel Perez to Estevan Miró, November 8, 1791, in Nasatir, ed., *Before Lewis and Clark*, 1:149–50; Gilbert C. Din and Abraham P. Nasatir, *The Imperial Osages: Spanish–Indian Diplomacy in the Mississippi Valley* (Norman: University of Oklahoma Press, 1983), 146–216.

31. Trudeau quoted in Willard H. Rollings, *The Osage: An Ethnohistorical Study of Hegemony on the Prairie-Plains* (Columbia: University of Missouri Press, 1992), 186; "Letter of Miró to Manuel Gayoso De Lemus, Enclosing a Letter from Lieut.-gov. Perez in Regard to Attack Made on Indians by Americans in 1789," in Houck, ed., *The Spanish Regime in Missouri*, 1:316–17.

32. Ekberg and Foley, eds., *An Account of Upper Louisiana*, 97.

33. This discussion of the impact of a century of colonialism on the Osages draws primarily on J. Frederick Fausz, "Becoming 'a Nation of Quakers': The Removal of the Osage Indians from Missouri," *Gateway Heritage* 21 (Summer 2000): 29–32; Rollings, *The Osage*, esp. 154–78; Thorne, *The Many Hands of My Relations*, esp. 102–105.

34. "Official Letters to Louis Lorimier, 1787–1793," in Houck, ed., *The Spanish Regime in Missouri*, 2:52. See also Perez to Miró, November 8, 1791, in Nasatir, ed., *Before Lewis and Clark*, 1:149–50; Trudeau to Carondelet, July 25, 1792, in ibid., 1:156–57; Trudeau to Carondelet, March 2, 1793, in ibid., 1:167–69; Trudeau to Carondelet, April 10, 1793, in ibid., 1:171–73; Trudeau to Carondelet, July 13, 1793, in ibid., 1:185–86.

35. Ekberg, *Colonial Ste. Genevieve*, 101.

36. Din and Nasatir, *The Imperial Osages*, 217–54.

37. "A Fort among the Troublesome Osages—1795," in Houck, ed., *The Spanish Regime in Missouri*, 2:104.

38. Foley and Rice, *The First Chouteaus*, 45–54; Foley and Rice, "Compounding the Risks: International Politics, Wartime Dislocations, and Auguste Chouteau's Fur Trading Operations, 1792–1815," *Bulletin of the Missouri Historical Society* 34 (April 1978): 132–34.

39. Fausz, "Becoming 'a Nation of Quakers,'" 32.

40. Thomas C. Danisi and Emily Troxell Jaycox, "A St. Louis River

Map Guides the Lewis and Clark Expedition," *Gateway Heritage* 24 (Fall 2003–Winter 2004): 12.

41. "Dealing of Americans with the Indians, 1795," from General Archives of the Indies, Seville, Department of Santo Domingo, Louisiana and Florida, case 87, drawer 1, bundle 22 (typescript in papers from Spain, Missouri Historical Society, St. Louis), 11, 16.

42. "Trudeau's Report Concerning the Settlements of the Spanish Illinois Country, 1798," in Houck, ed., *The Spanish Regime in Missouri,* 2:255; see also "Expedition under Don Carlos Howard to Upper Louisiana, 1796," in ibid., 2:127; "Fear of English Invasion of Upper Louisiana, . . . 1800," in ibid., 2:285, 290.

43. "Trudeau's Report Concerning the Settlements of the Spanish Illinois Country, 1798," in Houck, ed., *The Spanish Regime in Missouri,* 2:256; Pierre Charles de Hault Delassus Deluzieres, *An Official Account of the Situation, Soil, Produce, &c. of That Part of Louisiana Which Lies between the Mouth of the Missouri and New Madrid, or L'Anse a La Graise, and on the West Side of the Mississippi* (Lexington, Ky.: Printed by J. Bradford, 1796), 3–6.

44. Schroeder, *Opening the Ozarks,* 99; George P. Garrison, ed., "A Memorandum of M. Austin's Journey from the Lead Mines in the Country of Wythe in the State of Virginia to the Lead Mines in the Province of Louisiana West of the Mississippi, 1796–1797," *American Historical Review* 5 (April 1900): 542; C. F. Volney, *View of the Climate and Soil of the United States of America* (Philadelphia: Printed by T. & G. Palmer, 1804), 339. On Moses Austin, see David B. Gracy II, "Moses Austin and the Development of the Missouri Lead Industry," *Gateway Heritage* 1 (Spring 1981): 45; James Alexander Gardner, *Lead King: Moses Austin* (St. Louis: Sunrise, 1980). On the migration of the Boone family, see Ben L. Emmons, Letter [1926?], Western Historical Manuscripts Collection, C995, vol. 1, no. 16; Neal O. Hammon, ed., *My Father, Daniel Boone: The Draper Interviews with Nathan Boone* (Lexington: University Press of Kentucky, 1999), 107–15; John K. Hulston, "Daniel Boone's Sons in Missouri," *Missouri Historical Review* 47 (July 1947), 361–64; Hazel Atterbury Spraker, *The Boone Family: A Genealogical History of the Descendants of George and Mary Boone Who Came to America in 1717* (1922; repr., Baltimore: Genealogical Publishing, 1974), 127; R. Douglas Hurt, *Nathan Boone and the American Frontier* (Columbia: University of Missouri Press, 1998), 23–29; Faragher, *Daniel Boone,* 274–85.

45. Ekberg and Foley, eds., *An Account of Upper Louisiana,* 52; "Trudeau's Report Concerning the Settlements of the Spanish Illinois

Country, 1798," in Houck, ed., *The Spanish Regime in Missouri*, 2:255; Russell L. Gerlach, "Population Origins in Rural Missouri," *Missouri Historical Review* 71 (October 1976): 13; James R. Shortridge, "The Expansion of the Settlement Frontier in Missouri," *Missouri Historical Review* 75 (October 1980): 67; Conevery Bolton Valencius, *The Health of the Country: How American Settlers Understood Themselves and Their Land* (New York: Basic Books, 2002).

46. Ekberg and Foley, eds., *An Account of Upper Louisiana*, 50, 55, 65; M. Perrin du Lac, *Travels through the Two Louisianas, and among the Savage Nations of the Missouri; Also, in the United States along the Ohio, and the Adjacent Provinces, in 1801, 1802, & 1803* (London: Printed by J. G. Barnard, 1807), 44; for similar considerations of Creole ways and contrasts with American customs, see Volney, *View of the Climate and Soil of the United States of America*, 337–47; Georges-Victor Collot, *A Journey in North America, Containing a Survey of the Countries Watered by the Mississippi, Ohio, Missouri, and Other Affluing Rivers; With Exact Observations on the Course and Soundings of These Rivers; And on the Towns, Villages, Hamlets and Farms of that Part of the New-World; Followed by Philosophical, Political, Military and Commercial Remarks and A Projected Line of Frontiers and General Limits*, 2 vols. (Paris: A. Bertrand, 1826), 1:233, 248, 277.

47. Schroeder, *Opening the Ozarks*, 10.

48. Dick Steward, " 'With the Scepter of a Tyrant': John Smith T and the Mineral Wars," *Gateway Heritage* 14 (Fall 1993): 28–29; Ekberg and Foley, eds., *An Account of Upper Louisiana*, 124.

49. "Trudeau's Report Concerning the Settlements of the Spanish Illinois Country, 1798," in Houck, ed., *The Spanish Regime in Missouri*, 2:256.

50. David B. Gracy II, *Moses Austin: His Life* (San Antonio: Trinity University Press, 1987), 114–15; John C. Boone to Lyman C. Draper, November 20, 1890, Draper Mss. 16C132, State Historical Society of Wisconsin, Madison; James F. Keefe and Lynn Morrow, eds., *The White River Chronicles of S. C. Turnbo: Man and Wildlife on the Ozarks Frontier* (Fayetteville: University of Arkansas Press, 1994), 1–13; Lynn Morrow, "New Madrid and Its Hinterland," 241–42; Morrow, "Trader William Gilliss," 147–51; Usner, "An American Indian Gateway," 42–51; Stephen Aron, "The Legacy of Daniel Boone: Three Generations of Boones and the History of Indian–White Relations," *Register of the Kentucky Historical Society* 95 (Summer 1997): 225–30.

51. On the emergence of syncretic cultural elements in eighteenth-century Pennsylvania, see Faragher, *Daniel Boone*, 17–23; Terry G.

Jordan and Matti Kaups, *The American Backwoods Frontier: An Ethnic and Ecological Interpretation* (Baltimore: Johns Hopkins University Press, 1989). For the furthering of this process of cultural borrowings between Indians and Anglo-Americans in the Ohio valley, see Stephen Aron, "Pigs and Hunters: 'Rights in the Woods' on the Trans-Appalachian Frontier," in Andrew R. L. Cayton and Fredrika J. Teute, eds., *Contact Points: American Frontiers from the Mohawk Valley to the Mississippi, 1750–1830* (Chapel Hill: University of North Carolina Press, 1998), 175–204; Aron, *How the West Was Lost*, 1–57, 102–23. And for the fruition of these developments in the confluence region, see John Mack Faragher, "'More Motley than Mackinaw': From Ethnic Mixing to Ethnic Cleansing on the Frontier of the Lower Missouri, 1783–1833," in Cayton and Teute, eds., *Contact Points*, 304–26.

52. Ekberg and Foley, eds., *An Account of Upper Louisiana*, 34–35; Document no. 79, Manuel Gayoso de Lemos to chiefs and considered men of Shawnee Nation in the Illinois territory, May 17, 1799, in Collins, comp., "Ste. Genevieve Archives"; Perrin du Lac, *Travels through the Two Louisianas*, 45–46; Amos Stoddard, *Sketches, Historical and Descriptive, of Louisiana* (Philadelphia: Mathew Carey, 1812), 210, 215; Keefe and Morrow, eds., *The White River Chronicles of S. C. Turnbo*, 7; Schroeder, *Opening the Ozarks*, 374–75.

53. Aron, "Pigs and Hunters," 175–204.

54. Schroeder, *Opening the Ozarks*, 375–77.

55. Foley and Rice, *The First Chouteaus*, 54; Ekberg and Foley, eds., *An Account of Upper Louisiana*, 90, 98; Zenon Trudeau to Baron Carondelet, March 12, 1795, in Nasatir, ed., *Before Lewis and Clark*, 1:317–19; "Trudeau's Report Concerning the Settlements of the Spanish Illinois Country, 1798," in Houck, ed., *The Spanish Regime in Missouri*, 2:251; Thorne, *The Many Hands of My Relations*, 105; Rollings, *The Osage*, 191.

4. Transfers

1. Thomas Jefferson to Robert Livingston, April 18, 1802, in Paul Leicester Ford, ed., *The Writings of Thomas Jefferson*, 10 vols. (New York: G. P. Putnam's Sons, 1892–99), 8:144–45.

2. This paragraph and the next draws principally on Richard E. Oglesby, *Manuel Lisa and the Opening of the Missouri Fur Trade* (Norman: University of Oklahoma Press, 1963), 22–27; William E. Foley and C. David Rice, *The First Chouteaus: River Barons of Early St.*

Louis (Urbana: University of Illinois Press, 1983), 62; Tanis C. Thorne, *The Many Hands of My Relations: French and Indians on the Lower Missouri* (Columbia: University of Missouri Press, 1996), 106.

3. Dorothy Penn, ed., "The Missouri Reader: The French in the Valley," pt. 2, *Missouri Historical Review* 40 (January 1946): 274–75; Amos Stoddard to H. Dearborn, June 3, 1804, in "Papers of Captain Amos Stoddard," Missouri Historical Society, *Glimpses of the Past* 2 (May–September 1935): 105–106; Willard H. Rollings, *The Osage: An Ethnohistorical Study of Hegemony on the Prairie-Plains* (Columbia: University of Missouri Press, 1992), 184.

4. Neal O. Hammon, ed., *My Father, Daniel Boone: The Draper Interviews with Nathan Boone* (Lexington: University Press of Kentucky, 1999), 122–23; R. Douglas Hurt, *Nathan Boone and the American Frontier* (Columbia: University of Missouri Press, 1998), 34–39; John Mack Faragher, *Daniel Boone: The Life and Legend of an American Pioneer* (New York: Holt, 1992), 79–82; H. M. Brackenridge, *Views of Louisiana; Together with a Journal of a Voyage up the Missouri River, in 1811* (Pittsburgh: Cramer, Spear and Eichbaum, 1814), 218; George P. Garrison, ed., "A Memorandum of M. Austin's Journey from the Lead Mines in the Country of Wythe in the State of Virginia to the Lead Mines in the Province of Louisiana West of the Mississippi, 1796–1797," *American Historical Review* 5 (April 1900): 519.

5. Document no. 89, "Petition of inhabitants of New Bourbon to order the Peoria Indians not to settle within two or three miles of their town owing to Indian depredations, August 19, 1801," in A. Lloyd Collins, comp., "Ste. Genevieve Archives: Translated from the Original French Language into English," typescripts in Western Historical Manuscripts Collections, State Historical Society of Missouri, Columbia.

6. R. Douglas Hurt, *Agriculture and Slavery in Missouri's Little Dixie* (Columbia: University of Missouri Press, 1992), 27–28; Lemont K. Richardson, "Private Land Claims in Missouri," pt. 1, *Missouri Historical Review* 50 (January 1956): 134; William E. Foley, *The Genesis of Missouri: From Wilderness Outpost to Statehood* (Columbia: University of Missouri Press, 1989), 143; Walter A. Schroeder, *Opening the Ozarks: A Historical Geography of Missouri's Ste. Genevieve District, 1760–1830* (Columbia: University of Missouri Press, 2002), 109.

7. Amos Stoddard, *Sketches, Historical and Descriptive, of Louisiana* (Philadelphia: Mathew Carey, 1812), 245–55; Dick Steward, " 'With the Scepter of a Tyrant': John Smith T and the Mineral Wars," *Gateway Heritage* 14 (Fall 1993): 24–25.

8. Stephen Aron, *How the West Was Lost: The Transformation of*

Kentucky from Daniel Boone to Henry Clay (Baltimore: Johns Hopkins University Press, 1996), 58–101, 150–69; Christopher Waldrep, "Opportunity on the Frontier South of the Green," in Craig Thompson Friend, *The Buzzel about Kentuck: Settling the Promised Land* (Lexington: University Press of Kentucky, 1999), 153–72; Ruby Matson Robins, ed., "The Missouri Reader: Americans in the Valley," pt. 1, *Missouri Historical Review* 45 (October 1950): 2–5; Russel L. Gerlach, *Settlement Patterns in Missouri: A Study of Population Origins with a Wall Map* (Columbia: University of Missouri Press, 1986), 15.

9. Peter J. Kastor, " 'Motives of Peculiar Urgency': Local Diplomacy in Louisiana, 1803–1821," *William and Mary Quarterly*, 3rd ser., 58 (October 2001): 819.

10. Jerry W. Knudsen, "Newspaper Reaction to the Louisiana Purchase; 'This New, Immense, Unbounded World,' " *Missouri Historical Review* 63 (January 1969): 184–85, 194–98. For the most recent comprehensive treatment of the making of the Louisiana Purchase, see Jon Kukla, *A Wilderness So Immense: The Louisiana Purchase and the Destiny of America* (New York: Knopf, 2003).

11. Richardson, "Private Land Claims in Missouri," pt. 1, 136; Schroeder, *Opening the Ozarks*, 109.

12. John Francis McDermott, "Captain Stoddard Discovers St. Louis," *Bulletin of the Missouri Historical Society* 10 (April 1954): 332; William E. Foley, *A History of Missouri*, vol. 1: *1673–1820* (Columbia: University of Missouri Press, 1971), 72; "Summary by Delassus of Trade Licenses Issued at St. Louis, 1799–1804," in Abraham P. Nasatir, *Before Lewis and Clark: Documents Illustrating the History of the Missouri, 1785–1804*, 2 vols. (1952; repr., Lincoln: University of Nebraska Press, 1990), 2:592.

13. J. Stille to Nathaniel Leonard, July 5, 1804, Army Papers, Missouri Historical Society, St. Louis; William Clark, May 31, 1804, in Gary E. Moulton, ed., *The Journals of the Lewis and Clark Expedition*, 13 vols. (Lincoln: University of Nebraska Press, 1983–2001), 1:266; John F. Darby, *Personal Recollections of Many Prominent People Whom I Have Known, and of Events—Especially of Those Relating to the History of St. Louis—during the First Half of the Present Century* (St. Louis: G. I. Jones, 1880), 223–24; Harvey Wish, "The French of Old Missouri (1804–1821): A Study in Assimilation," *Mid-America: An Historical Review* 23 (July 1941): 168.

14. The text of the treaty is printed in Henry S. Geyer, ed., *A Digest of the Laws of Missouri Territory* (St. Louis: Printed for the publisher by Joseph Charless at the Missouri Gazette Office, 1818), 21.

15. Frederick Bates to Henry Dearborn, May 30, 1807, in Thomas Maitland Marshall, ed., *The Life and Papers of Frederick Bates,* 2 vols. (St. Louis: Missouri Historical Society, 1926), 1:133; Frederick Bates to Richard Bates, December 17, 1807, in ibid., 1:243, 241.

16. Stoddard, *Sketches, Historical and Descriptive, of Louisiana,* 325, 310. For a further examination of the emotional differences between French and American ideals about marriage and childrearing, see Martha Saxton, "The Moral Minority: Prescriptive Literature in Early St. Louis," *Gateway Heritage* 21 (Fall 2000): 18–31.

17. William E. Foley, "James A. Wilkinson: Territorial Governor," *Bulletin of the Missouri Historical Society* 25 (October 1968): 14–15; Donald Jackson, *Thomas Jefferson and the Stony Mountains: Exploring the West from Monticello* (Urbana: University of Illinois Press, 1981), 34; Bernard Sheehan, *Seeds of Extinction: Jeffersonian Philanthropy and the American Indian* (Chapel Hill: University of North Carolina Press, 1973), 245–50; Anthony F. C. Wallace, *Jefferson and the Indians: The Tragic Fate of the First Americans* (Cambridge: Belknap Press of Harvard University Press, 1999), 224, 248–57.

18. Rufus King to Christopher Gore, September 6, 1803, in Charles R. King, ed., *The Life and Correspondence of Rufus King,* 6 vols. (New York: G. P. Putnam's Sons, 1897), 4:303.

19. Schroeder, *Opening the Ozarks,* 166.

20. "Papers of Captain Amos Stoddard," 103–105.

21. Ibid., 117; Maximilian Richard, "Black and White on the Urban Frontier: The St. Louis Community in Transition, 1800–1830," *Bulletin of the Missouri Historical Society* 33 (October 1976): 3–17.

22. Wallace, *Jefferson and the Indians,* 255; Schroeder, *Opening the Ozarks,* 164–73.

23. "Papers of Captain Amos Stoddard," 89, 112; Amos Stoddard to General Henry Dearborn, June 3, 1804, in McCarter & English Indian Claim Cases, Mudd Library, Princeton University, box 17, folder 7, exhibit 22 (original in Amos Stoddard Collection, Missouri Historical Society, St. Louis).

24. "Papers of Captain Amos Stoddard," 117; Stoddard, *Sketches, Historical and Descriptive, of Louisiana,* 332–33.

25. William Henry Harrison (St. Louis) to Jonathan Dayton, October 29, 1804, in McCarter & English Indian Claim Cases, Mudd Library, Princeton University, box 18, folder 12, exhibit 22; Harrison to Jefferson, November 6, 1804, in Logan Esarey, ed., *Governors' Messages and Letters: Messages and Letters of William Henry Harrison, 1800–1816,* 2 vols. (Indianapolis: Indiana Historical Commission, 1922),

1:110–11; Harrison to Chouteau, December 21, 1804, in ibid., 1:113–14; Gary W. Pond, "William Henry Harrison (1773–1841)," in Lawrence O. Christensen, William E. Foley, Gary R. Kremer, and Kenneth H. Winn, eds., *Dictionary of Missouri Biography* (Columbia: University of Missouri Press, 1999), 381–83.

26. Wish, "The French of Old Missouri," 169.

27. Foley, *A History of Missouri*, 97–99.

28. For recent evaluations of Wilkinson's checkered career, see John Thornton Posey, "Rascality Revisited: In Defense of General James Wilkinson," *Filson Club History Quarterly* 74 (Fall 2000): 309–51; M. R. Montgomery, *Jefferson and the Gun-men: How the West Was Almost Lost* (New York: Crown Publishers, 2000), 20–28, 199–209, 251–54; Richard H. Kohn, "General Wilkinson's Vendetta with General Wayne: Politics and Command in the American Army, 1791–1796," *Filson Club History Quarterly* 45 (October 1971): 361–72.

29. Dick Steward, "James Wilkinson (1757–1825)," in Christensen, Foley, Kremer, and Winn, eds., *Dictionary of Missouri Biography*, 800–801.

30. Foley, "James A. Wilkinson," 4–5.

31. Ronald L. F. Davis, "Community and Conflict in Pioneer Saint Louis, Missouri," *Western Historical Quarterly* 10 (July 1979): 338–39.

32. For Jefferson's view of land problems in Kentucky, see Anthony Marc Lewis, "Jefferson and Virginia's Pioneers, 1774–1781," *Mississippi Valley Historical Review* 34 (March 1948): 551–88; Stanley N. Katz, "Thomas Jefferson and the Right to Property in Revolutionary America," *Journal of Law and Economics* 19 (October 1976): 467–88.

33. Samuel M. Wilson, *The First Land Court of Kentucky* (Lexington, Ky.: n.p., 1923), 1–13, 32–45; William Ayres, "Land Titles in Kentucky," *Proceedings of the Eighth Annual Meeting of the Kentucky State Bar Association* (Louisville, Ky.: n.p., 1909), 160–91.

34. Foley, "James A. Wilkinson," 12–13.

35. Frederick Bates to William Hull, St. Louis, June 17, 1807, in Marshall, ed., *The Life and Papers of Frederick Bates*, 1:145; Dick Steward, " 'With the Scepter of a Tyrant,' " 24–37. For a complete biography of this most colorful of Missouri pioneers, see Dick Steward, *Frontier Swashbuckler: The Life and Legend of John Smith T* (Columbia: University of Missouri Press, 2000).

36. Ada Paris Klein, ed., "The Missouri Reader: Ownership of the Land under France, Spain, and the United States," *Missouri Historical Review* 44 (April 1949–1950): 288.

37. Jefferson quoted in Betty Houchin Winfield, "Public Percep-

tion of the Expedition," in Alan Taylor, ed., *Lewis and Clark: Journey to Another America* (St. Louis: Missouri Historical Society Press, 2003), 187. A report on the reception given Lewis and Clark upon their return to St. Louis appeared in the Frankfort, Kentucky, newspaper *The Western World* on October 11, 1806, and is reprinted in James P. Ronda, ed., *Voyages of Discovery: Essays on the Lewis and Clark Expedition* (Helena: Montana Historical Society Press, 1998), 203–205. See also Anne L. Hunt, "Early Recollections," Missouri Historical Society, *Glimpses of the Past* 1 (May 1934): 48; Glenn E. Holt, "After the Journey Was Over: The St. Louis Years of Lewis and Clark," *Gateway Heritage* 2 (Winter 1981–82): 42; William E. Foley, "After the Applause: William Clark's Failed 1820 Gubernatorial Campaign," *Gateway Heritage* 24 (Fall 2003–Winter 2004): 104.

38. Lewis to Jefferson, April 7, 1805, in Gunther Barth, ed., *The Lewis and Clark Expedition: Selections from the Journals Arranged by Topic* (Boston: Bedford Books, 1998), 64; James P. Ronda, *Finding the West: Explorations with Lewis and Clark* (Albuquerque: University of New Mexico Press, 2001), 12.

39. Thomas Jefferson to Meriwether Lewis, January 22, 1804, in Clarence E. Carter, ed., *The Territorial Papers of the United States*, vol. 13: *The Territory of Louisiana–Missouri, 1803–1806* (Washington, D.C.: Government Printing Office, 1948), 15.

40. Jay H. Buckley, "William Clark: Superintendent of Indian Affairs at St. Louis, 1813–1838" (Ph.D. dissertation, University of Nebraska, 2001), 27; James Ronda, *Lewis and Clark among the Indians* (Lincoln: University of Nebraska Press, 1984), 1–16; John Logan Allen, "Imagining the West: The View from Monticello," in James P. Ronda, ed., *Thomas Jefferson and the Changing West* (St. Louis: Missouri Historical Society Press, 1997), 3–23; William E. Foley, "The Lewis and Clark Expedition's Silent Partners: The Chouteau Brothers of St. Louis," *Missouri Historical Review* 77 (January 1983): 131–46.

41. Clark quoted in Buckley, "William Clark," 113. For evidence of evolution in the diplomacy of Lewis and Clark, compare Lewis and Clark to the Oto Indians, August 4, 1804, in Donald Dean Jackson, ed., *Letters of the Lewis and Clark Expedition, with Related Documents, 1783–1854*, 2nd ed. with additional documents and notes, 2 vols. (Urbana: University of Illinois Press, 1978), 1:203–208, with Meriwether Lewis's journal entries in August 1805, excerpted in Barth, ed., *The Lewis and Clark Expedition*, 130–44.

42. Carolyn Gilman, "A World of Women," *Gateway Heritage* 24

(Fall 2003–Winter 2004): 46; Ronda, *Lewis and Clark among the Indians*, 36–37, 62–64, 106–107, 208–10, 232–33. For a Nez Perce version of the Lewis and Clark expedition, including details about William Clark's reputed offspring, see "William Clark's Nez Perce Son: A Tsoopnitpeloo Legend as Told by Otis Halfmoon of the Nez Perce Tribe," Discovering Lewis and Clark: A Legacy Website, http://www.lewis-clark.org/index.htm.

43. Barth, ed., *The Lewis and Clark Expedition*, 50; Meriwether Lewis, February 20, 1806, in Moulton, ed., *The Journals of the Lewis and Clark Expedition*, 6:331; Meriwether Lewis to Lucy Marks, March 31, 1805, in Tim Grove, ed., "Letters Home: Meriwether Lewis to His Mother," *Gateway Heritage* 24 (Fall 2003–Winter 2004): 63.

44. Russell M. Maghnaghi, "The Belle Fontaine Indian Factory, 1805–1808," *Missouri Historical Review* 75 (July 1981): 396–401; Stoddard, *Sketches, Historical and Descriptive, of Louisiana*, 263–64; Henry Dearborn to Amos Stoddard, May 4, 1804, and May 8, 1804, in Amos Stoddard Papers, Missouri Historical Society, St. Louis.

45. Geyer, ed., *A Digest of the Laws of Missouri Territory*, 23; "Papers of Captain Amos Stoddard," 102.

46. Willian E. Foley, "Different Notions of Justice: The Case of the 1808 St. Louis Murder Trials," *Gateway Heritage* 9 (Winter 1988–89): 2–13.

47. Thorne, *The Many Hands of My Relations*, 111; Rollings, *The Osage*, 220–21. Among the Sac and Fox, the bad feelings growing from the 1804 treaty instigated conflicts into the 1830s. See Thomas Forsyth, "Report of Original Causes of the Troubles with a Party of Sauk and Fox Indians under the Direction or Command of the Black Hawk Who Is No Chief," October 1, 1832, in McCarter & English Indian Claim Cases, Mudd Library, Princeton University, box 10, folder 10, exhibit 372.

48. Christian Schultz, *Travels on an Inland Voyage through the States of New York, Pennsylvania, Virginia, Ohio, Kentucky, and Tennessee, and through the Territories of Indiana, Louisiana, Mississippi, and New Orleans; Performed in the Years 1807 and 1808; Including a Tour of Nearly Six Thousand Miles*, 2 vols. (New York: Printed by Isaac Riley, 1810), 2:94; Stoddard, *Sketches, Historical and Descriptive, of Louisiana*, 215; Frederick Bates to Meriwether Lewis, April 28, 1807, in Marshall, ed., *The Life and Papers of Frederick Bates*, 1:105; Daniel H. Usner Jr., "An American Indian Gateway: Some Thoughts on the Migration and Settlement of Eastern Indians around Early St. Louis," *Gateway Heritage* 11 (Winter 1990–91): 43; Nathaniel Sheidley, "Unruly Men: Indians, Settlers, and the Ethos of Frontier Patriarchy in the

Upper Tennessee Watershed, 1763–1815" (Ph.D. dissertation, Princeton University, 1999), 230.

49. Mackay Wherry to Amos Stoddard, September 12, 1804, in Clarence E. Carter, ed., *The Territorial Papers of the United States,* vol. 13: *The Territory of Louisiana–Missouri, 1803–1806* (Washington, D.C.: Government Printing Office, 1948), 63; James Bruff to James Wilkinson, March 12, 1805, in ibid., 13:101–103; Frederick Bates to Henry Dearborn, May 15, 1807, in Marshall, ed., *The Life and Papers of Frederick Bates,* 1:119; Frederick Bates to Henry Dearborn, August 2, 1807, in ibid., 1:168–69.

50. Governor Wilkinson to the Secretary of War, October 8, 1805, in Carter, ed., *Territorial Papers,* 13:234; Governor Wilkinson to Secretary of War, December 10, 1805, in ibid., 13:298; Governor Wilkinson to Secretary of War, September 22, 1805, in ibid., 13:229; Frederick Bates to Secretary of War, May 15, 1807, in Marshall, ed., *The Life and Papers of Frederick Bates,* 1:119.

51. David J. Weber, *The Spanish Frontier in North America* (New Haven: Yale University Press, 1992), 291–95; Peter J. Kastor, *The Nation's Crucible: The Louisiana Purchase and the Creation of America* (New Haven: Yale University Press, 2004), 55–75.

52. James R. Bentley, ed., "Two Letters of Meriwether Lewis to Major William Preston," *Filson Club History Quarterly* 44 (April 1970): 172.

53. Frederick Bates to Richard Bates, March 24, 1808, in Marshall, ed., *The Life and Papers of Frederick Bates,* 1:316–17.

54. Governor Lewis to Nicholas Boilvin, May 14, 1808, in Clarence E. Carter, ed., *The Territorial Papers of the United States,* vol. 14: *The Territory of Louisiana–Missouri, 1806–1814* (Washington, D.C.: Government Printing Office, 1949), 217; Governor Lewis to the Secretary of War, August 20, 1808, in ibid., 14:214.

55. Jefferson quoted in J. Frederick Fausz, "Becoming 'a Nation of Quakers': The Removal of the Osage Indians from Missouri," *Gateway Heritage* 21 (Summer 2000): 32. See also Wallace, *Jefferson and the Indians,* 268–69.

56. Kate L. Gregg, ed., *Westward with Dragoons: The Journal of William Clark on His Expedition to Establish Fort Osage, August 25 to September 22, 1808* (Fulton, Mo.: Printed by the Ovid Bell Press, 1937), 58; Hammon, ed., *My Father, Daniel Boone,* 126; John K. Hulston, "Daniel Boone's Sons in Missouri," *Missouri Historical Review* 47 (July 1947): 366.

57. Gregg, ed., *Westward with Dragoons,* 39, 41. See Gregg, 64–68,

for the full text of Clark's 1808 treaty with the Osages. See also William Clark to the Secretary of War, September 23, 1808, in Carter, ed., *Territorial Papers*, 14:224; Jerome O. Steffen, *William Clark: Jeffersonian Man on the Frontier* (Norman: University of Oklahoma Press, 1977), 64–65.

58. Meriwether Lewis to Pierre Chouteau, October 3, 1808, in Carter, ed., *Territorial Papers*, 14:229; Meriwether Lewis to Thomas Jefferson, December 15, 1808, in McCarter & English Indian Claim Cases, box 18, folder 4, exhibit 144; Rollings, *The Osages*, 227–29.

59. Meriwether Lewis to Thomas Jefferson, December 15, 1808, in McCarter & English Indian Claim Cases, box 18, folder 4, exhibit 144.

60. Louis Lorimier to Acting Governor Browne, February 19, 1807, in Carter, ed., *Territorial Papers*, 14:112; Proclamation by Governor Lewis, April 6, 1809, in ibid., 261; "Petition of Louis Lorimier in the name and behalf of the Shawnee and Delaware Indians, settled within the Territory of Louisiana, August 16, 1806," Indian Collections, Missouri Historical Society, St. Louis; Schultz, *Travels on an Inland Voyage*, 35; Fortescue Cuming, *Sketches of a Tour to the Western Country, Through the States of Ohio and Kentucky; A Voyage Down the Ohio and Mississippi Rivers, and a Trip through the Mississippi Territory, and Part of West Florida* (Pittsburgh: Cramer, Spear & Eichbaum, 1810), 259; John Bradbury, *Travels in the Interior of America in the Years 1809, 1810, 1811* (1819; repr., Lincoln: University of Nebraska Press, 1986), 257; Stoddard, *Sketches, Historical and Descriptive, of Louisiana*, 210; Ruby Matson Robins, ed., "The Missouri Reader: Americans in the Valley," pt. 5, *Missouri Historical Review* 46 (October 1951): 53–54.

61. Proclamation by Governor Lewis, April 6, 1809, in Carter, ed., *Territorial Papers*, 14:261.

62. Frederick Bates to Richard Bates, July 14, 1809, in Marshall, ed., *The Life and Papers of Frederick Bates*, 2:68; Hurt, *Agriculture and Slavery*, 2.

63. Holt, "After the Journey Was Over," 44; Lemont K. Richardson, "Private Land Claims in Missouri," pts. 2 and 3, *Missouri Historical Review* 50 (April 1956): 282–83; 50 (July 1956): 387–90; Frederick Bates to Meriwether Lewis, January 26, 1808, in Marshall, ed., *The Life and Papers of Frederick Bates*, 1:268; Bates to Albert Gallatin, February 9, 1808, in ibid., 1:282; Bates to James Abbot, February 23, 1808, in ibid., 1:300.

64. Stuart Banner, *Legal Systems in Conflict: Property and Sover-*

eignty in Missouri, 1750–1860 (Norman: University of Oklahoma Press, 2000), 90, 93.

65. Ibid., 98.

66. William Carr to Charles Carr, August 25, 1809, William C. Carr Papers, Missouri Historical Society, St. Louis.

67. William Clark to Jonathan Clark, October 28, 1809, in James J. Holmberg, ed., *Dear Brother: Letters of William Clark to Jonathan Clark* (New Haven: Yale University Press, 2002), 216, 218; Larry E. Morris, *The Fate of the Corps: What Became of the Lewis and Clark Explorers after the Exploration* (New Haven: Yale University Press, 2004), 54–74, 203–209; Gary E. Moulton, "Meriwether Lewis," in Christensen et al., eds., *Dictionary of Missouri Biography*, 486; Paul Aron, *Unsolved Mysteries of American History* (New York: J. Wiley, 1997), 79–84; Kathryn Moore, "The Lost Years of Meriwether Lewis," *Journal of the West* 42 (Summer 2003): 62–65. Although suicide is currently the dominant view of Lewis's death, see J. Frederick Fausz and Michael A. Gavin, "The Death of Meriwether Lewis: An Unsolved Mystery," *Gateway Heritage* 24 (Fall 2003–Winter 2004): 66–79, for an interrogation of the evidence that suggests the case should not yet be considered closed.

68. Clark quoted in Fausz, "Becoming 'a Nation of Quakers,' " 37.

5. Quakes

1. Ruby Matson Robins, ed., "The Missouri Reader: Americans in the Valley," pt. 4, *Missouri Historical Review* 45 (July 1951): 392–93, 396, 390–91; "The Reminiscences of General Bernard Pratte Jr.," *Bulletin of the Missouri Historical Society* 6 (October 1949): 64; Timothy Flint, *Recollections of the Last Ten Years in the Valley of the Mississippi*, ed. George R. Brooks (1826; repr., Carbondale: Southern Illinois University Press, 1968), 161; Margaret Ross, "The New Madrid Earthquake," *Arkansas Historical Quarterly* 27 (Summer 1968): 83–104; Samuel W. Watkins, "The Causes and Cure of Earthquakes: Methodists and the New Madrid Earthquakes, 1811–1812," *Methodist History* 30 (July 1992): 242–50. Interestingly, the first earthquakes received very little attention in St. Louis, where the *Missouri Gazette* ran only short notices of their occurrences in the issues of December 16 and 21, 1811.

2. Rufus Babcock, ed., *Forty Years of Pioneer Life: Memoir of John Mason Peck, D.D.* (Carbondale: Southern Illinois University Press, 1965), 146.

3. Census figures in Frederic L. Billon, ed., *Annals of St. Louis in Its*

Territorial Days from 1804 to 1821 (St. Louis: Printed for the author, 1888), 34, 66.

4. William E. Foley, *The Genesis of Missouri: From Wilderness Outpost to Statehood* (Columbia: University of Missouri Press, 1989), 222–23, 283–84; Billon, ed., *Annals of St. Louis*, 22.

5. Landon Y. Jones Jr., "The Council That Changed the West: William Clark at Portage des Sioux," *Gateway Heritage* 24 (Fall 2003–Winter 2004): 89.

6. Quotation in Christian Wilt, Letter book, August 6, 1814, War of 1812 Papers, Missouri Historical Society, St. Louis. For other reports of Indians poised to attack, see the entries in Wilt's letter book for July 19, 1812, September 13, 1812, August 7, 1813, September 14, 1813, and *Missouri Gazette*, July 25, 1812; Billon, ed., *Annals of St. Louis*, 57–58; Jerome O. Steffen, *William Clark: Jeffersonian Man on the Frontier* (Norman: University of Oklahoma Press, 1977), 89–91. For conditions in the Boon's Lick Country during the War of 1812, see Edity S. Burris, "Patsy the Pioneer," undated manuscript in Western Historical Manuscripts Collections, C2947, State Historical Society of Missouri, Columbia; Nicholas Patterson and John Mason Peck, "The Boon's Lick Country: Two Gospel Preachers Explore a New Settlement," *Bulletin of the Missouri Historical Society* 6 (July 1950): 456; Ruby Matson Robins, ed., "The Missouri Reader: Americans in the Valley," pt. 8, *Missouri Historical Review* 46 (July 1952): 373–74; *Missouri Gazette*, May 14, 1814; Gary Bynum Letter, May 28, 1814, Western Historical Manuscripts Collections, C995, vol. 8, no. 212; R. Douglas Hurt, *Nathan Boone and the American Frontier* (Columbia: University of Missouri Press, 1998), 99.

7. Joseph Thorp, ed., *Early Days in the West: Along the Missouri One Hundred Years Ago—Letters by Judge Joseph Thorp* (Liberty, Mo.: I. Gilmer, 1924), 14–15.

8. Ibid.; "David Murphy's Book," October 13, 1813, Missouri Historical Society, St. Louis; Christian Wilt, Letter book, War of 1812 Papers, August 6, 1812, August 23, 1812; Kate L. Gregg, "The War of 1812 on the Missouri Frontier," pts. 1–3, *Missouri Historical Review* 33 (October 1938): 3–22; 33 (January 1939): 184–202; 33 (April 1939): 326–48.

9. Gregory Evans Dowd, *A Spirited Resistance: The North American Indian Struggle for Unity, 1745–1815* (Baltimore: Johns Hopkins University Press, 1992), 123–47.

10. Governor Howard to Pierre Chouteau, April 1813, in Clarence E. Carter, ed., *The Territorial Papers of the United States*, vol. 14: *The Territory of Louisiana–Missouri, 1806–1814* (Washington, D.C.: Gov-

ernment Printing Office, 1949), 674; William Clark to the Secretary of War, August 20, 1814, in ibid., 14:786; Benjamin Howard to Alexander Craighead, September 17, 1812, Craighead Papers, Missouri Historical Society, St. Louis; Jones, "The Council That Changed the West," 92.

11. Christian Wilt to Joseph Hertzog, August 6, 1814, Christian Wilt, Letter book; Joseph Persinger, *The Life and Adventures of Jacob Persinger* (Sturgeon, Mo.: Printed for the author by Moody & M'Michael, 1861), 17.

12. *Missouri Gazette*, April 8, 1815, and April 29, 1815, in Charles Van Ravenswaay Papers, Western Historical Manuscripts Collections, C3873; Steffen, *William Clark*, 95. See also Extract of a letter from William Clark to the Secretary of War, April 17, 1815, William Clark Papers, Missouri Historical Society.

13. Extract of a letter from Messers Clark, Edward & Chouteau, commissioners to treat with the Indian, May 22, 1815, William Clark Papers, Missouri Historical Society; G. C. Sibley to Samuel H. Sibley, August 20, 1815, Lindenwood Collection, Missouri Historical Society.

14. Governor William Clark, A Proclamation, December 4, 1815, in Clarence E. Carter, ed., *The Territorial Papers of the United States*, vol. 15: *The Territory of Louisiana–Missouri, 1815–1821* (Washington, D.C.: Government Printing Office, 1951), 192; Jones, "The Council That Changed the West," 95.

15. Justus Post to John Post, November 20, 1816, Justus Post Papers, Missouri Historical Society, St. Louis.

16. Walter A. Schroeder, *Opening the Ozarks: A Historical Geography of Missouri's Ste. Genevieve District, 1760–1830* (Columbia: University of Missouri Press, 2002), 146–47.

17. William Clark, "A Report of the Names and probable Number of the Tribes of Indians in the Missouri Territory, the Amount of Annuities paid them, the Amount of Expences of provisions issued to them at the Distribution of their Annuities and on every other occasion of the Amount of Presents other than provisions which ought to be distributed among them," November 4, 1816, Indian Collections, Missouri Historical Society, St. Louis; "The State of the Indians of Missouri Territory from Information 1817," Western Historical Manuscripts Collections, C1628, State Historical Society of Missouri, Columbia.

18. Ruby Matson Robins, ed., "The Missouri Reader: Americans in the Valley," pt. 3, *Missouri Historical Review* 45 (April 1951): 279; John C. Hudson, "North American Origins of Middlewestern Frontier Populations," *Annals of the Association of American Geographers* 78 (September 1988): 400.

19. Milton D. Rafferty, ed., *Rude Pursuits and Rugged Peaks: Schoolcraft's Ozark Journal, 1818–1819* (Fayetteville: University of Arkansas Press, 1996), 54, 98, 74. For a recent excavation of the material culture of Ozark pioneers, see Cynthia R. Price and James E. Price, "Investigation of Settlement and Subsistence Systems in the Ozark Border Region of Southeast Missouri during the First Half of the Nineteenth Century: The Widow Harris Cabin Project," *Ethnohistory* 28 (Summer 1981): 237–58. Among other findings, the Prices dispute the claim that Ozark pioneers depended primarily on wild game. Instead, their excavation of faunal assemblages showed a high proportion of hog bone. Pigs, though, were only semi-domesticated. In the Ozarks, as in earlier backcountries, hogs foraged on the open range.

20. Rafferty, ed., *Rude Pursuits and Rugged Peaks*, 78, 79, 70.

21. George Sibley letter from Fort Osage, October 1, 1820, in Rev. Jedidiah Morse, *A Report to the Secretary of War of the United States on Indian Affairs, Comprising a Narrative of a Tour Performed in the Summer of 1820, under a Commission from the President of the United States, for the Purpose of Ascertaining for the Use of the Government the Actual State of the Indian Tribes in Our Country* (New Haven: Converse, 1822), 207; George Sibley, "Indian Mode of Life in Missouri and Kansas," *Missouri Historical Review* 9 (October 1914): 48.

22. James F. Keefe and Lynn Morrow, eds., *The White River Chronicles of S.C. Turnbo: Man and Wildlife on the Ozarks Frontier* (Fayetteville: University of Arkansas Press, 1994), 1–13; Foley, *The Genesis of Missouri*, 217; Lynn Morrow, "Trader William Gilliss and Delaware Migration in Southern Missouri," *Missouri Historical Review* 75 (January 1981): 147–67.

23. Jay H. Buckley, "William Clark: Superintendent of Indian Affairs at St. Louis, 1813–1838" (Ph.D. dissertation, University of Nebraska, 2001), 136; Governor Clark to the President, January 22, 1816, in Carter, ed., *Territorial Papers*, 15:105.

24. John G. Heath to Frederick Bates, January 14, 1816, in Thomas Maitland Marshall, ed., *The Life and Papers of Frederick Bates*, 2 vols. (St. Louis: Missouri Historical Society, 1926), 2:297; Resolutions of the Territorial Assembly, January 22, 1816: To the Honourable the Senate and House of Representatives of the United States of America in Congress, in Carter, ed., *Territorial Papers*, 15:106–107; Resolutions of the Territorial Assembly Referred, January 24, 1817: Resolutions Concerning the Indian Title in the Counties of Ste. Genevieve and Cape Ger-

ardeau, in ibid., 235; Memoirs of David Meriwether, typescript at Filson Historical Society, Louisville, 71–72.

25. Copy of letter from Mr. Welch, Baptist Missionary to Corresponding Secretary, June 20, 1818, Robert McClure Snyder Jr. Papers, Western Historical Manuscripts Collections, Missouri State Historical Society, C3524, folder 62.

26. Schroeder, *Opening the Ozarks*, 379–80.

27. Nicholas Perkins Hardeman, *Wilderness Calling: The Hardeman Family in the American Westward Movement, 1750–1900* (Knoxville: University of Tennessee Press, 1977), 71; Frederic L. Billon, "Reminiscences of Our Removal to St. Louis," ed. Dana O. Jensen, *Bulletin of the Missouri Historical Society* 12 (April 1956): 278; Flint, *Recollections*, 147; Samuel R. Brown, *The Western Gazetteer; or, Emigrant's Directory. Containing a Geographical Description of the Western States and Territories, viz. The States of Kentucky, Indiana, Louisiana, Ohio, Tennessee, and Mississippi: and the Territories of Illinois, Missouri, Alabama, Michigan, and North-Western* (Auburn, N.Y.: Printed by H.C. Southwick, 1817), 192; Elijah Iles, *Sketches of Early Life and Times in Kentucky, Missouri, and Illinois* (Springfield, Ill.: Springfield Printing Co., 1883), 11–14.

28. "Journal of Henry Bousfield of a trip through Missouri in 1819," Journals and Diaries Envelope, Missouri Historical Society, St. Louis, 14; Iles, *Sketches of Early Life and Times in Kentucky, Missouri and Illinois*, 15; R. Douglas Hurt, "Seeking Fortune in the Promised Land: Settling the Boon's Lick Country, 1808–1825," *Gateway Heritage* 13 (Summer 1992): 4–19; Michael J. O'Brien et al., *Grassland, Forest, and Historical Settlement: An Analysis of Dynamics in Northeast Missouri* (Lincoln: University of Nebraska Press, 1984), 75; Leslie Hewes and Christian L. Jung, "Early Fencing on the Middle Western Prairie," *Annals of the Association of American Geographers* 71 (June 1981): 187; Terry G. Jordan, "Between the Forest and the Prairie," *Agricultural History* 38 (October, 1964): 205–16.

29. R. Douglas Hurt, *Agriculture and Slavery in Missouri's Little Dixie* (Columbia: University of Missouri Press, 1992), 24–37, 45–46; Stuart F. Voss, "Town Growth in Central Missouri, 1815–1880: An Urban Chaparral," pt. 1, *Missouri Historical Review* 64 (October 1969): 69–70.

30. Memorial quoted in William E. Foley, *A History of Missouri*, vol. 1: *1673–1820* (Columbia: University of Missouri Press, 1971), 172; Babcock, ed., *Forty Years of Pioneer Life*, 147; David Manchester to Sister, April 19, 1819, David Manchester Letters, Western Historical Manuscripts Collection, C2064, Missouri State Historical Society, Columbia; Marie George

Wendell, ed., "The Road West in 1818, The Diary of Henry Vest Bingham," pt. 1, *Missouri Historical Review* 40 (1945–46): 186.

31. James W. Goodrich and Lynn Wolf Gentzler, eds., "'I Well Remember': David Holmes Conrad's Recollections of St. Louis, 1819–1823," pt. 1, *Missouri Historical Review* 90 (October 1995): 25; Justus Post to Brother, December 5, 1817, Justus Post Letter, Western Historical Manuscripts Collection, C1976, Missouri State Historical Society, Columbia; Wendell, ed., "The Road West in 1818," 30; Ruby Matson Robins, ed., "The Missouri Reader: Americans in the Valley," pt. 5, *Missouri Historical Review* 46 (October 1951): 63; Flint, *Recollections,* 137; Dorothy B. Dorsey, "The Panic of 1819 in Missouri," *Missouri Historical Review* 29 (January 1935): 79–80.

32. The poem, which was published in the *Missouri Intelligencer,* August 20, 1819, was found in the Charles Van Ravenswaay Papers, Western Historical Manuscripts Collection, C3873, Missouri State Historical Society, 58–59.

33. Hudson, "North American Origins of Middlewestern Frontier Populations," 399–400; Richard Maxwell Brown, "Backcountry Rebellions and the Homestead Ethic in America, 1740–1799," in Richard Maxwell Brown and Don E. Fehrenbacher, eds., *Tradition, Conflict, and Modernization: Perspectives on the American Revolution* (New York: Academic Press, 1977), 73–99; Stephen Aron, *How the West Was Lost: The Transformation of Kentucky from Daniel Boone to Henry Clay* (Baltimore: Johns Hopkins University Press, 1996), 58–81; Daniel Blake Smith, "'This Idea in Heaven': Image and Reality on the Kentucky Frontier," in Craig Thompson Friend, ed., *The Buzzel about Kentuck: Settling the Promised Land* (Lexington: University Press of Kentucky, 1999), 77–98; John R. Finger, *Tennessee Frontiers: Three Regions in Transition* (Bloomington: Indiana University Press, 2001), 99–124.

34. Stephen Aron, "Pioneers and Profiteers: Land Speculation and the Homestead Ethic in Frontier Kentucky," *Western Historical Quarterly* 23 (May 1992): 192–98.

35. Glen E. Holt, "St. Louis's Transition Decade, 1819–1830," *Missouri Historical Review* 76 (July 1982): 367; Lloyd A. Hunter, "Slavery in St. Louis, 1804–1860," *Bulletin of the Missouri Historical Society* 30 (July 1974): 235–36; Richard C. Wade, *The Urban Frontier: Pioneer Life in Early Pittsburgh, Cincinnati, Lexington, Louisville, and St. Louis* (Chicago: University of Chicago Press, 1959), 125; Jeffrey S. Adler, *Yankee Merchants and the Making of the Urban West: The Rise and Fall of Antebellum St. Louis* (New York: Cambridge University

Press, 1991), 17; Maximilian Richard, "Black and White on the Urban Frontier: The St. Louis Community in Transition, 1800–1830," *Bulletin of the Missouri Historical Society* 33 (July 1976): 3–17.

36. Christian Wilt to Joseph Hertzog, March 19, 1814, Christian Wilt Letter book; Henry R. Schoolcraft, *Travels in the Central Portions of the Mississippi Valley: Comprising Observations on Its Mineral Geography, Internal Resources, and Aboriginal Population* (New York: Collins and Hannay, 1825), 227–28; William Darby, *The Emigrant's Guide to the Western and Southwestern States and Territories* (New York: Kirk and Mircein, 1818), 143.

37. Foley, *The Genesis of Missouri*, 244–45.

38. John Darby, *Personal Recollections of Many Prominent People Whom I Have Known, and of Events—Especially of Those Relating to the History of St. Louis—during the First Half of the Present Century* (St. Louis: G. I. Jones, 1880), 5; Goodrich and Gentzler, eds., "I Well Remember," 9–10; Wendell, ed., "The Road West in 1818," 182–83; Harvey Wish, "The French of Old Missouri (1804–1821): A Study in Assimilation," *Mid-America: An Historical Review* 23 (July 1941): 188; Marshall Smelser, "Housing in Creole St. Louis, 1764–1821: An Example of Cultural Change," *Louisiana Historical Quarterly* 21 (April 1938): 347–48.

39. Jerome O. Steffen, "William Clark: A New Perspective of Missouri Territorial Politics, 1813–1820," *Missouri Historical Review* 47 (January 1973): 171–97; Foley, *The Genesis of Missouri*, 257.

40. Edward Bates to Frederick Bates, December 18, 1815, in Marshall, ed., *The Life and Papers of Frederick Bates*, 2:295–96; Foley, *The Genesis of Missouri*, 287; Steffen, *William Clark*, 105–109.

41. Darby, *Personal Recollections*, 5.

42. Arvarh E. Strickland, "Aspects of Slavery in Missouri, 1821," *Missouri Historical Review* 65 (July 1971): 505–26; Hunter, "Slavery in St. Louis," 235–36; Wade, *The Urban Frontier*, 125; Donnie D. Bellamy, "Free Blacks in Antebellum Missouri, 1820–1860," *Missouri Historical Review* 67 (January 1973): 200.

43. Flint, *Recollections*, 201; Frederick Bates to Caroline M. Bates, July 19, 1812, in Marshall, ed., *The Life and Papers of Frederick Bates*, 2:228; Lucy Witcher Blythe, "The Early Settlers of Missouri: My Grandparents Emigrating to This State," Western Historical Manuscripts Collections, State Historical Society of Missouri, Columbia, C995, vol. 12, no. 351; Michael J. Cassity, *Defending a Way of Life: An American Community in the Nineteenth Century* (Albany: State University of New York Press, 1989), 28–31; Samuel Bannister Harding,

Life of George R. Smith: Founder of Sedalia, Mo. (Sedalia, Mo.: Privately printed, 1904), 49–52.

44. Harding, *Life of George R. Smith*, 20; William Clark to Jonathan Clark, May 28, 1809, in James J. Holmberg, ed., *Dear Brother: Letters of William Clark to Jonathan Clark* (New Haven: Yale University Press, 2002), 201; William Clark to Jonathan Clark, December 10, 1808, in ibid., 184; William Clark to Jonathan Clark, November 9, 1808, in ibid., 160; James J. Holmberg, " 'A Notion about Freedom': The Relationship of William Clark and York," *Gateway Heritage* 24 (Fall 2003–Winter 2004): 80–87.

45. Robert B. Betts, *In Search of York: The Slave Who Went to the Pacific with Lewis and Clark*, rev. ed. (Boulder: University Press of Colorado, 2000), 106–32, 151–70; Holmberg, ed., *Dear Brother*, 13, 158–59, 161, 193, 197, 199; Larry E. Morris, *The Fate of the Corps: What Became of the Lewis and Clark Explorers after the Exploration* (New Haven: Yale University Press, 2004), 139–48; Thomas P. Slaughter, *Exploring Lewis and Clark: Reflections on Men and Wilderness* (New York: Knopf, 2003), 114–33; Foley, *The Genesis of Missouri*, 255–56.

46. Babcock, ed., *Forty Years of Pioneer Life*, 90; William G. Bek, trans., "Gottfried Duden's 'Report,' 1824–1827," Fifth Article, *Missouri Historical Review* 13 (October 1918): 53; Alice H. Finckh, ed., "Gottfried Duden Views Missouri 1824–1827," pt. 1, *Missouri Historical Review* 43 (July 1949): 334–43; Hunter, "Slavery in St. Louis," 234, 244.

47. Troen and Holt, eds., *St. Louis*, 32; Henry S. Geyer, ed., *A Digest of the Laws of Missouri Territory* (St. Louis: Printed for the publisher by Joseph Charless at the Missouri Gazette Office, 1818), 376; for a full listing of the Territory's slave code, see ibid., 373–84; Bellamy, "Free Blacks," 198–200; Richard, "Black and White on the Urban Frontier," 7.

48. William Clark to Jonathan Clark, January 2, 1809, in Holmberg, ed., *Dear Brother*, 190; Foley, *The Genesis of Missouri*, 256.

49. Jefferson penned these lines in a letter, dated April 22, 1820, to Congressman John Holmes. Quoted in Stuart Leibiger, "Thomas Jefferson and the Missouri Crisis: An Alternative Interpretation," *Journal of the Early Republic* 17 (Spring 1997): 124.

50. Perry McCandless, *A History of Missouri*, vol. 2, *1820–1860* (Columbia: University of Missouri Press, 1972), 1–2; David D. March, "The Admission of Missouri," *Missouri Historical Review* 65 (July 1971): 427–49.

51. McCandless, *A History of Missouri*, 6; John D. Morton, " 'This

Magnificent New World': Thomas Hart Benton's Westward Vision Reconsidered," *Missouri Historical Review* 90 (April 1996): 297–302; Robert J. Brugger, *Beverley Tucker: Heart over Head in the Old South* (Baltimore: Johns Hopkins University Press, 1978), 54; Walter Williams and Floyd Calvin Shoemaker, *Missouri: Mother of the West*, 5 vols. (Chicago: American Historical Society, 1930), 1:345–64.

52. David Manchester, Letter, 1819, Western Historical Manuscripts Collection, C2064, State Historical Society of Missouri, Columbia; Morton, " 'This Magnificent New World,' " 303.

53. Thomas H. Benton to Thomas Claiborne, December 15, 1817, O'Fallon Family Papers, Western Manuscripts Historical Collection, SUNP2984, State Historical Society of Missouri, Columbia; Morton, " 'This Magnificent New World,' " 304.

54. Junius P. Rodriguez, ed., *The Louisiana Purchase: A Historical and Geographical Encyclopedia* (Santa Barbara: ABC-CLIO, 2002), 228–29; Glover Moore, *The Missouri Controversy, 1819–1821* (Lexington: University of Kentucky Press, 1953).

55. Leibiger, "Thomas Jefferson and the Missouri Crisis," 121.

56. Bellamy, "Free Blacks," 199.

57. Gerald T. Dunne, *The Missouri Supreme Court: From Dred Scott to Nancy Cruzan* (Columbia: University of Missouri Press, 1993), 9.

58. Steffen, *William Clark*, 122–23; Hurt, *Nathan Boone*, 116–17; William E. Foley, "The Political Philosophy of David Barton," *Missouri Historical Review* 58 (April 1964): 278–79; Aron, *How the West Was Lost*, 89–100; Joan Wells Coward, *Kentucky in the New Republic: The Process of Constitution Making* (Lexington: University Press of Kentucky, 1979); John Barnhart, *Valley of Democracy: The Frontier versus the Plantation in the Ohio Valley, 1775–1818* (Bloomington: Indiana University Press, 1953).

59. Steffen, *William Clark*, 125.

60. William E. Foley, "After the Applause: William Clark's Failed 1820 Gubernatorial Campaign," *Gateway Heritage* 24 (Fall 2003–Winter 2004): 108; Buckley, "William Clark," 143; Frances Lea McCurdy, *Stump, Bar, and Pulpit: Speechmaking on the Missouri Frontier* (Columbia: University of Missouri Press, 1969), 86–87.

61. The quotation and the full text of the March 2, 1821, "Resolution providing for the admission or the state of Missouri into the Union on a certain condition" can be found on the web. See John Wallis, NBER/Maryland State Constitutions Project, http://129.2.168.174/Constitution/Thorpe/display.aspx?ID=66. This Web site also includes the full text of the Missouri constitution of 1820 and President James

Monroe's proclamation of August 10, 1821, which formally admitted Missouri as a state.

62. George Sibley to William Clark, February 2, 1819, in McCarter & English Indian Claim Cases, box 2, folder 15, exhibit 5, Mudd Library, Princeton University.

6. Closings

1. Governor John Miller, Second Inaugural Address, November 18, 1828, in Buel Leopard and Floyd C. Shoemaker, eds., *The Messages and Proclamations of the Governors of the State of Missouri* (Columbia: University of Missouri Press, 1922), 1:131. For an interpretation of the closing of the frontier in Missouri as a example of state-sponsored ethnic cleansing, see John Mack Faragher, " 'More Motley than Mackinaw': From Ethnic Mixing to Ethnic Cleansing on the Frontier of the Lower Missouri," in Andrew R. L. Cayton and Fredrika J. Teute, eds., *Contact Points: American Frontiers from the Mohawk Valley to the Mississippi, 1750–1830* (Chapel Hill: University of North Carolina Press, 1998), 304–26.

2. Adams quoted in Richard H. Brown, "The Missouri Crisis, Slavery, and the Politics of Jacksonianism," *South Atlantic Quarterly* 65 (Winter 1966): 57.

3. Donald J. Abramoske, "The Public Lands in Early Missouri Politics," *Missouri Historical Review* 53 (July 1959): 295–96; "Descriptions of St. Louis: Report of French Staff Officer—1796," Missouri Historical Society, *Glimpses of the Past* 1 (March 1934): 28.

4. *Missouri Gazette*, July 14, 1819; Glen E. Holt, "St. Louis's Transition Decade, 1819–1830," *Missouri Historical Review* 76 (July 1982): 369–71.

5. Dorothy B. Dorsey, "The Panic of 1819 in Missouri," *Missouri Historical Review* 29 (January 1935): 82.

6. Harry S. Gleick, "Banking in Early Missouri," pt. 1, *Missouri Historical Review* 61 (July 1967): 427–28; William E. Foley, "Justus Post: Portrait of a Frontier Land Speculator," *Bulletin of the Missouri Historical Society* 36 (October 1979): 22–25; James Neal Primm, *Economic Policy in the Development of a Western State: Missouri, 1820–1860* (Cambridge: Harvard University Press, 1954), 1–17.

7. "Descriptions of St. Louis," 28; Jeffrey S. Adler, *Yankee Merchants and the Making of the Urban West: The Rise and Fall of Antebellum St. Louis* (New York: Cambridge University Press, 1991), 18–21, 17. The full text of Missouri's 1820 Constitution, including Article VIII (dealing with banks and stockholder liability) is available on the Web.

See John Wallis, NBER/Maryland State Constitutions Project, http://129.2.168.174/Constitution/Thorpe/display.aspx?ID=66.

8. Dorsey, "The Panic of 1819 in Missouri," 85–87; Samuel H. Rezneck, "The Depression of 1819–1822: A Social History," *American Historical Review* 39 (October 1933): 28–47; Murray N. Rothbard, *The Panic of 1819: Reactions and Policies* (New York: Columbia University Press, 1962); Charles Sellers, *The Market Revolution: Jacksonian America, 1815–1846* (New York: Oxford University Press, 1991), 103–71.

9. Primm, *Economic Policy*, 11.

10. Robert J. Brugger, *Beverley Tucker: Heart over Head in the Old South* (Baltimore: Johns Hopkins University Press, 1978), 62–63.

11. Ibid., 63.

12. *Missouri Republican*, September 4, 1822; Arndt Stickles, *The Critical Court Struggle in Kentucky, 1819–1829* (Bloomington: Indiana University Press, 1929); Matthew Gerard Schoenbachler, "The Origins of Jacksonian Politics: Central Kentucky, 1790–1840" (Ph.D. dissertation, University of Kentucky, 1996).

13. Abramoske, "The Public Lands in Early Missouri Politics," 296–97; Perry McCandless, *A History of Missouri*, vol. 2: *1820–1860* (Columbia: University of Missouri Press, 1972), 71.

14. Ronald L. F. Davis, "Community and Conflict in Pioneer Saint Louis, Missouri," *Western Historical Quarterly* 10 (July 1979): 353–55; Robert E. Shalhope, "Thomas Hart Benton and Missouri State Politics: A Re-examination," *Bulletin of the Missouri Historical Society* 25 (April 1969): 171–91. For biographies of Benton, see William N. Chambers, *Old Bullion Benton: Senator from the West* (Boston: Little, Brown, 1956), and Elbert B. Smith, *Magnificent Missourian: The Life of Thomas Hart Benton* (Philadelphia: Lippincott, 1958).

15. *Gales and Seaton's Register of Debates in Congress, Comprising the Leading Debates and Incidents of the First Session of the Nineteenth Congress* (Washington, D.C.: Gales and Seaton, 1826), 727–29; *Gales and Seaton's Register of Debates in Congress, Comprising the Leading Debates and Incidents of the First Session of the Twentieth Congress* (Washington, D.C.: Gales and Seaton, 1828), 23; Perry McCandless, "Benton v. Barton: The Formation of the Second-Party System," *Missouri Historical Review* 79 (February 1985): 431.

16. *Gales and Seaton's Register of Debates . . . Twentieth Congress*, 486; William E. Foley, "The Political Philosophy of David Barton," *Missouri Historical Review* 58 (April 1964): 283–86; McCandless, "Benton v. Barton," 425–32.

17. Thomas Hart Benton, *Thirty Years' View; or, A History of the*

Working of the American Government for Thirty Years, from 1820 to 1850, 2 vols. (New York: D. Appleton, 1854–56), 1:103; R. Douglas Hurt, *Agriculture and Slavery in Missouri's Little Dixie* (Columbia: University of Missouri Press, 1992), 48; McCandless, *A History of Missouri*, 85; Byron G. Lander, "Missouri and the Presidential Election of 1828," *Missouri Historical Review* 71 (June 1977): 419–35.

18. Elmer T. Clark, ed., *The Journal of the Reverend Jacob Lanius*, January 17, 1834, typescript at Filson Historical Society, Louisville.

19. Hattie M. Anderson, "Missouri, 1804–1828: Peopling a Frontier State," *Missouri Historical Review* 31 (January 1937): 174.

20. Russell L. Gerlach, *Settlement Patterns in Missouri: A Study of Population Origins* (Columbia: University of Missouri Press, 1986); Russell L. Gerlach, "Population Origins in Rural Missouri," *Missouri Historical Review* 71 (October 1976): 1–21; James R. Shortridge, "The Expansion of the Settlement Frontier in Missouri," *Missouri Historical Review* 75 (October 1980): 64–90.

21. "Views of Missouri by an Anglo-American," *Bulletin of the Missouri Historical Society* 28 (October 1971): 47–48; Marie George Windell, ed., "Westward along the Boone's Lick Trail in 1826: The Diary of Colonel John Glover," *Missouri Historical Review* 39 (January 1945): 184; "Two Letters from St. Charles," *Missouri Historical Review* 55 (October 1960): 33–34; Charles Augustus Murray, *Travels in North America during the Years 1834, 1835, & 1836*, 2 vols. (New York: Harper, 1839), 1:174; Hurt, *Agriculture and Slavery*, 80–124, 187–88, 215–44; Michael J. Cassity, *Defending a Way of Life: An American Community in the Nineteenth Century* (Albany: State University of New York Press, 1989), 3–19.

22. Frederick S. Klein, ed., "Letters of a Young Surveyor, 1828–1829," *Missouri Historical Review* 23 (October 1928): 70; Sealsfield and Flint quoted in Holt, "St. Louis's Transition Decade," 379.

23. Adler, *Yankee Merchants*, 23–24.

24. For Astor and his operations, see James P. Ronda, *Astoria and Empire* (Lincoln: University of Nebraska Press, 1990); John D. Haeger, "Business Strategy and Practice in the Early Republic: John Jacob Astor and the American Fur Trade," *Western Historical Quarterly* 19 (May 1988): 183–202; Richard E. Ogelsby, "John Jacob Astor: 'A Better Businessman than the Best of Them,'" *Journal of the West* 25 (January 1986): 8–14; David Lavender, "Some American Characteristics of the American Fur Company," *Minnesota History* 40 (Winter 1966): 178–87. For the entrance of New York and Boston firms and the migration of "Yankee" traders, see Adler, *Yankee Merchants*, 25–29.

25. James W. Goodrich and Lynn Wolf Gentzler, eds., "'I Well Remember': David Holmes Conrad's Recollections of St. Louis, 1819–1823," pt. 1, *Missouri Historical Review* 90 (October 1995): 32–33. On Ashley and the reorganization of the fur trade, see Dale L. Morgan, ed., *The West of William H. Ashley* (Denver: Old West, 1965), and Richard M. Clokey, *William H. Ashley: Enterprise and Politics in the Trans-Mississippi West* (Norman: University of Oklahoma Press, 1980).

26. McCandless, *A History of Missouri*, 129; James W. Covington, ed., "Correspondence between Mexican Officials at Santa Fe and Officials in Missouri, 1823–1825," *Bulletin of the Missouri Historical Society* 16 (October 1959): 21–22; David Meriwether, "Memoirs," typescript at Filson Historical Society, Louisville, see esp. 50–65.

27. Lewis E. Atherton, "The Santa Fe Trader as Mercantile Capitalist," *Missouri Historical Review* 77 (October 1982): 1–12; Mark L. Gardner, ed., "The Mexican Road: Trade, Travel, and Confrontation on the Santa Fe Trail," *Journal of the West* 28 (April 1989): 3–87; Holt, "St. Louis's Transition Decade," 376.

28. Jeffrey S. Adler, "Yankee Colonizers and the Making of Antebellum St. Louis," *Gateway Heritage* 12 (Winter 1992): 7.

29. William G. Bek, trans., "Gottfried Duden's 'Report,' 1824–1827," Second and Third Articles, *Missouri Historical Review* 12 (January 1918): 87, 82; 12 (April 1918): 171, 177; Alice H. Finckh, ed., "Gottfried Duden Views Missouri, 1824–1827," pts. 1 and 2, *Missouri Historical Review* 43 (July 1949): 334–43; 44 (October 1949): 21–30; James W. Goodrich, "Gottfried Duden: A Nineteenth-Century Missouri Promoter," *Missouri Historical Review* 75 (January 1981): 131–46; William E. Lass, "Tourists' Impressions of St. Louis, 1766–1859," pt. 1, *Missouri Historical Review* 52 (July 1958): 331.

30. Rev. Jedidiah Morse, *A Report to the Secretary of War of the United States on Indian Affairs, Comprising a Narrative of a Tour Performed in the Summer of 1820, under a Commission from the President of the United States, for the Purpose of Ascertaining for the Use of the Government the Actual State of the Indian Tribes in Our Country* (New Haven: Converse, 1822), 366; "Statement Showing the Names and Numbers of the Different Tribes of Indians Now Remaining within the Limits of the Several States and Territories, and the Quantity of Land Claimed by Them, Respectively," Department of War, Office of Indian Affairs, December 21, 1824, in McCarter & English Indian Claim Cases, box 3, folder 10, Mudd Library, Princeton University.

31. Graham quoted in Willard H. Rollings, *The Osage: An Ethnohis-*

torical Study of Hegemony on the Prairie-Plains (Columbia: University of Missouri Press, 1992), 235; Speech of Keokuck to the Secretary of War, December 8, 1823, with Remarks in Council for Treaty of August 4, 1824, in McCarter & English Indian Claim Cases, box 18, folder 1, exhibit 87; James R. Christianson, "The Early Osage: 'The Ishmaelites of the Savages,'" *Kansas History* 11 (1988): 11–15.

32. William Clark to John C. Calhoun, April 29, 1824, in Letters Received by the Office of Indian Affairs, 1824–81, roll 747, St. Louis Superintendency, 1824–51, National Archives (copies in U.S. Superintendency of Indian Affairs, St. Louis, Records, 1824–51, Western Historical Manuscripts Collection, C2970, State Historical Society of Missouri, Columbia); Richard Graham to Anderson, Chief of the Delawares, March 1826, and John Campbell to Major Richard Graham, March 16, 1826, in Richard Graham Papers, Missouri Historical Society, St. Louis; Rollings, *The Osage*, 250–51, 278.

33. John C. Calhoun to Richard Graham, April 22, 1822, Richard Graham Papers; William Clark to Secretary of War, October 20, 1827, McCarter & English Indian Claim Cases, box 2, folder 9, exhibit 96; Richard W. Cummins to William Clark, February 18, 1833, U.S. Superintendency of Indian Affairs, St. Louis Records, 1807–55, Kansas State Historical Society, Topeka; Stephen A. Warren, "The Baptists, the Methodists, and the Shawnees: Conflicting Cultures in Indian Territory, 1833–34," *Kansas History* 17 (Autumn 1994): 149–61.

34. S.P. Pettis to President James Monroe, March 20, 1821, McCarter & English Indian Claim Cases, box 18, folder 1, exhibit 71. For additional examples of disputes between whites and Indians over property damages and thefts, as well as personal injuries, see William F. McMurtry to A. T. Crawford, January 31, 1824, Woods-Holman Family Papers, Western Historical Manuscripts Collection, C191, State Historical Society of Missouri, Columbia; and the following correspondence from the Richard Graham Papers: Richard Graham to Mr. Owings, April 29, 1823; Richard Graham to Col. R. Easton, September 18, 1823; R. Easton to Richard Graham, September 30, 1823.

35. Jay H. Buckley, "William Clark: Superintendent of Indian Affairs at St. Louis, 1813–1838" (Ph.D. dissertation, University of Nebraska, 2001), 203.

36. John Campbell (Anderson's Village) to Major R. Graham, October 1, 1825, Richard Graham Papers. See also Tanis C. Thorne, "'Liquor Has Been Their Undoing': Liquor Trafficking and Alcohol Abuse in the Lower Missouri Fur Trade," *Gateway Heritage* 13 (Fall 1992): 4–23.

37. "Mr. Benton, . . . communicating the Memorial of the General Assembly of the State of Missouri, on the subject of Indians residing within that state," May 14, 1824, 18th Cong., 1st sess., 1824, S. Doc. 79, 1.

38. Sally Dodge to Mary Gale, January 23, 1825, and Philena Modrel to Betsey Gale, May 17, 1829, in Missouri Pioneer Letters, 1822–36, vol. 14, no. 424, Western Historical Manuscripts Collection, C995, State Historical Society of Missouri, Columbia; Sarah J. Gregory, ed., "Pioneer Housewife: The Autobiography of Sally Dodge Morris," *Gateway Heritage* 3 (Spring 1983): 26; McCandless, *A History of Missouri*, 52.

39. S. G. Hopkins to Major Richard Graham, August 6, 1825, Richard Graham Papers.

40. William Clark to John C. Calhoun, April 29, 1824, U.S. Superintendency of Indian Affairs, St. Louis, Records, 1824–51.

41. Benton, *Thirty Years' View*, 1:28. My thanks to Louise Pubols for pointing me to this reference.

42. "Mr. Benton, . . . communicating the Memorial of the General Assembly of the State of Missouri, on the subject of Indians residing within that state," May 14, 1824, 18th Cong., 1st sess., 1824, S. Doc. 79, 1.

43. Ibid., 2–3; David Barton to John C. Calhoun, September 6, 1822, McCarter & English Indian Claim Cases, box 18, folder 4, exhibit 150; Duff Green to Calhoun, December 9, 1821, Indian Collections, Missouri Historical Society, St. Louis.

44. Governor Alexander McNair, Second Annual Message, November 4, 1822, in Leopard and Shoemaker, eds., *Messages and Proclamations*, 1:33; Governor John Miller, First Inaugural Address, January 20, 1826, in ibid., 1:113; Governor John Miller, Second Inaugural Address, November 18, 1828, in ibid., 1:131.

45. Timothy Flint, *Recollections of the Last Ten Years in the Valley of the Mississippi*, ed. George R. Brooks (1926; repr., Carbondale: Southern Illinois University Press, 1968), 117, 119.

46. John Scott to the Secretary of War, September 21, 1820, in Clarence E. Carter, ed., *The Territorial Papers of the United States*, vol. 15: *The Territory of Louisiana–Missouri, 1815–1821* (Washington, D.C.: Government Printing Office, 1951), 646.

47. J. Frederick Fausz, "Becoming 'a Nation of Quakers': The Removal of the Osage Indians from Missouri," *Gateway Heritage* 21 (Summer 2000): 38; Walter A. Schroeder, *Opening the Ozarks: A Historical Geography of Missouri's Ste. Genevieve District, 1760–1830* (Columbia: University of Missouri Press, 2002), 194, 381–82.

48. William Clark (St. Louis) to the Secretary of War, December 8, 1823, McCarter & English Indian Claim Cases, box 18, folder 2, exhibit

91; William Clark to Secretary of War, June 1, 1829, ibid., box 24, folder 2, exhibit 205.

49. William Clark to Secretary of War, March 1, 1826, in Walter Lowrie and Walter Franklin, eds., *American State Papers*, Class II: *Indian Affairs*, 2 vols. (Washington, D.C.: Gales and Seaton, 1834), 2:653.

50. William Clark to Secretary of War, June 1, 1829, McCarter & English Indian Claim Cases, box 24, folder 2, exhibit 205.

51. For a fresh perspective on Indian activism during the era of removal, see John Bowes, "Opportunity and Adversity: Indians and American Expansion in the Nineteenth-Century Trans-Mississippi West" (Ph.D. dissertation, University of California, Los Angeles, 2003).

52. Governor John Miller, "To the Senate," November 29, 1830, in Leopard and Shoemaker, eds., *Messages and Proclamations*, 1:202.

53. Fausz, "Becoming 'a Nation of Quakers,'" 38.

54. Tanis C. Thorne, *The Many Hands of My Relations: French and Indians on the Lower Missouri* (Columbia: University of Missouri Press, 1996); Thorne, "'Liquor Has Been Their Undoing,'" 5–7.

55. Maximilian Richard, "Black and White on the Urban Frontier: The St. Louis Community in Transition, 1800–1830," *Bulletin of the Missouri Historical Society* 33 (October 1976): 11–12; Donnie D. Bellamy, "Free Blacks in Antebellum Missouri, 1820–1860," *Missouri Historical Review* 67 (January 1973): 200, 208; Lloyd A. Hunter, "Slavery in St. Louis, 1804–1860," *Bulletin of the Missouri Historical Society* 30 (July 1974): 232–65.

56. Conevery Bolton Valencius, *The Health of the Country: How American Settlers Understood Themselves and Their Land* (New York: Basic Books, 2002), 254; Bellamy, "Free Blacks," 201, 211, 219; Gerald T. Dunne, *The Missouri Supreme Court: From Dred Scott to Nancy Cruzan* (Columbia: University of Missouri Press, 1993), 27–28; Robert Moore Jr., "A Ray of Hope, Extinguished: St. Louis Slave Suits for Freedom," *Gateway Heritage* 14 (Winter 1993–94): 4–15.

57. Moore, "A Ray of Hope, Extinguished," 8–10.

58. Flint, *Recollections*, 110; Governor John Miller, "To the Senate," January 15, 1831, in Leopard and Shoemaker, eds., *Messages and Proclamations*, 1:189; Governor John Miller, "Third Biennial Address," November 20, 1832, in ibid., 171. See also William F. Switzler, "Diary of a Trip to the South," 4, Missouri Historical Society, St. Louis; William G. Bek, trans., "Gottfried Duden's 'Report,'" Fourth Article, *Missouri Historical Review* 12 (July 1918): 269–70.

Epilogue

1. Jay H. Buckley, "William Clark: Superintendent of Indian Affairs at St. Louis, 1813–1838" (Ph.D. dissertation, University of Nebraska, 2001), 268.

2. On the waning and waxing of popular interest in Lewis and Clark, see Betty Houchin Winfield, "Public Perception of the Expedition," in Alan Taylor, ed., *Lewis and Clark: Journey to Another America* (St. Louis: Missouri Historical Society Press, 2003), 178–99; John Spencer, " 'We Are Not Dealing Entirely with the Past': Americans Remember Lewis and Clark," in Kris Fresonke and Mark Spence, eds., *Lewis and Clark: Legacies, Memories, and New Perspectives* (Berkeley: University of California Press, 2004), 159–83.

3. For the wonderful companion volume to the bicentennial exhibition, see Carolyn Gilman, *Lewis and Clark: Across the Divide* (Washington, D.C.: Smithsonian Institution, 2003). For recent studies of Sacagawea, see Virginia Scharff, *Twenty Thousand Roads: Women, Movement, and the West* (Berkeley: University of California Press, 2003), 11–33; Thomas P. Slaughter, *Exploring Lewis and Clark: Reflections on Men and Wilderness* (New York: Knopf, 2003), 86–113; Laura McCall, "Sacagawea: A Historical Enigma," in Kriste Lindenmeyer, ed., *Ordinary Women, Extraordinary Lives: Women in American History* (Wilmington, Del.: SR Books, 2000), 39–54.

4. Thomas Maitland Marshall, ed., *The Life and Papers of Frederick Bates*, 2 vols. (St. Louis: Missouri Historical Society, 1926), 1:30.

5. Buckley, "William Clark," 114; John L. Loos, "William Clark: Indian Agent," *Kansas Quarterly* 3 (Fall 1971): 29–38.

6. "Boon's Lick Folk Tales," *Bulletin of the Missouri Historical Society* 6 (July 1950): 483; Sarah J. Gregory, "Pioneer Housewife: The Autobiography of Sally Dodge Morris," *Gateway Heritage* 3 (Spring 1983): 31; John Francis McDermott, ed., *Tixier's Travels on the Osage Prairies*, trans. Albert J. Salvan (Norman: University of Oklahoma Press, 1940), 99–100; R. Douglas Hurt, *Nathan Boone and the American Frontier* (Columbia: University of Missouri Press, 1998), 187; Willard H. Rollings, *The Osage: An Ethnohistorical Study of Hegemony on the Prairie-Plains* (Columbia: University of Missouri Press, 1992), 280.

7. John Dougherty to William Clark, September 10, 1828, in John A. Dougherty, Letter book, 1826–29, Western Historical Manuscripts Collection, State Historical Society of Missouri, Columbia, C2292, Letter 65. See also Landon Y. Jones Jr., *William Clark and the Shaping of the West* (New York: Hill and Wang, 2004), 296–334; William E. Foley,

Wilderness Journey: The Life of William Clark (Columbia: University of Missouri Press, 2004), 226–64.

8. For these letters, see James J. Holmberg, ed., *Dear Brother: Letters from William Clark to Jonathan Clark* (New Haven: Yale University Press, 2002).

9. R. David Edmunds, "Potawatomis in the Platte Country: An Indian Removal Incomplete," *Missouri Historical Review* 68 (1974): 375–78; Dorothy Neuhoff, "The Platte Purchase," 310–11, in McCarter & English Indian Claim Cases, Mudd Library, Princeton University, box 7, folder 2, exhibit 519; J. Calvin Berry Letter, April 16, 1842, Western Historical Manuscripts Collection, State Historical Society of Missouri, Columbia, C1461; Thomas C. Duggins, Letter, 1840, Western Historical Manuscripts Collection, State Historical Society of Missouri, Columbia, C995, vol. 3, no. 111.

10. Indian Agent Dougherty to Senator Linn, January 26, 1835, in McCarter & English Indian Claim Cases, box 12, folder 3, exhibit C-2; Governor John Miller, "Third Biennial Address," November 20, 1832, in Buel Leopard and Floyd C. Shoemaker, eds., *The Messages and Proclamations of the Governors of the State of Missouri* (Columbia: University of Missouri Press, 1922), 1:170.

11. Neuhoff, "The Platte Purchase," 318–19.

12. Edmunds, "Potawatomis in the Platte Country," 382–84; Bert Anson, "Variations of the Indian Conflict: The Effect of the Emigrant Indian Removal Policy, 1830–1854," *Missouri Historical Review* 59 (October 1964): 81–82.

13. Andrew S. Hughes to Governor Dodge, May 12, 1837, in McCarter & English Indian Claim Cases, box 24, folder 1, exhibit 160; Neuhoff, "The Platte Purchase," 340–41; Anthony F. C. Wallace, "The Iowa and Sac and Fox Indians in Iowa and Missouri," October 20, 1954, in McCarter & English Indian Claim Cases, box 39, folder 11.

14. W. Darrell Overdyke, ed., "A Southern Family on the Missouri Frontier: Letters from Independence, 1843–1855," *Journal of Southern History* 17 (May 1951): 216–18; W.J.J. Morrow to Col. John Drennen, October 1, 1852, W.J.J. Morrow Papers, Western Historical Manuscripts Collection, State Historical Society of Missouri, Columbia, C2051; Samuel Lewis to Lewis Jones, December 18, 1842, Lewis Jones Papers, Missouri Historical Society, St. Louis; Tanis C. Thorne, *The Many Hands of My Relations: French and Indians on the Lower Missouri* (Columbia: University of Missouri Press, 1996), 195–96.

15. Eugene T. Wells, "The Growth of Independence, Missouri, 1827–1850," *Bulletin of the Missouri Historical Society* 16 (October 1959): 33–46; Jane Hamill Sommer, "Outfitting for the West, 1849," *Bulletin of*

the Missouri Historical Society 24 (1968): 340–47; Mitchel Roth, "Cholera Summer: Independence, St. Joseph, and the Path of Contagion," *Gateway Heritage* 15 (Summer 1994): 20–22; A. Theodore Brown, *Frontier Community: Kansas City to 1870* (Columbia: University of Missouri Press, 1963), 53–59.

16. A. Wislizensus, "Memoirs of a Tour to Northern Mexico," *Western Journal* 1 (July 1848): 363; Perry McCandless, *A History of Missouri*, vol. 2: *1820–1860* (Columbia: University of Missouri Press, 1972), 35–36, 137–38.

17. Donnie D. Bellamy, "Free Blacks in Antebellum Missouri, 1820–1860," *Missouri Historical Review* 67 (January 1973): 200.

18. For a poignant case study of a woman's reluctance, see Edward D. Jervey and James E. Moss, eds., "From Virginia to Missouri in 1846: The Journal of Elizabeth Ann Cooley," *Missouri Historical Review* 60 (January 1966): 162–206. For broader studies of this gender divide, see John Mack Faragher, *Women and Men on the Overland Trail* (New Haven: Yale University Press, 1979); Lillian Schlissel, ed., *Women's Diaries of the Westward Journey* (New York: Schocken Books, 1992). For evidence of the same reluctance among a previous generation of westering women, see Joan E. Cashin, *A Family Venture: Men and Women on the Southern Frontier* (New York: Oxford University Press, 1991), 32–52.

19. Shirley Christian, *Before Lewis and Clark: The Story of the Chouteaus, the French Dynasty That Ruled America's Frontier* (New York: Farrar, Straus and Giroux, 2004), 250–436; Thorne, *The Many Hands of My Relations*, 177–244.

20. Jeffrey S. Adler, *Yankee Merchants and the Making of the Urban West: The Rise and Fall of Antebellum St. Louis* (New York: Cambridge University Press, 1991), 93–94; McCandless, *A History of Missouri*, 38.

21. Adler, *Yankee Merchants*, 91; John Darby, *Personal Recollections of Many Prominent People Whom I Have Known, and of Events—Especially of Those Relating to the History of St. Louis—during the First Half of the Present Century* (St. Louis: G. I. Jones, 1880), 301.

22. Bruce A. Van Orden, "From Kirtland to Missouri," in S. Kent Brown, Donald Q. Cannon, and Richard H. Jackson, eds., *Historical Atlas of Mormonism* (New York: Simon and Schuster, 1994), 26; Stephen C. LeSueur, *The 1838 Mormon War in Missouri* (Columbia: University of Missouri Press, 1987); R. J. Robertson Jr., "The Mormon Experience in Missouri, 1830–1839," *Missouri Historical Review* 68 (1973–74): 280–98, 393–415; Dean C. Jessee and David J. Whittaker, eds., "The Last Months of Mormonism in Missouri: The Albert Perry Rockwood Journal," *Brigham Young University Studies* 28 (1988): 5–

91; Richard E. Bennett, "Mormons and Missourians: The Uneasy Truce," *Midwest Review* 9 (1987): 12–21.

23. Clark V. Johnson, "The Missouri Redress Petitions: A Reappraisal of Mormon Persecutions in Missouri," *Brigham Young University Studies* 26 (1986): 31–44.

24. Durward T. Stokes, ed., "The Wilson Letters, 1835–1849," *Missouri Historical Review* 60 (July 1966): 504; William D. Hoyt, ed., "A Clay Countian's Letters of 1834," *Missouri Historical Review* 45 (July 1951): 353.

25. Robert Moore Jr., "A Ray of Hope, Extinguished: St. Louis Slave Suits for Freedom," *Gateway Heritage* 14 (Winter 1993–94): 4–15.

26. William G. Bek, trans., "Nicholas Hesse, German Visitor to Missouri, 1835–1837," pt. 4, *Missouri Historical Review* 41 (July 1947): 382; Donnie Duglie Bellamy, "Slavery, Emancipation, and Racism in Missouri, 1850–1865" (Ph.D. dissertation, University of Missouri, Columbia, 1971), 64–65; R. Douglas Hurt, *Agriculture and Slavery in Missouri's Little Dixie* (Columbia: University of Missouri Press, 1992), 257.

27. Moore, "A Ray of Hope, Extinguished," 12.

28. Bellamy, "Slavery," 50.

29. Governor Meredith M. Marmaduke, "First Biennial Message," November 18, 1844, in Leopard and Shoemaker, eds., *Messages and Proclamations*, 2:13; *St. Louis Daily Union*, January 20, 1847.

30. Governor Austin A. King, "Inaugural Address," December 27, 1848, in Leopard and Shoemaker, eds., *The Messages and Proclamations of the Governors of the State of Missouri*, 2:274; Hurt, *Agriculture and Slavery*, 274.

31. Nicole Etcheson, *Bleeding Kansas: Contested Liberty in the Civil War Era* (Lawrence: University Press of Kansas, 2004), 11.

32. Richard Lloyd Anderson, "Atchison's Letters and the Causes of Mormon Expulsion from Missouri," *Brigham Young University Studies* 26 (1986): 8.

33. Ibid., 3.

34. St. Louis Circuit Court, Dred Scott vs. Irene Emerson, 1847, in Dred Scott Collection, Missouri Historical Society, St. Louis; McCandless, *A History of Missouri*, 258–60; Walter Ehrlich, "Was the Dred Scott Case Valid?" *Journal of American History* 55 (September 1968): 256–65; Lea VanderVelde and Sandhya Subramanian, "Mrs. Dred Scott: Race and Gender Issues in Harriet Robinson Scott's Emancipation Claims," *Yale Law Journal* 106 (January 1997): 1033–1122; Walter Ehrlich, *They Have No Rights: Dred Scott's Struggle for Freedom* (Westport, Conn.: Greenwood Press, 1979), 9–88.

Index

Italicized page numbers indicate maps and illustrations.

STEPHEN ARON

Professor of History at the University of California, Los Angeles and Executive Director of the Institute for the Study of the American West at the Autry National Center, is a specialist in frontier and western American history. He is author of *How the West Was Lost: The Transformation of Kentucky from Daniel Boone to Henry Clay*, co-author of *Worlds Together, Worlds Apart: A History of the Modern World from the Mongol Empire to the Present*, and co-editor of *Trading Cultures: The Worlds of Western Merchants.*